Cargo Liners

An Illustrated History

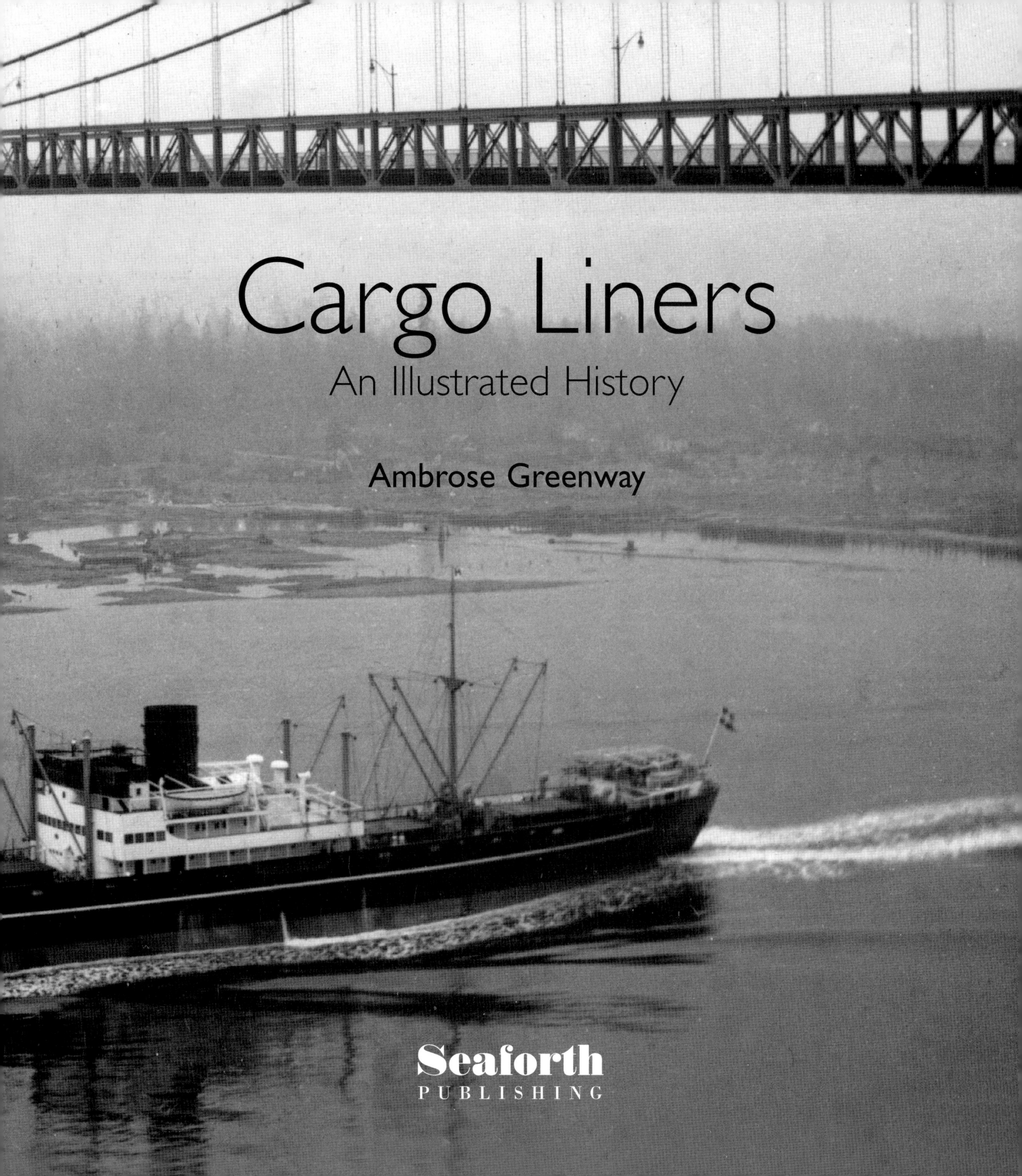

Cargo Liners

An Illustrated History

Ambrose Greenway

Seaforth
PUBLISHING

Half title page photo: Blue Funnel's *Antenor*, see page 90.
Title page photo: *Martin Bakke*, see page 79.

First published in Great Britain in 2009 by
Seaforth Publishing,
Pen & Sword Books Ltd,
47 Church Street,
Barnsley S70 2AS

www.seaforthpublishing.com

British Library Cataloguing in Publication Data
A catalogue record for this book is available from the British Library

ISBN 978 1 84832 006 2

Typeset and designed by Ian Hughes
Printed and bound in Thailand

Contents

Preface

I inherited a love of the sea and ships from my father and research into shipping history has become something of a lifelong passion. Although my interest has ranged across all areas of shipping, I have always had a particular fascination with the cargo liners that plied the seven seas on a regular basis, transporting all manner of goods and raw materials between nations and, in so doing, providing a vital link in the world trade chain. Characterised by a forest of masts and posts and often faster than many passenger liners, they had a grace and beauty all their own.

Many of the well-known companies that operated cargo liners are fast becoming memories but we should be thankful that almost all have been written about in one form or another, either in official company histories or illustrated fleet lists. A number of excellent larger versions of the latter have been published recently, notably in the United Kingdom, Germany, Holland and Denmark. A few more books have dealt with specific subjects relating to cargo ships but, as far as I am aware, no book has tackled the development of the cargo liner *per se*, a somewhat surprising omission when one considers the number of books produced on other types of ships. Perhaps the sheer size and complexity of the subject, involving as it does so many different variations, has put people off.

In seeking to go some way towards filling this gap, it is my hope that this illustrated history will provide a starting point that will encourage others to tackle the subject in somewhat greater depth. Much remains to be written and perhaps one day an equivalent to David MacGregor, that champion of the fast sailing ship, will emerge to produce a definitive work.

With so many ships to choose from, I have had to be fairly selective in my choice of subjects with the inevitable result that a number of 'favourites' have had to be omitted. I have endeavoured to take a broad approach but the predominance of the British merchant navy during most of the period under review is self-evident. The story starts in the second half of the nineteenth century and I have chosen to end it around 1970, when development of the traditional cargo liner had reached a peak. That date, more or less, coincides with the entry into service of the first generation of purpose-built cellular container ships that revolutionised the carriage of general cargo and quickly began to usurp the role of the cargo liner. 'Tween-deckers continued to be built for non-containerised trades for a further ten years or so, but these became increasingly container friendly and really fall into the multi-purpose ship category, which, for space reasons alone, is beyond the scope of this work.

I have consulted a large number of sources in the compilation of this work but would like to express my gratitude in particular to Lloyd's Register of Shipping Information Services, the Starke-Schell Registers and the Miramar Ship Index website sponsored by the New Zealand Ship & Marine Society.

All the illustrations are taken from my own collection, built up over many years, and those where the source is known are acknowledged. However, despite my best endeavours, it has proved impossible to ascertain the origin of many and I can only apologise if I have inadvertently infringed anyone's copyright.

AMBROSE GREENWAY. MOREBATH, January 2009

Introduction

The cargo liner has been described as the backbone of empire. For more than a century it was the main vehicle for transporting general cargo around the world, carrying manufactured goods from the industrialised nations on the outward voyage and bringing back foodstuffs and raw materials vital to the manufacturing processes on the return voyage. It could also, if required, be adapted to carry bulk cargoes, such as grain.

Unlike the tramp steamer, which worked the bulk trades and sailed on a random basis to wherever cargo was on offer, the cargo liner sailed on a regular schedule to named destinations, and its itinerary generally included more ports of call than the passenger liner.

An external feature that distinguished the cargo liner from the average tramp was its more extensive cargo-handling arrangements. These consisted of derricks and winches, the former being supported by the masts as well as a number of tall posts, usually mounted in pairs, which were known as kingposts or sampson posts. The cargo liner also had a greater number of cargo holds, which were subdivided horizontally by two or more between or 'tween decks, hence their often being referred to as ''tween-deckers'. This allowed several different layers of cargo to be carried, making much greater use of the hold space. Following a decline in the tramp trades from the 1920s, an increasing number of tramp-ship owners built 'tween-deckers that could be used for bulk cargoes, such as grain and fertiliser, but which were also suitable for charter to liner companies when bulk markets were depressed.

Another description widely used for cargo liners was 'shelter-deckers'. This term had its origin in an extra deck – the shelter-deck – which was created by 'filling in' the well-decks of a vessel with three separate island erections – forecastle, bridge and poop – on the main deck. As enclosed space counted towards the calculation of gross or net tonnage on which port dues were generally based, a device was employed which entailed leaving openings in the shelter-deck – tonnage openings – whereby the ship could operate in either an open or closed condition. The latter allowed the ship to be more deeply laden and was widely employed in wartime when maximum cargo capacity was required. Over time, additional deck erections came to be added to the shelter-deck, predominantly just a forecastle, but often various combinations of forecastle, bridge or poop.

Types of cargo

A cargo liner had to be capable of carrying almost any item of cargo, including the proverbial kitchen sink. Manufactured goods ranged from the smallest screws to household items, from explosives to steel products and from vehicles to railway engines. Imports, on the other hand, included all types of foodstuffs ranging from meat, dairy products and fruit to coffee, tea and sugar. Non-comestibles included raw materials such as lumber, jute, rubber, silk and wool, whilst provision was also made for the carriage of liquid cargoes, such as latex and vegetable oils. These required special tanks with heating facilities and were generally positioned at either ends of the ship or deep in the holds. If cereals such as grain were carried, shifting boards had to be installed to stop the cargo moving in rough weather.

Loading and discharge were the responsibility of the chief officer and posed a complex juggling problem, as cargo had to be arranged where it could be readily available at the correct port of discharge. Some cargoes were sensitive and therefore could not be juxtaposed or loaded on top of each other; in addition the ship's stability had to be taken into account, which necessitated heavier cargo being placed deeper in the ship. The means of achieving the correct balance was the cargo plan, which was hand drawn, using different coloured crayons, on a pre-printed elevation of the ship. On arrival in port, copies were distributed to those who required them, including the the stevedoring company that would be providing the shore-side labour.

Passengers

Because they operated as far as possible on fixed schedules, cargo liners were also attractive to a certain type of passenger, generally those who favoured a quieter and more leisurely mode of travel than was available in their larger and faster sisters, the passenger liners. In the early days, even the predominantly cargo-carrying ships still carried quite a number of passengers, but these were gradually whittled down to twelve after it was agreed that any ship carrying in excess of this number would be classed as a passenger ship and therefore had to carry a doctor. Cargo-liner accommodation was often the equivalent of first class and was generally pleasant and sometimes quite luxurious.*

Cargo handling

Derricks

Cargo liners were distinguished from tramp steamers by their extensive array of cargo-handling gear. Although comparatively common in Northern Europe, harbour cranes were by no means universal and, in many ports, particularly in the Far East and America, ships had to be capable of loading and discharging cargo directly onto open quaysides or into a variety of craft alongside. The gear consisted of an outfit of derricks and deck winches, the former often numbering more than twenty, with several different safe working loads and generally including one or two heavy derricks.

Derricks would be 'topped up' or raised from their stowage position before berthing, clearing the deck for working. If ship's gear was to be used rather than dockside cranes, the crew would rearrange the derricks abutting the holds needing to be worked in readiness for the arrival of dock labour gangs. The most widely adopted method of operation, known as 'union purchase', involved positioning the end of the outboard derrick over the hold and the end of the inboard derrick over the quay. By the dextrous use of guys and a pair of winches, the load could be raised from the hold and transferred ashore or visa versa in one seamless movement. This was a skilled operation performed by the stevedores, but things did not always run smoothly and accidents resulting in cargo damage often occurred. Cargo positioned in the wings of the hold required particularly careful manhandling, especially when using the lifting hook and bond at an oblique angle.

Derricks could also be operated singly, in the same way as a crane, but it was not until the 1950s, when new types of 'crane derricks' were developed, that this process became more widely used.

Different techniques were required for handling individual items of heavy cargo, such as railway engines and boilers, and most cargo liners were equipped with one or

*Note: The intermediate ship type referred to as a passenger/cargo ship or combi-liner bridged the gap between liner and cargo liner and carried up to fifty passengers. These are beyond the scope of this book, but a number of those fitted with between twelve and twenty berths have been included, because they appeared to all intents and purposes like most other cargo liners.

Ships discharging with derricks and crane.

A jumbo derrick hoisting a tank.

two heavy derricks referred to as 'jumbos'. These had to be rigged in a different way from the standard derrick, in itself a time-consuming process, and were operated more like a large crane with the derrick gently swinging the load over the side (see *Heavy-lift ships* at page 12).

Cargo handling was a time-consuming business, so much so that during the course of a year ships often spent as much time in port as they did at sea. The situation was not helped by additional interruptions caused by the vagaries of the weather or industrial action by stevedores.

Deck Cranes

Hydraulic, steam-operated deck cranes were widely used in the coastal and short-sea trades in the later decades of the nineteenth century but were comparatively rare in the liner trades. More flexible than the 'union purchase' method using winches and derricks and requiring only one operator, they could plumb any area below the hatch or on the quayside within the radius of their boom. In the 1930s, the German Hugo Stinnes group built a series of ships fitted entirely with electro-hydraulic cranes, but these were essentially for the bulk trades and their holds lacked 'tween-decks. The practice was resurrected in Johnson Line's fast *Seattle* class completed after World War II; gradually the use of cranes increased, tentatively at first, with just a single or two units, but becoming more widespread as the 1950s progressed. Some were mounted on rails and others on travelling pontoon-type hatch covers. Cranes really came into their own following the development of multiple hatches, which allowed cargo to be placed directly where it was required in the hold.

Hatches

Cargo liners generally had between five and seven holds served by a like number of hatches. The latter were generally not large and were raised above deck level by coamings to reduce the possibility of water entering in heavy seas. The traditional method of securing hatches was by means of baulks of timber known as hatchboards, which rested on steel hatch beams which fitted the inside edge of the coaming. The hatches were then sealed by two or three tarpaulins, which were secured around the side of the coaming by wedges. The reverse process had to take place before discharge could begin.

This time-consuming system lasted well into the 1950s but at the outset of that decade a new type of articulated steel cover was developed by the MacGregor Company, which had worked on steel hatch covers to minimise collier losses before the war. The cover was mounted on wheels running along either side of the coaming top,

Folding the steel hatch cover.

A Stülcken heavy-lift mast.

allowing it to fold up like a concertina for vertical stowage when pulled by a single wire mounted at one end of the hatch. This came to revolutionise the opening and closing of hatches, which could now be performed by one man in a matter of minutes. Other companies developed similar systems and folding hatch covers became more or less standard after 1960. MacGregor also developed flush-fitting folding hatches for the tween-decks, which enabled fork-lift trucks to be used to speed up cargo handling.

Another innovation that occurred, in 1957, was the use of multiple hatches. Johnson Line's *Rio de Janeiro* class had three hatches abreast serving individual compartments, and this idea developed into the 'open ship' concept whereby the hatch area covered almost the entire weather deck. The first applications were in the US twin-hatch *Del Rio* class in 1961 and the Russian *Poltava* type which appeared the following year. Triple hatches were subsequently used in many of the larger and faster cargo liners, but usually only for the two or three holds amidships where the hull was broadest.

Propulsion

The early types of cargo liner were propelled by compound steam engines, but the coming of the vastly more efficient and economical triple-expansion reciprocating engine soon became almost universal. Later, a number of quadruple-expansion plants were employed, but real changes that were to revolutionise cargo-liner propulsion did not occur until just before World War I. They resulted from two groundbreaking inventions that had occurred a decade or so earlier, namely Rudolf Diesel's internal-combustion engine which bore his name and Charles Parsons' steam turbine. The latter was first used commercially in the Clyde excursion steamer *Queen Alexandra* and thereafter in fast naval ships and passenger liners, such as *Lusitania* and *Mauretania*. In 1909, Parsons bought the old clipper-bowed steamer *Vespasian* from G Reid, Newcastle, and used her as a test-bed to perfect a system of gearing for his turbine, which made it suitable for use in cargo liners and other types of ship.

In 1912, Burmeister & Wain completed the world's first ocean-going motorship, *Selandia*, a cargo/passenger liner with accommodation for twenty-six passengers for the

Danish East Asiatic Company. Later that year it delivered the first diesel-driven cargo liner, *Suecia*, to Sweden's Johnson Line. Diesel development was aided by the greater availability of oil in the 1920s. Twin-screw installations were still necessary if high power was required, despite the increased use of turbo-charging. It was not until the 1950s that the use of single diesels accelerated rapidly, as larger bore engines with greater output per cylinder became available. By the time the cargo liner reached the peak of its development in the 1960s, the majority were driven by oil engines, some of which exceeded 20,000bhp.

Meanwhile, the United States had made great advances in steam turbine development, largely for use in warships during World War II, and it was not altogether surprising that the majority of its postwar cargo-liner replacements used this form of propulsion. The fact that most were built with government subsidy for use as naval auxiliaries with extra, built-in defence power probably also had something to do with this.

Other forms of propulsion were briefly tried in cargo liners, including diesel-electric engines in Hamburg-America Line's *Wuppertal* in 1936 and gas-turbine propulsion in the Soviet *Parizhskaya Kommuna* of 1968.

Refrigeration

The development of refrigeration had a huge impact on sea transport, opening up new markets for countries such as Argentina, Australia and New Zealand, which enjoyed rich grazing land yet had populations that were too small to consume all its meat and dairy products. However, the rapidly industrialising nations in Northern Europe were in urgent need of more meat to feed the growing numbers of workers who had left the land to seek their fortunes in the new manufacturing industries.

Freezer plants for preserving meat were operating in Australia from the early 1860s, but nigh on two decades were to pass before the process was successfully adapted for use at sea. In view of the shorter sea voyage to Europe, it was from Argentina that the first trial shipments of frozen beef and mutton were conducted by the Frenchmen Ferdinand Carré and Charles Tellier. The latter's initial attempt in 1868 with an ammonia absorption plant in the *City of Rio de Janeiro* failed when the machinery broke down, but almost a decade later he had limited success with an ammonia compression plant fitted in the small steamer *Frigorifique*, which arrived in Rouen early in 1877, with some meat in reasonable condition. The first truly successful carriage of frozen meat was achieved the following winter when the Chargeurs Réunis steamer *Paraguay*, fitted with a Carré ammonia compressor, delivered 5,500 carcasses from Buenos Aires to Le Havre in good condition.

The United Kingdom quickly took up the idea of refrigeration at sea and in 1879 the Glasgow firm of Bell, Coleman & Company installed one of its cold-air machines, invented two year earlier, in Charles Burrell's steamer *Strathleven*. She had been chartered by Andrew McIlwraith, a Queenslander who had previously inspected the *Paraguay*, and arrived back in London in February 1880 with forty tons of frozen beef and mutton representing the first successful shipment from Australia. Two years later Albion Line's similarly equipped sailing ship *Dunedin* brought the first successful shipment from New Zealand, and thereafter many existing ships were fitted with refrigeration plants and had their holds partially or fully insulated.

Insulation was necessary to prevent the cold air escaping and initially came in several forms, such as flake charcoal, silicate cotton and pumice, but in time granulated cork came to be the most widely employed. In the case of Bell, Coleman & Company and, later, Haslam machines, cold air was circulated by means of fans and wooden ducts, but in compression and absorption machines, a cooled liquid – usually brine to prevent it freezing – was circulated through an extensive piping system arranged in grids on either side or on the ceiling of each insulated chamber. The complexity of the system required additional crew in the form of 'fridge engineers' to run it. This combined with the high initial expense of fitting refrigeration and the need for adequate speed margins to minimise the risk of cargo deterioration in the event of unforeseen delay to make these special types of cargo liners considerably more expensive to build than general cargo carriers.

The first purpose-built refrigerated steamer was the *Elderslie*, built for Turnbull, Martin & Company's Scottish Shire Line, which entered the Antipodean meat trade in 1884. Others soon followed for the same owners, as well as the New Zealand Shipping Company, Federal Steam Navigation Company, the 1882-merged Shaw, Savill & Albion, James P Corry & Company and Tyser & Company, the latter two later being absorbed into the Commonwealth & Dominion Line, soon to become known as Port Line. In the River Plate trade, Lamport & Holt set the pace and was quickly joined by Houlder Line, Nelson Line and Royal Mail Steam Packet Company. The shorter voyage time of around three weeks from Argentina was about half that taken by ships coming from the Antipodes, and allowed meat carcasses to be transported on hooks in chilled form at between 28.5°F and 29.5°F, which resulted in their being almost indistinguishable from home-killed produce. This method had originally been developed for the extensive transatlantic meat trade, which declined after 1910 following a rapid increase in US home consumption.

It was not until 1930 that chilled meat was successfully transported from Australia in *Port Fairy*. Earlier trials as far back as the 1890s had brought mixed results, and even five reasonably successful voyages made by Aberdeen Line's *Marathon* in 1910–11 using a Linley sterilising system – which kept beef in good condition for up to seventy days – had failed to elicit much support. The problem was eventually solved by government-backed research in the 1920s, which discovered that the answer lay in injecting small amounts of CO_2 into gas-tight compartments. The same research showed that frozen apples could be carried from Tasmania and New Zealand by circulating air in the temperature-controlled chambers.

A number of large refrigerated motor ships were built in the 1930s, those trading to Australasia becoming known as the 'Empire Food Ships'. Many became casualties during World War II, necessitating replacement during the 1940s and 1950s, a period that also witnessed the emergence of more efficient forms of insulation. Construction of these specialised ships slowed in the 1960s but, nevertheless, some fine examples were built, culminating in Port Line's *Port Caroline* and *Port Chalmers* in 1968, just one year before the containerisation of the trade began, with the entry into service of the first new cellular ships operated by the Overseas Container Line and the Associated Container Transportation consortia.

Heavy-lift ships

Shortly after World War I, Norwegian naval officer Captain Christen Smith successfully transported two hundred railway locomotives from the United Kingdom to Belgium in two specially fitted steamers. He went on to design the first purpose-built heavy-lift ship, the 2,406gt *Beldis*, which was completed by Armstrong Whitworth at Low Walker-on-Tyne in 1924. She had long uncluttered decks, three very large strengthened hatches and open pillarless holds, being in essence a tramp steamer with heavy-lift capability, which could sail to wherever heavy items of cargo were on offer.

In 1927, Germany's Hansa Line built a series of special cargo liners fitted with 120t derricks; a number of other companies, including Elder Dempster and Ellerman, also invested in special ships of this type. During World War II, the British government ordered eight fifteen-knot heavy-lift ships fitted with three 120t derricks, which were similar in concept to Christen Smith's *Bel* ships with large open holds. A number of these were later purchased by Ben Line but their lack of 'tween-decks made them rather unsuitable for the carriage of normal break-bulk cargoes.

In the 1950s, Germany's Hansa Line was quick to rebuild its heavy-lift fleet, starting with the *Braunfels* class fitted with a single 165t derrick but, in 1965, after collaboration with the Stülcken shipyard in Hamburg, it introduced an entirely new form of heavy-lift mast in the *Lichtenfels*. The Stülcken mast, as it became known, consisted of two heavy tapering masts splayed outwards at an angle of around fifteen degrees. The base of the heavy derrick was positioned midway between them, enabling it to pivot fore and aft and serve the holds on either side. Its operation was much quicker and simpler than that of the traditional 'jumbo', and it could be controlled by one person, initially from platforms half way up each mast, but later from a mobile control unit.

Lichtenfels was fitted with two Stülckens, one of 120t and one of 40t, and the new form of mast became a feature of subsequent series' of Hansa ships, whilst specialist ships such as *Treuenfels* of 1960 employed two derricks that could work in tandem with a single yoke to lift up to 280t. A number of British companies, starting with Thos & Jas Harrison, built heavy-lift ships with Stülcken masts, and Blue Star Line's *Australia Star*, when completed in 1966, had the largest single lifting capacity of 300t. Stülcken masts, together with variations on the same principle from other manufacturers, came in many different sizes and were increasingly substituted for traditional jumbo derricks in new cargo liner construction.

CHAPTER

1

Origins and Early Years

Two significant events brought a revolution in ocean transport in the nineteenth century; the first was the introduction of steam propulsion and the second the gradual replacement of the paddle by the screw propeller. Development tended to revolve around passenger ships in the North Atlantic trade, in which competition was fiercest, but it was competition in the West Indies trade that led Liverpool shipowner Alfred Holt and his brother Philip to change direction in 1864 and try their luck against the sailing ships engaged in the China trade. Alfred, a trained railway engineer, had designed a new type of compound tandem steam engine with high-pressure boilers, which proved to offer lower fuel consumption during tests in their steamer *Cleator*. The brothers established the Ocean Steam Ship Company and built three new 2,280gt steamships fitted with the new engines at Scott & Company of Greenock. *Agamemnon*, *Ajax* and *Achilles* were iron, three-masted ships with the somewhat unusual arrangement of the rudder being mounted forward of the screw. Their instant commercial success resulted in a decision to concentrate on the carriage of cargo, although all the early Holt ships continued to carry passengers for a number more years. The opening of the Suez Canal in 1869 reduced the voyage to and from the Far East by more than 3,000 miles and underlined the superiority of the steamship over sail. Thus were sown the first seeds of what later developed into the cargo liner.

The first successful shipment of live cattle across the Atlantic was made by the *European* (H N Hughes & Nephew) in July 1874 and subsequently many passenger/cargo ships had temporary stalling arranged on the upper deck. This in turn led to the development of a new type of purpose-built cattle carrier in the late 1880s but the trade declined shortly before World War II, when the fast-expanding United States needed to retain its livestock to feed its own burgeoning population. Meanwhile, developments in refrigerating techniques had finally enabled frozen meat to be transported long distances at sea, initially from the River Plate and later from Australia and New Zealand. Demand was such that the final decade of the nineteenth century saw increasing numbers of new insulated steamers coming off the ways, primarily for British owners.

Increasing availability of the new triple-expansion engines in the 1880s greatly aided the development of the cargo liner, which had become much more substantial and had almost tripled in size compared with the early Holt ships. In mainland Europe, liner companies from Germany and Holland, which had previously concentrated on ships carrying a mix of passengers and cargo, were also starting to invest in ships designed solely for the carriage of freight, as existing ships were unable to cope with the growing amounts of cargo on offer.

Note: An asterisk in a caption indicates the vessel shown in the photograph.

Far East beginnings

The origin of the cargo liner owes a great deal to the early steamers of that great British shipowner Alfred Holt. His 2,072gt *Antenor* completed by Andrew Leslie & Company, Hebburn-on-Tyne, in 1872 was the last of four sisters, which were two-masted developments of the pioneering *Agamemnon* trio. She measured 322ft and was driven at a modest ten knots by a two-cylinder compound tandem engine, speed being considered secondary to reliability and regularity of service by her fastidious owner. Like most early cargo steamers, she also carried a number of passengers, either on deck or in the 'tween deck. Along with *Patroclus* and *Glaucus* she was transferred to Holt's Dutch subsidiary N S M 'Oceaan' in the early 1890s and all three had been sold to Japan by 1898, *Antenor* serving as *Tateyama Maru* until broken up in 1929.

MacGregor, Gow & Company's Glen Line was one of Holt's great rivals in the UK–Far East trade. The 2,985gt *Glenfruin* and *Glenavon* were built of iron to a three-island design by London & Glasgow Engineering & Iron Shipbuilding Company, Govan, in 1880–1. They had a registered length of 360ft on a beam of 43ft and were considerably faster than the Holt ships, being capable of steaming at thirteen and a half knots by means of a two-cylinder compound inverted engine developing 3,000ihp. Like the Holt ships, however, they also carried a number of passengers. This view purports to show *Glenavon* loading at an anchorage in Japan shortly before she was wrecked off the Chinese coast on Lintang Rock near Sa Mun in December 1898. *Glenfruin* became McIlwraith McEacharn's *Kalgoorlie* in 1897 and was laid up after grounding at Singapore in 1910. Sold to local owners, she was hulked but was rebuilt in 1917 for Ho Hong Steamship Company and renamed *Hong Hwa* a year later. She was finally broken up in Osaka in 1934 after a remarkable fifty-four-year-long career. Glen Line concentrated on speed and some of its later ships could steam at up to fifteen knots, making a number of record passages. This proved expensive and, coupled with fierce competition with P&O in the passenger business, led the company to switch to slower, more economical, cargo-only ships at the turn of the century.

Established in Liverpool in 1877, the firm of Greenshields, Cowie operated the Knight Line to the Far East and its *Knight Errant*, shown in the Suez Canal, was a typical example of an early cargo steamer still retaining crossed yards. She was completed by Palmers, Jarrow, in the last month of 1885 and measured 3,471gt on dimensions of 330ft overall by 43ft. Propulsion was by means of a 350nhp reciprocating engine. In 1897, she was renamed *Kensington* by new owners and was broken up in the first quarter of 1910. A second *Knight Errant*, built by Charles Connell & Company, Glasgow, in 1898, was a much larger (470 x 57ft), four-masted steamer which, after sale in 1914, passed through four different ownerships until 1925, when she was converted into the whale factory/tanker *Lancing* by Melsom & Melsom of Larvik. She was notable in being the first of this type to be fitted with a stern ramp, and was eventually torpedoed by *U522* on 7 April 1942 in the vicinity of Cape Hatteras. The Knight Line was sold to Alfred Holt in 1917.

Charles Hill's Bristol City Line ran a service from its West Country homeport to the US east coast. Its 2,140gt *Exeter City*, seen here negotiating the Avon Gorge, was built by Blyth Shipbuilding & Dry Docks Company in 1887 and represented the smaller type of cargo steamer engaged in regular liner trade. Her hull was built on the three-island principle, a design widely favoured by tramp-ship owners and at that time there was not much to differentiate the two types, except for *Exeter City* and her consorts having more lifeboats. Length was 289ft between perpendiculars on a beam of 39ft and she was driven by triple-expansion machinery at around ten knots. After an uneventful career, she was broken up in Genoa in the summer of 1925.

Cattle carriers

White Star Line's 4,639gt *Cufic* was a ship of several firsts. Not only was she the company's first cargo ship and first to be driven by triple-expansion engines, but also she was the first North Atlantic ship to incorporate specific stabling facilities for the transportation of live cattle. Completed in Belfast by Harland & Wolff in the final month of 1888, she operated in the Liverpool–New York trade and was joined by sister *Runic** the following year, both being capable of transporting 1,000 head. Over the following seven years, Harlands delivered six increasingly large, twin-screw 'cattle boats': *Nomadic* and *Tauric* (461 x 49ft) in 1891, *Naronic* and *Bovic* (470 x 53ft) in 1892, *Cevic* (500 x 60ft) in 1894 to replace *Naronic*, which had gone missing in February 1893, and finally *Georgic* in 1895, which was the largest of all the transatlantic cattle carriers at 10,077gt on dimensions of 559 x 60ft. *Cufic* was chartered to Spain's Cia Transatlántica as *Nuestra Senora de Guadaloupe* during 1896–8; in 1901 she became Dominion Line's *Manxman*, retaining the name through two more ownerships until foundering in the Atlantic a week before Christmas in 1919. Sister *Runic* became West India & Pacific Steamship Company's *Tampican* in 1895 and was transferred to Leyland Line in 1899. In 1913 she was converted to the whale-oil tanker *Imo* by South Pacific Whaling and on 6 December 1917 was involved in a massive tragedy in Halifax, Nova Scotia, after colliding with the French steamer *Mont Blanc*. The latter's ammunition cargo exploded, killing some 3,500 and wounding another 8,000, as well as destroying 3,000 homes. Miraculously, *Imo* survived and in 1918 became the Norwegian *Guvornoren*, but she was lost on 30 November 1921 after grounding in the Falklands.

In 1895, Cunard Line built its first cargo/cattle carriers, the twin-screw *Sylvania** and *Carinthia*, for Liverpool–Boston service. They were constructed on the Clyde by the London & Glasgow company and measured 5,598gt on a registered length of 445 x 49ft. Two sets of triple-expansion engines provided a sea speed of thirteen knots and they had flush-decked hulls with boats carried on the weather deck. *Carinthia* was chartered by the British government in 1899 to carry mules from New Orleans to South Africa for the Boer War campaign but was wrecked in May 1900 on Gravois Point, Haiti. *Sylvania* was broken up in Italy in 1910.

Elder Dempster Lines built a number of cargo/cattle steamers for a new North Atlantic service, which it inaugurated in 1894. Depicted here is the 8,644gt four-master *Montreal* completed by C S Swan & Hunter, Newcastle, late in 1899. She measured 470 x 56ft and her twin-screw triple-expansion machinery gave a speed of thirteen knots. Employed initially as a Boer War horse and mule transport, she was transferred to Canadian Pacific Railway along with Elder Dempster's other North Atlantic ships in April 1903. In 1915, she served for a while as a World War I troop transport before resuming her Liverpool–Canada service, but was rammed by the White Star liner *Cedric* in Liverpool Bay on 29 January 1918 and sank under tow the following day, fourteen miles from the Bar light vessel. Her single-screw sister *Mount Royal* (1898) was broken up at Rosyth in 1933 after a more eventful career, which included acting as the dummy battleship HMS *Marlborough* at the outset of World War I and in 1915 being converted to the Admiralty oiler *Rangol*. She was renamed *Mapleleaf* in 1916 and in 1919 was sold to the British Tanker Company, becoming *British Maple*. She acted as a bunkering ship in Southampton from June 1922 until broken up at Rosyth in 1932–3.

Early refrigerated ships

Houlder Brothers had been trading to Australia since 1861 but its association with the River Plate meat trade arose out of a contract to ship materials for the construction of Buenos Aires harbour. Chartered tonnage was employed from January 1884 but in 1890 the company took delivery of two new refrigerated steamers, *Hornby Grange* and *Ovingdean Grange**, from Wigham, Richardson, Newcastle and Sir Raylton Dixon, Middlesbrough, respectively. Unusually for cargo steamers, they were given two funnels and measured a shade over 2,400gt on a registered length of 300ft, their insulated capacity being around 40,000cu ft. *Hornby Grange* became *Evald* in 1920 and was scrapped in Barcelona seven years later, whilst her sister was sold to Russia in 1907 and renamed *Roman*. She passed to Japanese owners as *Tamon Maru No 16* in 1915 and disappeared without trace en route to Wakamatsu in September 1917.

Pakeha was an early Shaw, Savill & Albion refrigerated steamer built for the Antipodean meat trade. Built by R Ropner & Son, Stockton-on-Tees, in 1890, she was a three-island vessel and measured 4,331gt on dimensions of 365 x 47ft. A triple-expansion engine gave her a speed of ten knots but compared with the many sailing ships still involved in the trade, she had the advantage of being able to steam a straight course at all times. Subsequently she became the first vessel purchased by Vestey Brothers, who renamed her *Lizanka* in 1909 and then *Broderick* in 1911, following a year's charter as a mother ship for the Siberian salmon fishing fleet. Vesteys formed Blue Star Line to manage its *Brod* ships in 1912 but *Broderick* became a late-World War I loss, being torpedoed by *UB57* seven miles SSE of Hastings on 2 April 1918.

Indian traders

Thos & Jno Brocklebank had been trading to India for three-quarters of a century when they took delivery of their first steamship, *Ameer* (4,127gt/401ft), from Harland & Wolff, Belfast, in 1889. She and sister *Gaekwar* were only 1,000gt larger than the company's final sailing ships *Sindia* and *Holkar* delivered by Harlands in the preceding two years. They were three-island ships with four masts, the foremast being fully rigged. Four larger steamers followed: *Pindari* (pictured at Sharpness, where she was one of the largest regular traders); *Mahratta* from Harlands in 1891–2; and *Marwarri* and *Bengali* from Gourlay Bros & Company, Dundee, in 1900–1 – the latter differing in layout with No 3 hatch placed between bridge and funnel and a seventh hold added aft. *Pindari* measured 5,713gt on dimensions of 446 x 49ft and she and her sister were alone in being driven by twin screws for a slightly higher service speed of eleven knots, but as a result were less economical to run. In 1906, all but *Mahratta* were briefly transferred to Jenkins' Shire Line, *Pindari* as *Breconshire*, *Marwarri* as *Glamorganshire* and *Bengali* as *Montgomeryshire*, all four being modernised at this time with boats raised in davits. The inward-bound *Mahratta* was wrecked on the Goodwin Sands on 19 April 1909 and *Pindari* became the Japanese *Shinyo Maru* in 1911, being broken up in 1925. *Bengali* was torpedoed by *UC34* 115 miles north of Derna on 13 September 1917 and beached, but after engine repairs in Tobruk she was struck a second time by *UC34* on 8 April 1918 within sight of Alexandria and sank under tow in the buoyed channel. *Marwarri* went to Italy as *Sant'Andrea* in 1920 and was scrapped five years later.

In the 1890s, Liverpool shipowners Thomas & James Harrison decided to concentrate on three main cargo liner types; 10,000dwt ships for the Calcutta and seasonal New Orleans (cotton) trades; 7,600dwt vessels for the Mexican, Caribbean, South African and North Pacific services and shallow-draught 6,000dwt ships to serve Brazil, the Caribbean and Mexico. *Statesman**, delivered by Workman Clark & Company, Belfast, in July 1895, was the first ship in the larger category and inaugurated a fine series of four-masters that eventually numbered twenty-two ships built over a twenty-five-year period. By no means identical, their tonnages ranged from 9,100 to 12,600dwt and length from 450 to 505ft, the majority being of three-island construction with just three vessels, including the largest of the series, *Wayfarer* (1903), having flush hulls and twin-screw propulsion. All were driven by triple-expansion engines save the final pair, completed after World War I, which had geared turbines. *Statesman* measured 6,153gt on dimensions of 411ft between perpendiculars by 48ft and was capable of steaming at thirteen knots. She was one of six Harrison four-masters lost during World War I, being torpedoed between the Azores and the Iberian peninsula on 3 November 1916.

Deutsche Dampschifffahrts Gesellschaft 'Hansa' (Hansa Line), established in Bremen in 1881, was one of the first German companies to operate steamers outside the European–North American sphere, in particular to India. Sailings were random at first but in 1888 a regular 'Asiatic Line' to Bombay and Calcutta was instigated to meet the growing needs of European cotton manufacturers and the rice and jute industries. The 3,589gt *Ockenfels*, built by Sir Raylton Dixon, Middlesbrough in 1895, was one of three sisters from UK northeast coast yards, which ranked amongst the company's largest ships at that time. Sails and yards had been dispensed with and the basic three-island design featured two masts and no kingposts. *Ockenfels* was sunk in collision with *Duart* off Gibraltar in July 1909 and her sisters *Steinberger* and *Goldenfels* were sold off shortly afterwards. The former became the Italian *Italia* in 1910 and was mined off Savona in June 1917, whilst *Goldenfels* was renamed *Ingeborg* in 1911 and went through four more names changes in quick succession, finally being torpedoed as *Polar Prince* in September 1917, not far from where *Ockenfels* had been lost earlier.

British India Steam Navigation Company's *Obra* of 1895 marked the start of a major expansion of its cargo services, no less than twenty-eight ships being delivered by five different shipyards over the next seven years: William Denny & Bros, Dumbarton (thirteen), A & J Inglis, Glasgow (seven), Sir James Laing, Sunderland (four) and A Stephen & Sons, Linthouse and Sir Raylton Dixon, Middlesbrough, a pair each. Tonnage figures averaged around 5,300gt (8,200dwt) and they were built in four separate series of seven ships, distinguished by names beginning with the letters O, U, I and S. They all shared the same hull dimensions of 410 x 51ft and were driven by triple-expansion engines giving around ten knots. The O class, designed for the Australian trade, had a fairly basic design with forecastle and bridge deck, but subsequent series had longer forecastles, more raking funnels and carried boats one deck higher. The greatest difference, however, lay in the more elaborate cargo gear consisting of several pairs of short kingposts as evidenced in this view of *Uganda* (1898). The S class had accommodation for around twenty passengers and up to 1,400 emigrants. They were used on most of the company's Indian, Australian and South Pacific cargo services and many acted as transports during the Boer War and Boxer Rebellion. *Ikhona* (1900) was sunk by the Russian cruiser *Terek* in 1905 and *Onipenta* (1896) was wrecked whilst leaving Calcutta in 1909. During World War I, five were lost as a result of enemy action, *Islanda* (1900) was wrecked on Malta in 1917 and *Itria* (1901) sank following collision with *Clan Chisholm* in a Mediterranean convoy in April 1918. Fifteen were sold for further trading during 1922–4, eleven going to Japan, where some survived until broken up in 1935. *Okara* (1895) foundered in a cyclone in 1923 but the last to go was *Urlana* (1899), which was wrecked on Lundy Island in July 1937 as the Italian *Carmine Filomena*.

Eastern contrasts

RIGHT: Alfred Holt's *Dardanus*, delivered in 1894 by the company-owned shipyard Scott & Company of Greenock, was the third of the six-ship *Orestes* class, the other three being completed by Workman, Clark & Company in Belfast. At around 4,650gt, they were the company's largest yet and had a registered length of 492ft on a beam of 47ft. Cargo gear comprised an impressive array of twenty-two derricks, including two for heavier lifts on each mast. Previous Blue Funnel ships had all been developments of the pioneering *Agamemnon*, but this class introduced a new look with a three-island hull and several pairs of short kingposts that doubled as ventilators, setting a trend that would still be discernible in the 1950s. Her three-cylinder triple-expansion machinery provided a speed of twelve knots. *Dardanus* was transferred to the Dutch subsidiary N S M 'Oceaan' in 1911, followed by sister *Sarpedon* three years later. In 1923, she was sold to Kiel-based Paulsen & Ivers as *Fingal* and was sold to Italy in 1926, being broken up a year later as *Fortunato Secondo*.

LEFT: Although crossed yards would soon be dropped on new steamers, one liner company – William Thomson of Leith – remained faithful to another vestige of the sailing era – the clipper bow. Operating a service to the Far East, the company built no fewer than twenty steamers with this feature between 1881 and 1914. Known as the 'Leith Yachts', they were broadly similar in appearance but gradually increased in size from 2,200 to 4,800gt, half being built on the Clyde and the other half at northeast coast yards. Although advertised as sailing for the Clipper Line of Steamers, their speed of ten to eleven knots was anything but clipper-like. *Benalder* (1895), which measured 3,044gt, depicted here working cargo at an Eastern anchorage, was the fifth and last unit built by A Stephen & Sons, Linthouse. Some fifty feet shorter than *Dardanus*, she certainly looked small in comparison. She became *General Allenby* in 1919 and *Ganda* the following year, her career ending in Savona in 1929 after stranding. Some of the later clipper-bowed Ben Line steamers survived into the 1950s as Soviet fish-cannery ships.

North and South Atlantic designs

The Liverpool firm of Edward Bates & Son, whose chairman, Sir Percy Bates, later became chairman of Cunard Line, ran a cargo service between Liverpool and Boston. *Istrar** and her sister *Imani* were built by Harland & Wolff, Belfast, in 1896 and 1897 and measured 4,582gt on hull dimensions of 400 x 46ft. Triple-expansion machinery provided a service speed of twelve knots. Both ships were chartered out in 1914 to Brocklebank Line, which acquired them two years later. *Istrar* was torpedoed on 2 December 1916 but her sister survived until broken up in 1929 at Hendrik-Ido-Ambacht. Bates also owned three four-masted, twin-screw ships, the largest of which was the 6,250gt *Iran* built by Harland & Wolff in 1896. She also passed into Brocklebank ownership in 1916 but was sunk by *U155* on 19 January 1917 some 200 miles southeast of Santa Maria, Azores, after her stern had been severed by two torpedo hits.

Established in 1845 by William Lamport and Alfred Holt's elder brother George, Lamport & Holt initially operated sailing ships to the Mediterranean and did not enter the UK–South American east coast trade until 1863, later adding services from Antwerp and New York. Something of an innovator, Lamport & Holt pioneered the Brazil–New York coffee trade in 1869 and started carrying frozen meat from Argentina in 1887. The 5,366gt *Canning*, seen here on trials, remained its largest ship for ten years, following delivery by D & W Henderson in 1896. At 425ft, she was 15ft longer than the three *Canova*-class ships built by the same yard a year previously and the line of development could be traced back to Lamport's first three-island-type steamer *Caxton* purchased in 1885. As with so many ships of this period, *Canning* served as a transport during the Boer War and was again called up for duty in World War I, acting first as a Royal Navy balloon protection ship and later as a Royal Flying Corps depot ship. Sold to Greece in 1921, she passed to Genoa-based D Pittaluga three years later and was scrapped locally in 1925.

Continental awakenings

Deutsche-Australische Dampschiffs-Gesellschaft (DADG or German Australia Line) commenced trading in July 1889 with seven 2,700gt passenger/cargo steamers built in British and German yards. Several cargo ships followed but *Meissen**, delivered by Flensburger Schiffsbau-Gesellschaft (Flensburg Shipbuilding Company) in 1897, was the first of a series of ten larger vessels that were unusual in having two closely spaced funnels. Design-wise, they had a forecastle and long combined bridge and poop. Main particulars were 5,209gt (7,100dwt) on dimensions of 388 x 48ft and a 2,500ihp triple-expansion engine gave a speed of twelve knots. Around 100,000cu ft of the cargo space was insulated. A larger pair – the 5,467gt *Apolda* and *Rostock*, measuring 391 x 48ft – came from Flensburg in 1901, with quadruple-expansion machinery developing 3,400hp for an extra knot of speed. All twelve became familiar sights in South African (added 1900) and Australian ports, being nicknamed 'The Black Germans' in the latter, presumably on account of their colouring, despite the funnel bearing red and white rings. Initially they loaded homewards in Batavia. *Laeisz* (1901, Flensburg) was wrecked in the Red Sea in March 1908 and *Bergedorf* (1900, Sir Raylton Dixon, Middlesbrough) near Cape Town in April 1911 but most were seized by the Allies during World War I and then broken up in the 1920s. *Kiel* (1900, Flensburg) became the US Shipping Board's *Camden* in 1917 and was converted to a naval submarine tender two years later. Used as an accommodation ship from 1940, she was handed to the USMC in 1946 but was not broken up until 1949 in Baltimore. An afterthought, intended to be named *Muhlhausen* but completed by A G Neptun, Rostock in 1915 as the 4,972gt, 420ft long *Lennep*, became Bergen Steamship Company's *Brant County* in 1921 and ran in North Atlantic service until torpedoed in March 1943 by *U757*.

Amongst the first purpose-built Dutch cargo liners were Nederland Line's 3,351gt *Madura** built by Nederlandsche Scheepsbouw Maats. (NSM), Amsterdam in 1897 and Rotterdam Lloyd's 3,621gt *Bogor*, delivered by Blohm & Voss, Hamburg a year later. Despite differences in length (*Bogor* was 11ft longer at 333ft), their designs were remarkably similar in appearance with forecastle and bridge deck and they doubled up as pilgrim carriers during the annual six-week Hadj season. Propulsion was by means of three-cylinder reciprocating engines of 1,500ihp for ten knots. *Madura*'s sisters, *Bali* (built in the UK) and *Soembawa*, were followed by three stretched versions (3,600gt, 340ft), *Flores* and *Timor* from NSM and *Ambon* from De Schelde, Flushing. In similar vein, *Bogor* and her Wigham Richardson-built sisters *Malang* and *Solo* were succeeded by the twelve-feet-longer *Besoeki* and *Kediri*, which were completed in Dutch yards due to industrial problems at Blohm & Voss. *Bogor* was wrecked near Leixoes in December 1914 and *Kediri* was torpedoed off the Canaries by *U47* in November 1916, but all bar one of the remainder, although sold on, had careers of around twenty-five to thirty years' duration. The exception was *Madura*, which passed through several ownerships after 1912 and survived until her sixtieth year as the Russian *Komsomolets Arktikiy*.

CHAPTER

2

Consolidation

The coming of the new century saw steady progress in cargo liner development, particularly in refrigerated ships, which continued to be built in long series for the Australia and New Zealand frozen-meat trade. On the North Atlantic, Leyland Line came up with some interesting new designs, whilst P&O built a series of ships with deck cranes in place of the usual derricks. Several companies, including Holt's Blue Funnel Line, introduced a new form of twin mast arrangement, which when joined by a crosspiece was generally referred to as goalpost masts, although rugby posts might be a more appropriate description in some instances. As a result, the attached derricks had a longer outreach, which helped when loading heavier items of cargo such as timber.

Clan Line, alone amongst liner companies, continued to construct turret ships for general cargo use, profiting from their unique construction, which reduced net tonnage and saved on dues. On the Continent, yet another well-established liner shipping company, Norddeutscher Lloyd, took its first tentative steps into the cargo-liner business.

In terms of propulsion, the reciprocating engine held sway and despite the invention of the direct-drive steam turbine by Charles Parsons in 1901, it would be some time before it could be suitably adapted for cargo liner use.

Note: An asterisk in a caption indicates the vessel shown in the photograph.

New Atlantic design

Leyland Line built five four-masted livestock carriers between 1888 and 1891 but in 1900 it broke away from this traditional design with the 4,986gt *Caledonian*. Delivered by Caledon Shipbuilding & Engineering Company, Dundee, for Liverpool–Boston service, she had three continuous decks and a central deckhouse set on a raised bridge deck that separated the three forward and two after hatches. In addition to the foremast, a prominent pair of kingposts was placed on the foredeck between Nos 2 and 3 hatches, completing a layout that would later be widely emulated. A single three-cylinder reciprocating engine supplied by four single-ended boilers working at 200psi drove her at the then relatively high speed of thirteen knots. She was broken up in 1930 at Hendrik-Ido-Ambacht.

Series-built refrigerated ships for the Australasian trade

R & W Hawthorn, Leslie's Hebburn shipyard was responsible for one of the earliest standard cargo-liner designs, a partially refrigerated steamer for the Australasian meat trade. Starting with Turnbull, Martin's *Perthshire* in 1893, the series ended with Federal Steam Navigation Company's *Durham* in 1904 and during which period sixteen ships were delivered: four to Turnbull Martin, six to Federal Steam Navigation, four to New Zealand Shipping, *Karamea* (laid down as *Sussex*) to Shaw, Savill & Albion and *Waipara* (launched as *Port Jackson*) to British India Steam Navigation. Concurrently, Barclay, Curle & Company delivered the similar *Mataura* to New Zealand Shipping; Clydebank Engineering & Shipbuilding Company delivered *Fifeshire* and *Nairnshire* to Turnbull, Martin; Sunderland Shipbuilding Co delivered *Suffolk* and *Norfolk* to Federal Steam Navigation Company and Sir James Laing delivered *Indradevi* to Thomas B Royden & Company, resulting in a grand total of twenty-two ships. Gross measurement varied between 5,300t and 5,900t and their 420 x 54ft hulls had three insulated holds forward of the machinery for the homeward carriage of meat and dairy produce. Triple-expansion engines of 3,000–4,000ihp gave a service speed of around eleven knots. Shown here is *Whakatane* (1900), measuring 5,902gt, the last of four delivered to New Zealand Shipping Company by R & W Hawthorn, Leslie & Company, which was also responsible for a quartet of four-masted variants for Federal Steam Navigation Company. As built, some had passenger and emigrant accommodation but this was later removed. Many were broken up between the wars but *Durham* lasted until 1950 as Lloyd Brasileiro's *Minasloide* and the former *Morayshire* (1898) even longer, not being broken up until 1952 as Ignazio Messina's *Lugano*.

Federal Steam Navigation Company received four similar but larger twin-screw steamers with four masts from John Brown & Company, Clydebank, in 1902–3. *Suffolk*, *Essex**, *Dorset* and *Somerset* measured around 7,500gt on dimensions of 460 x 58ft and were driven at thirteen knots by twin reciprocating engines. The large deckhouse under the mainmast and the Manchester Ship Canal platform on the funnel distinguished them from the Hawthorn, Leslie-built four-masters *Kent*, *Surrey*, *Suffolk*, *Norfolk*, *Karamea* and *Sussex* (II). *Somerset* was torpedoed on 26 July 1917, 230 miles west of Ushant and the others were sold in 1927, *Suffolk* and *Dorset* to P & W MacLellan for scrap, whilst *Essex* became the Belgian *Van* and was broken up in 1933.

Parallel with the Hawthorn, Leslie design, fourteen similar ships were built by Workman, Clark & Company, Belfast (eleven), Sir James Laing, Sunderland (two) and Charles Connell & Company, Glasgow (one) for three other companies engaged in the Australian trade, namely James P Corry & Co (five), Thomas B Royden & Company (two) and G D Tyser & Co (seven) – companies that would join forces with W Milburn & Company in 1914 to form the Commonwealth & Dominion Line, later restyled Port Line. The series began with G D Tyser & Co's 5,987gt *Tomoana* built by Laing in 1899, closely followed by James P Corry & Co's *Star of Australia** from Workman, Clark & Co, which also delivered *Mimiro* to Tyser a year later. Hull dimensions were 440 x 54ft and reciprocating machinery gave them a speed of twelve knots. The next group of steamers from Belfast with 1ft greater beam were the twin-screw 6,444gt *Niwaru* and *Marere* for Tyser in 1902 and single-screw 6,230gt *Star of Scotland* and *Star of Japan* for Corry in 1904 and 1906. Meanwhile back in 1901, Charles Connell & Company had completed the 451ft-long *Indralema* for Thomas B Royden & Co, which was followed in 1907 by *Whakarua* and *Nerehana*, a similar pair built for Tyser in Belfast. Dimensions were further increased by 58ft to 470ft in length for three final twin-screw ships from Workman, Clark & Company in 1909–10, the thirteen-knot, 7,280gt *Star of Canada*, *Muritai* and *Star of India*, which had more compact superstructures. *Tomoana* was sold to Vestey Brothers in 1912 becoming *Brodvale*, then *Tudorstar* and *Tudor Star* and was scrapped in Savona in 1934. Two were wrecked – *Star of Japan* at Pedro de Galha, West Africa, in August 1908, and *Star of Canada* at Gisborne in June 1912. *Marere* was sunk by *U35* in the Eastern Mediterranean in January 1916 but all the others took on new 'Port' names later that year. *Star of Scotland* and *Nerehana* were torpedoed in 1918 and all bar one of the rest were scrapped in the 1930s. *Whakarua*, which with *Mimiro* had been sold to Genoa-based Andrea Zanchi in 1926–7 and renamed *Norge*, was the last to go, being bombed by Allied aircraft off the Tunisian coast on 21 December 1940.

Other refrigerated tonnage

Built by W Denny & Brothers, Dumbarton, in the same year as Tyser & Company's *Tomoana*, Shaw, Savill & Albion's 6,237gt *Waiwera** and her C S Swan & Hunter-built sister *Kumara* were unusual for the Australasian trades in having three masts mounted on a flush hull. They originally mounted yards on the foremast as shown and had extremely tall funnels and a split superstructure around No 3 hatch, the latter features also being incorporated in the larger *Mamari* trio, which followed from Belfast shipyards between 1904 and 1907. They measured 426 x 54ft and just more than half their total cargo capacity of 440,800cu ft was insulated in Nos 2, 3 and 4 holds, the others being reserved for general cargo. Propulsion was by a single triple-expansion engine giving twelve knots. Following Boer War service, they concentrated on the frozen-meat trade and *Waiwera* was sold to Ellerman as *City of Pretoria* in 1926, and was broken up in Barrow-in-Furness in 1928, the same year that her sister was demolished in Venice.

The 4,538gt *Pardo* was one of a trio of insulated steamers completed by Harland & Wolff, Belfast in 1904 for the Royal Mail Steam Packet Company's South American meat trade. They were three-island, two-deck ships with the somewhat unusual arrangement of long forecastle and bridge deck and measured 375 x 48ft. A single three-cylinder triple-expansion engine gave a speed of twelve knots. *Potaro* was the first to be lost, being captured off Pernambuco on 10 January 1915 by North German Lloyd's four-funnelled liner *Kronprinz Wilhelm*, which was acting as a commerce raider, and scuttled a few weeks later. *Parana* was broken up at Blyth in 1933 and *Pardo* was demolished in Genoa a year later, after completing thirty years of useful if unremarkable service.

Deck cranes and turrets

P&O was already a large liner company with more than sixty years of trading behind it when it built its first true cargo liner, the 6,482gt *Candia*, at Caird & Co, Greenock in 1896. She was unusual on two counts, being the company's first large twin-screw vessel and one of the first deep-sea cargo ships to be fitted with steam cranes for cargo handling. Designed for the Australian service, her dimensions of 451 x 52ft on a draught of just more than 30ft were the largest that could reach Adelaide at the time. Sister *Socotra* followed from Palmers, Jarrow, in 1897 and during 1903–5 five larger versions bearing P names – three from Barclay, Curle & Company, Whiteinch and two from Workman, Clark & Company, Belfast – were constructed for the company's Indian and Far Eastern services. *Pera*, shown here, was the first of the Belfast-built ships. Her career was cut short by a torpedo on 19 October 1917 when bound for Calcutta in convoy some sixty miles off the Tunisian coast. *Peshawur* had succumbed to the same fate southeast of Ballyquintin Head, Northern Ireland ten days previously; the three surviving sisters were all broken up in Italy in 1924.

The Doxford turret ships were based on the Great Lakes whaleback ships. Their strange construction, which resembled a surfaced submarine when viewed from ahead, reduced deck area by around 50 per cent, resulting in a considerable saving on Suez Canal dues and also provided a 20 per cent reduction in net tonnage – which was used by most ports to calculate harbour dues. In all, 182 turret ships were built before these loopholes were closed, the majority being employed in the tramp trades or for transporting iron ore, but their tonnage advantages also attracted liner companies, the best known being Clan Line, which acquired no less than thirty of varying sizes between 1896 and 1907. These were much larger than previous Clans and all but three were two-deckers, only the *Clan Colquhoun* trio of 1899, which were the largest at 5,856gt on dimensions of 440 x 52ft, having an added shelter deck. The final trio, delivered in 1907, were the 5,212gt *Clan Graham, Clan Sinclair* and *Clan Buchanan* (illustrated in Cape Town), which were slightly smaller than *Clan Colquhoun* at 400 x 52ft. Their three-cylinder reciprocating machinery developed 2,800ihp and gave a speed of eleven knots. *Clan Graham* was torpedoed by *UC74* in the Kassos Strait on 4 March 1918 but survived and was eventually towed to Mudros, where she lay until towed to Rotterdam for repairs in August 1919. On 11 November 1920, only eight months after re-entering service, she collided in fog in the Scheldt with the *Cholmley*, was beached and later caught fire, being declared a constructive total loss (CTL) after being refloated and towed to Antwerp. *Clan Sinclair* and *Clan Buchanan* were broken up at Blyth in 1933–4.

West Africa and Persian Gulf traders

Elder Dempster Lines had established a service from Plymouth to Freetown as far back as 1852 and by 1900 was one of a number of companies trading to West Africa. *Benue*, delivered by Swan, Hunter & Wigham Richardson, Newcastle in 1905, was the second of four 3,150gt *Sapele*-class steamers and the only one not to be built by Palmer's, Jarrow. Registered to British & African Steam Navigation Company, they were constructed to the same design as the passenger ships *Zaria* and *Muraji* delivered by Clyde Shipbuilding & Engineering in 1904 but without a raised poop. They measured 350 x 48ft and could maintain twelve knots by means of three-cylinder reciprocating machinery. *Sapele* and *Adda* were both sunk by submarines in 1917 and *Benue* was sold in 1930 to Compagnia Genovese and renamed *Capo Pino*, being lost in collision in the Dardanelles in February 1937. Her sister, *Chama*, had gone to Naples owners as *Assunzione* in 1930 but rejoined her erstwhile sister in 1933 as Genovese's *Capo Arma*, under which name she was torpedoed by HMS *Turbulent* off Benghazi on 29 May 1942 whilst acting as a government supply ship.

The 4,508gt *Gorjistan* (shown in the Scheldt) was the second of a pair of ships completed in 1905 by W Gray & Company, West Hartlepool, for Frank Strick's Anglo-Algerian Steamship Company. Measuring 373 x 50ft, she and *Turkistan* were the precursors of more than a dozen similar-looking ships of varying sizes ordered by Strick before World War I, many of which were sold before delivery. Three-island ships, their main identifying feature was a pair of kingposts placed close to the bridge front at the forward end of a short No 3 hatch, which in most cases was incorporated into an extended bridge deck. Both were sold to Hamburg-Amerika Linie in 1910 and renamed *Persepolis* and *Ekbatana* respectively, the former running to Brazil with a grey-painted hull. *Ekbatana* was scuttled on 5 April 1914 by Turkish forces in the Shatt al Arab to slow the British advance; *Persepolis* was interned by Italy at Massawah in 1915 and renamed *Belluno*. In 1920 she was sold to S A Cooperativa Garibaldi, becoming first *Pietro Gori*, then *Patria* in 1926 and finally *Ordino* in 1931, being broken up in Savona a year later. Near sisters *Nigaristan* and another *Gorjistan*, completed by W Gray & Co in 1911, also went to Hamburg-Amerika in 1913, as *Liguria* and *Ninive*. The former was scrapped in Hamburg in 1933 but *Ninive* was bought back by Strick from the Shipping Controller after internment at Padang, becoming the seventh *Shahristan*. Sold to Finland in 1934 as *Atlanta* and then *Equator* in 1938, she sank after stranding near Sundsvall at the end of 1941 but was raised and changed hands three more times before being wrecked in the Scheldt in February 1959 after a remarkable forty-eight-year career. (Note: Strick repeated names several times leading to some confusion, for instance three *Shahristans* were ordered consecutively in 1913, all being sold to British India Steam Navigation Company and completed as *Chantala, Ozarda* and *Orna*).

Twin masts

Prentice, Service & Henderson's Crown Line was possibly the first company to employ twin masts in its 4,500gt *Crown of Castile** and *Crown of Aragon* built on Clydeside by D & W Henderson & Co in 1905. The advantage lay in greater derrick outreach and the similarly fitted 5,149gt *Crown of Galicia* followed a year later from A Stephen & Sons, Linthouse. A sister vessel, *Ormiston*, was delivered in 1907 to R & C Allan of Glasgow but joined Crown Line as a second *Crown of Castile* (her forebear having been torpedoed thirty-one miles southwest of Bishop Rock on 30 March 1915), the company having in the meantime received two larger twin-masters, the 5,900gt *Crown of Toledo* and *Crown of Seville* from Russell & Co, Port Glasgow in 1911–12. The remaining *Crowns* were acquired by T & J Harrison in 1920, becoming *Centurion*, *Candidate*, *Craftsman* and *Collegian* respectively, the former having notched up thirty-six years when finally wrecked as *Gladys Moller* off the east coast of Ceylon on 7 November 1942.

Twin half-height masts, with just the forward pair linked by a cross-piece in goalpost fashion, were also adopted by Alfred Holt's 9,000gt *Bellerophon*, completed by Workman, Clark & Company Belfast in 1906 for the transpacific trade, which the company had acquired four years earlier through its acquisition of China Mutual Steam Navigation Company. Lumber was a staple cargo from North American west coast ports to China and the new mast arrangement coupled with large hatches assisted in the loading of the heavy baulks. *Teucer* and *Antilochus** followed from R & W Hawthorn, Leslie & Company, Hebburn, and the final pair *Cyclops* and *Titan* were delivered by D & W Henderson & Company, Glasgow all in 1906. No beauties, they retained the distinctive Holt upright funnel and split superstructure but had less sheer than normal and only a short forecastle in place of the traditional three islands. Their 485 x 58ft hulls incorporated three full decks and they could maintain the comparatively high service speed of thirteen to fourteen knots with twin three-cylinder triple-expansion machinery driving twin screws. Hawthorn, Leslie delivered the slightly modified *Protesilaus* in 1910, which was two feet beamier and had full-height rugby-post masts. The initial three ships survived both world wars and were broken up in the United Kingdom in 1948 but *Titan* and *Cyclops* were torpedoed in 1940 by *U47* and 1942 by *U123* respectively. *Protesilaus* was mined off Swansea on 21 January 1940, never repaired and broken up at Briton Ferry two years later. Goalpost masts were also used in eight subsequent Blue Funnel ships, beginning with *Talthybius* in 1912, which could be distinguished by a longer forecastle extending to the forward pair of posts, whilst the final ship *Achilles*, completed in 1920, had full-height masts. The last Holt ships to have twin masts were the four *Calchas*-class ships built between 1921 and 1923, which had three island hulls and more raked, soft-nosed stems.

Nederland Line shipped a lot of hardwood, such as mahogany, from the Netherlands East Indies and *Celebes** of 1907 followed the lead of Alfred Holt in mounting twin goalpost-type masts. The first of a class of five, she and sister *Lombok* were British-built by Furness Withy & Company, West Hartlepool and William Hamilton & Company, Port Glasgow in 1907. The remaining ships were completed in Holland – a pair, *Sumatra* and *Billiton*, from De Schelde, Flushing, in 1908 and *Nias* from Nederlandsche Scheepsbouw Maats. (NDSM), Amsterdam, in 1909. They measured 5,900gt and 8,250dwt tons on dimensions of 394 x 51ft and were driven at eleven knots by a three-cylinder reciprocating engine developing 2,300ihp. Due to Dutch neutrality, none were lost in World War I. In its aftermath, *Lombok* and *Nias* were fitted with basic accommodation for 195 and 100 persons respectively to meet an urgent need for passenger accommodation to and from the East Indies. All were sold after around twenty years' service, four going to United Netherlands Navigation Company, which scrapped them in Italy and Japan in 1931, while *Lombok* went to Holland Steamship Company. Renamed *Ijstroom*, she went to Belgian breakers in 1934.

New German ships

Norddeutscher Lloyd's first purpose-built cargo liner was *Franken*, completed at Vegesack by Bremer Vulkan in 1905. Together with sisters *Hessen* and *Westfalen* from J C Tecklenborg, Geestemünde, she opened a new Australian cargo service via Suez and the Dutch East Indies but lack of support led to it being changed to a direct service via the Cape of Good Hope in 1907. A short well-deck by way of No 1 hatch and long combined bridge and poop distinguished these three vessels from the three-island type *Schwaben*, *Lothringen* and *Thüringen*, which were delivered in 1906 by Bremer Vulkan (one) and A G 'Weser', Bremen (two). Measurement was just over 5,000gt on hull dimensions of 431 x 53ft and quadruple-expansion machinery developed 2,750ihp for eleven knots in the first three ships and 3,200ihp for twelve knots in the second three. Insulated space was provided for the carriage of meat and fruit. Illustrated is *Westfalen*, which was rebuilt as a catapult ship for Deutsche Lufthansa in 1932 and stationed in mid-South Atlantic waters under Norddeutscher Lloyd management. She was eventually mined in Swedish waters in September 1944 whilst operating for the Luftwaffe. Of the others, three were taken by Australia at the start of World War I, *Franken* by Brazil as *Taubate* and *Schwaben* by the United Kingdom, becoming *Cragness* then *Oakwin* before being lost in 1924. *Taubate* outlived her sisters and was not broken up until 1955.

A three-island design with long bridge deck was employed by Hansa Line for more than sixty cargo ships of differing sizes. From around the turn of the century, ships were also distinguished by a single kingpost aft as depicted here by the war prize *Kingsmere*, built as *Lindenfels* in 1906 by Swan, Hunter & Wigham Richardson along with three sisters. She was one of eight, the others coming from Flensburger Schiffsbau-Gesellschaft (Flensburg Shipbuilding Company) (two), J C Tecklenborg and A G 'Weser' and they shared the same particulars of 5,500gt and 8,600dwt on dimensions of 422 x 55ft. Propulsion was by quadruple-expansion engines. Later Hansa vessels were similar but could be distinguished by having twin kingposts aft. *Kingsmere* became the Greek *Agios Ioannis* in 1922 and passed through several different ownerships under the same name before being broken up in Italy in 1933.

Following its earlier twin-funnelled ships, Deutsche-Australische Dampschiffs-Gesellschaft (DADG) built a long series of ships with only single funnels and a short well-deck between forecastle and foremast, a feature common to many German ships. Depicted here in the Tasmanian port of Burnie is *Plauen*, one of seven sisters built at Flensburg in 1906–7. Measuring 4,210gt on dimensions of 393 x 52ft, they were driven at eleven knots by triple-expansion machinery developing 2,200ihp. *Plauen* became Ellerman's *City of Milan* in 1921 and ten years later the Portuguese *Ganda*; she was shelled and sunk by *U123* west of the Strait of Gibraltar on 20 June 1941. Several different yards were responsible for the next batch of ships, which were similar in design but six feet longer and had taller kingposts. The theme was continued for a number of DADG ships built after World War I.

A large transatlantic series

The 6,305gt *Median** was the lead ship of the largest group of shelter-deckers ever built for North Atlantic cargo service. Fourteen similar ships were built for Leyland Line, part of the International Mercantile Marine Company, between 1908 and 1914 and a further eight between 1921 and 1923. The first four came from Harland & Wolff, Belfast in 1908–9, the remaining ships following between 1912 and 1914 from Scotts' Shipbuilding & Engineering Co (two), D & W Henderson (three), Hawthorn, Leslie (three) Caledon Shipbuilding & Engineering Co (one) and Napier & Miller (one). Sturdy looking ships, the first group were unusual in having two bridge decks separated by No 3 hatch but these were combined into a single structure in the postwar ships. They measured 400 x 52ft and were driven by quadruple-expansion engines giving twelve knots in the first group and fourteen knots, due to higher installed power, in the second. Three of the earlier group were lost during World War I and of the survivors, nine were broken up in the United Kingdom and Italy in 1933 and the remaining pair, which had been sold to Donaldson Line in 1934, went to Italian breakers a year later. Regarding the postwar deliveries, six were sold to T & J Harrison and two to Donaldson in 1934, the latter going on to acquire two of the Harrison ships in 1936. The last to go was *Norwegian*, lead ship of the second group, which became *Maria Elene* in 1954 and was broken up in Osaka in 1959.

CHAPTER

3

Innovations in Machinery and German Competition

The six years leading up to the outbreak of World War I witnessed a number of advances in ship propulsion, beginning in 1908 with the first installation of a new triple-screw system whereby a direct-drive steam turbine positioned on the centreline was run off the waste steam from triple-expansion engines on either side. The idea came from the inventor of the turbine, Charles Parsons, who the following year purchased the old steamer *Vespasian*, built as *Eastern Prince* in 1887, and began a series of trials to perfect the geared steam turbine. Success opened up the way for steam turbines – previously confined to fast passenger ships or warships – to be used in cargo liners. A development of perhaps even greater magnitude – one that would in the course of time have a profound influence on world shipping – concerned the first application in 1912 of an internal-combustion oil engine, named after its inventor Rudolf Diesel, to power a vessel engaged in ocean trade.

By the end of the first decade of the twentieth century, shipping was starting to recover from a prolonged slump. As confidence grew, orders were placed for new cargo ships and a number of those for the Ellerman Group would be the first to incorporate cruiser sterns. Although the United Kingdom still operated by far the largest cargo liner fleet, it was faced with increasing competition from an expanding Germany, which for nationalistic reasons was striving to enhance its global influence; one of the best ways of doing this was to increase its merchant fleet.

Note: An asterisk in a caption indicates the vessel shown in the photograph.

New Zealand meat carriers

New Zealand Shipping Company's *Otaki*, which followed her 1906 W Denny & Brothers-built sisters *Orari* and *Opawa* into service in 1908, had the distinction of being one of the few cargo liners to earn a place in shipping history on account of her novel form of propulsion. This consisted of two three-cylinder triple-expansion engines exhausting into a centreline steam turbine which drove a third screw, an arrangement patented by Charles Parsons that resulted in a 12 per cent reduction in fuel consumption. It would later be used in a number of famous liners, including *Olympic*, *Titanic* and *Britannic*. Denny had to lengthen *Otaki* by five feet at its own expense to guarantee the same 556,000cu ft capacity as her sisters, around half of which was insulated. She measured 7,420gt on hull dimensions of 465 x 60ft and could steam at fourteen knots. She gained further notoriety when she put up a gallant fight against the German commerce raider *Möwe* some 420 miles southwest of Lisbon on 10 March 1917, eventually succumbing, but not before she had inflicted considerable damage on her adversary. Of her sisters, *Orari* was broken up at Glasgow in 1927 and a year later *Opawa* was sold to Norwegian owners in Tønsberg and converted into the whale factory *Antarctic*. She became the Japanese *Antarctic Maru* in 1935 and Nippon Suisan Kisen Kaisha's *Tonan Maru* in 1937 but was torpedoed by USS *Bowfin* off Indo-China in November 1943.

Completed by Workman, Clark & Company, Belfast for Shaw, Savill & Albion in 1909, the twin-screw *Rangatira* was the first of five large frozen-meat carriers for the New Zealand trade. *Waimana* (1913) and *Mahia* (1917) came from the same yard, *Pakeha* from Harland & Wolff in 1910 and *Raranga* from the Tyne yard of Armstrong Whitworth in 1916. They were developments of the earlier *Mamari* class, with the addition of raised forecastle and long bridge deck and an extra hold abaft the machinery. As built, they had rudimentary berthing for 1,000 emigrants in the 'tween decks and measured around 10,100gt, length being 478ft and beam 63ft. Propulsion was by twin triple-expansion engines developing 5,600ihp for a sea speed of thirteen knots, or quadruple-expansion units in the case of *Raranga*. They undertook trooping duties during World War I and the lead ship was wrecked on Robben Island off Cape Town on 31 March 1916. *Waimana* was temporarily transferred to the South American run in 1915 and between 1926 and 1932 ran for Aberdeen Line as *Herminius**. Both *Pakeha* and *Waimana* were taken up by the Admiralty in 1939 and converted to the dummy battleships HMS *Revenge* and HMS *Resolution* respectively, reverting to Ministry of War Transport cargo ships with *Empire* prefixes in 1941. Although bought back by Shaw, Savill & Albion after the war, they were chartered to the British government for meat storage and were both broken up at Briton Ferry in 1950. *Raranga* was scrapped at Blyth in the same year and *Mahia* at Faslane in 1953.

A powerful Blue Funnel series

With shipping going through a slump, Alfred Holt took advantage of low building prices to embark on a long series of powerful cargo liners. *Perseus* (6,728gt) was the first to be delivered by Workman, Clark & Company, Belfast in 1908, followed by *Theseus** and seven more sisters had been completed by 1913. They measured 443 x 53ft and were followed by ten broadly similar but slightly larger ships (455 x 57ft) starting with *Lycaon* in 1913 and ending with *Elpenor* in 1917. All nineteen vessels had a distinctive donkey funnel on the forward side of the main stack and continued the Holt three-island theme with short kingposts topped by ventilator cowls, which became a familiar feature on the Eastern trade routes. Reliable triple-expansion machinery provided a sea speed of fourteen knots when required. Six, including *Perseus*, were lost during World War I and a further five in the course of World War II. *Demodocus* (Workman, Clark, 1912) survived a torpedo attack in 1918 and went on to outlive the other World War II survivors, trading from 1951 as D Pittaluga's *Ircania* and from 1956 as *Miriam* for other Italian owners, until scrapped in Trieste two years later. The broadly similar eleven-ship *Machaon* class, completed between 1920 and 1923, were again a few feet longer and, *Machaon* apart, mounted their donkey exhausts aft of the funnel. The fifteen-knot motorships *Orestes* and *Idomeneus*, built by Workman, Clark in 1926, had similar hulls but funnel and machinery were placed slightly further aft. The latter was equipped in 1933 to carry chilled beef from Australia.

Advanced refrigerated ships for the River Plate

In April 1912, Houlder Brothers introduced a completely new type of twin-screw refrigerated meat carrier to the weekly Liverpool–River Plate service operated in conjunction with Royal Mail Steam Packet Company and Furness Withy. *El Paraguayo** and *El Uruguayo* were products of Irvine's Ship Building & Dry Docks Company, Hartlepool, and Alexander Stephen & Sons respectively and were followed by three more sisters, *La Rosarina* and *La Negra* from Palmers, Jarrow, in 1912–13 and *La Correntina* from Irvine's in November 1912. Gross measurement was 8,508t on dimensions of 440 x 59ft and their insulated capacity of around 400,000cu ft made them the largest of their type. Twin triple-expansion engines gave a speed of twelve knots and basic accommodation was initially provided for 400 steerage passengers. The design was modified for five subsequent ships ordered before the outbreak of World War I. Beginning with *Condesa* in 1916, they were larger at 451 x 61ft and had extended bridge decks incorporating all but No 1 and No 5 hatches. Of the original five ships, *La Correntina* was captured and sunk by the Norddeutscher Lloyd liner *Kronprinz Wilhelm* 320 miles east of Montevideo on 7 October 1914, while the inbound *La Negra* was torpedoed by *UC50* on 3 September 1917 in mid-Channel, WSW of Start Point. The others survived the war and were broken up in 1937, *El Paraguayo* at Newport and *El Uruguayo* in Japan, after sailing out as *Rosarina*.

Early cruiser sterns

The Ellerman Group was one of the first to make use of the cruiser stern, which provided greater waterline length and better buoyancy aft. A particularly full form was adopted as shown in this view of Hall Line's 6,382gt *City of Norwich*, wearing the colours of Bucknall Steamship Lines, which was effectively acquired by John Ellerman in 1908 and re-titled Ellerman & Bucknall Steamship Company in 1914.

She and sister *Kathlamba*, which was built for Bucknall, measured 449ft overall on a beam of 55ft and were products of William Gray, West Hartlepool in July and August 1913. Although in some respects continuing an earlier counter stern design with three long islands and a split superstructure, they set the pattern for around thirty subsequent ships built by a number of yards, principally William Gray, over a fourteen-year period. Very few were actual sisters, and the length of the separate islands also varied. *City of Winchester* delivered by Palmers in 1917 had her forecastle and bridge combined, leaving just a short well at No 5 hatch and this layout applied to more than twenty ships. *City of Norwich* was one of many with three-cylinder reciprocating engines, but exhaust turbines were added to a number of ships from 1915 and full steam turbine propulsion introduced with *City of Canton* in 1916. *City of Norwich* was sold to Italy in 1953 and as *Marinucci* was scrapped at Mukaishima in 1959. *Kathlamba* became *City of Carlisle* in 1927 and was demolished by Arnott Young at Dalmuir in 1934.

African services

T & J Harrison first adopted a three-island design with five holds and a split superstructure with *Barrister* (4,750gt) in 1893. Apart from the company's large four-masted steamers, this concept would become almost standard, subject to increases in size and different positioning of kingposts, until the late 1930s. The first of the more substantial versions began with the 5,421gt *Architect**, completed by Charles Connell in 1912. She and her five sisters carried another Harrison trademark, namely a cowl-topped funnel, and measured 417ft between perpendiculars by 54ft beam. The same dimensions were used for the *Governor* group of ships built between 1918 and 1925, which, apart from the lead ship, carried their pair of posts at the break of the forecastle, whilst the subsequent *Wayfarer* class (1925–6, 396ft) and *Planter* class (1927–30, 420ft) had no posts but retained counter sterns. *Architect*, a twelve-knot steamer driven by a single reciprocating engine, survived World War I but broke her back after stranding on Pluckington Bank off Liverpool's Brunswick Dock on 29 October 1933.

Advanced tonnage spearheads German expansion

Norddeutscher Lloyd's 6,588gt *Rheinland* of 1912 was the first of a dozen cargo liners designed to be interchangeable between the Australian and Far East routes. They had flush decks, something of a rarity in German-built tonnage, and a deadweight measurement of 11,000t on dimensions of 473 x 59ft. Propulsion was by triple-expansion engines developing 4,000ihp for a speed of twelve and a half knots. Some of the later ships were fitted with an extra pair of posts abaft the superstructure, and the final ship *Lippe* (1915) had her mainmast positioned one hatch further forward. The first seven were delivered by Bremer Vulkan, Vegesack, with Flensburger Schiffsbau-Gesellschaft and J C Tecklenborg, Geestemünde, each being responsible for a further pair. World War I soon disrupted the careers of these advanced ships but not before two of them had opened a new service to the River Plate. None were lost during World War I but several were seized – *Elsass, Pommern* and *Mark* by the United States, the latter two ending up in the Luckenbach fleet, *Mark* having operated as *Poznan* for the Polish-American Navigation Corporation between 1920 and 1922; *Pfalz* was taken by Australia in 1914 and renamed *Boorara* and, *Posen* by Brazil in 1917, becoming *Belmonte* then *Mandu*. War reparations saw *Waldeck* and *Altenburg* passing to Chargeurs Réunis as *Dalny* and *Camranh* (wrecked in September 1920 off Singapore) and *Meiningen* to Messageries Maritimes as *Si Kiang*. *Rheinland* became United Netherlands Navigation Company's *Abbekerk** and *Lippe* became Hain Steamship Company's *Tresithney*, passing to Federal Steam Navigation Company as *Pipiriki* in 1924 and being scrapped in Genoa in 1933. *Anholt*, which had spent the war in Java and then briefly been owned by H Hogarth & Sons and Sota y Aznar as *Aya-Mendi*, together with *Dessau*, which had been Thomas Dunlop & Sons' *Voreda*, were bought back by Norddeutscher Lloyd in 1924, *Dessau* being demolished in Hamburg in 1935. *Boorara* was sold to Greece as *Nereus* in 1926 but was wrecked off Vancouver in August 1937. Four were lost in World War II and of the survivors, *Elsass*, which had been named *Appeles, Kermit, Nebraksan* and *Sukhona* (USSR lend-lease) was finally broken up in Baltimore in 1948. *William Luckenbach* (ex-*Pommern*) became Costa Line's *Maria Costa* in 1946 and was scrapped at Savona in 1953. *Mandu*, which bore the name *Comandante Martini* from 1956 and *Bonnetra* from 1958 lasted until November 1966, when a fire at Macieo ended her career.

The *Rheinland* design was modified for seven *Remscheid*-class vessels expressly built for Far East service after Norddeutscher Lloyd had broken an agreement with Hamburg-Amerika and Rickmers Linie not to participate in the trade. Completed between 1915 and 1919, two by Kieler Howaldtswerke, one by Lübecker Flender-Werke and the final four by Bremer Vulkan, Vegesack, they were similar in length with marginally greater beam but differed in having three-island hulls with a long forecastle. Their four masts with pairs of kingposts forward and in front of the bridge completed a powerful-looking design and they were in fact about half a knot faster than the earlier class thanks to an extra 400 horsepower. Of those ceded to the UK Shipping Controller in 1919, three were bought in 1921 by David Steamship Company, a London company acting for the newly formed United Netherlands Navigation Company, which gave a number of ships temporary 'Abbey' names, illustrated here by *Eastminster Abbey* (ex-*Heilbronn*), which became *Aagtekerk* then *Oostkerk* in 1922. She was broken up in Yokohama in 1932, but her sister *Ouderkerk* (ex-*Orsino*, ex-*Gera*) was bought from Italian breakers by Italiani Trasporti Marittimi in 1934 and returned to service as *Gianfranco*. Seized by Argentina in 1941, she became Flota Mercante del Estado's *Rio Salado*, was laid up in 1949 and finally demolished at Barracas in 1955.

Prior to World War I, Deutsche-Australische Dampschiffs-Gesellschaft (DADG) embarked on an extensive new building programme that would make it the third largest ship owner in Hamburg and fifth largest in Germany. The 5,872gt *Fremantle* was the first of seven ships built by J C Tecklenborg, Geestemünde in 1911–12, an eighth *Stolberg* coming from the Flensburger Schiffsbau-Gesellschaft. Measuring 9,600dwt on dimensions of 451 x 57ft, they had seven hatches and a short well forward, a German feature unpopular with crew housed in the forecastle. Other German characteristics were a large funnel casing, tall masts and a pair of kingposts mounted right aft. Some of the class mounted the foremast immediately aft of the well, whilst others had it transposed with the next sets of posts; *Fremantle* had a composite superstructure. Triple-expansion machinery developing 3,600shp gave a sea speed of twelve and a half knots. *Essen* was seized by Portugal in 1916 and renamed *Inhambane*, and *Albany* became the Italian Navy's *Matteo Renato Imbriani* in 1917 but was mined off Planier Island near Marseilles in March 1918. The remaining vessels were surrendered after the war: *Freiberg* and *Düsseldorf* passed through Ellerman Hall hands as *City of Sydney* and *City of Boston* before reverting to German ownership, the former as Kosmos' *Lüneburg** in 1923, repeating the name of a sister that had gone to P&O as *Padua* in 1920 (demolished in Osaka 1933). *Düsseldorf* became Norddeutscher Lloyd's *Grandon* in 1927. *Stolberg* went to Union Steamship Company of New Zealand as *Waitapu* in 1919 and *Fremantle* and *Mannheim* to Messageries Maritimes in 1922 as *Andromède* (scrapped in Italy 1931) and *Lieutenant Saint-Loubert Bié*. *Lüneberg*, as *Sperrbrecher 9*, was mined off La Pallice on the last day of May 1943 and scuttled off Brest on 1 July 1944. After World War II, the damaged *Grandon*, which had been transferred to Hapag in 1934 and renamed *Patagonia* in 1937, was scuttled in the Skagerrak with gas ammunition in 1945. The former *Mannheim* was scrapped at La Seyne in 1950 after suffering mine damage in the Saigon River. *Stolberg* was sold to Hong Kong in 1946 as *Victoria Peak*, and briefly became Wallem & Company's *Shah Rokh* in 1947 before going to China as *Dah Hung*, and was scrapped in 1951. Finally, *Essen* was demolished in Hong Kong in 1959 as the Costa Rican *Vassiliki*.

Flensburger Schiffsbau-Gesellschaft was chosen by Deutsche-Australische Dampschiffs-Gesellschaft (DADG) for another new series of ships, which had fewer holds forward of the machinery than aft, producing a unique if somewhat unbalanced profile. Measuring around 5,900gt on dimensions of 450 x 58ft, they were propelled by three-cylinder reciprocating engines of 3,600ihp producing a sea speed of twelve and a half knots. *Adelaide*, *Sydney* and *Melbourne* were completed in 1911, *Hobart* in 1912 and *Cannstatt* in 1913. The last three were seized by Australia in 1914 and later sailed for Australian Commonwealth Line as *Boonah*, *Barambah* and *Bakara** respectively. *Adelaide* was taken by Portugal in 1916 becoming *Cunene*, and *Sydney* went to Lloyd Royal Belge as *Caucasier* in 1920, being scrapped at Pola in 1932. Postwar deliveries to a similar design in 1919 included *Tannenberg* (originally to be named *Ceylon*), which briefly held the name *Ardover* (David Steamship Company) before passing to Koninklijke Nederlandsche Stoomboot Maats. (KNSM) as *Amersfoort* in 1921, only to be lost through stranding on Antigua on 20 September 1927. The last of the type also passed through David Steamship Company's hands as *Cesario* before becoming United Netherlands' *Meliskerk* in 1921. She too was lost through stranding, on 8 January 1943 off Port St John's, Cape Province. Meanwhile *Boona* and *Bakara*, which had been sold to Roland Line as *Witram* and *Witell* in 1926, became Hamburg South America Line's *Buenos Aires* and *Rosario* in 1936. Taken up as naval transports in World War II, *Buenos Aires* was torpedoed by HMS *Narwhal* off the Skaw on 1 May 1940. *Rosario* survived in a damaged state at Hamburg and became the Finnish *Albertina* and then *Kotka*. In July 1956, two years after *Cunene* had been demolished at Dunston-on-Tyne, she was scuttled by the British Ministry of Transport in the North Atlantic with a cargo of gas ammunition and explosives.

Three larger Deutsch-Australische ships, the 7,500gt *Australia*, *Sumatra* and *Tasmania**, also came from the Flensburg shipyard, in 1912–13, with a fourth unit, *Java*, being completed by Bremer Vulkan in 1912. These had a long forecastle incorporating No 1 hatch and a short well at No 2. Their dimensions were 484 x 63ft and quadruple-expansion engines developing 4,500ihp gave a speed of thirteen and a half knots. *Sumatra* was seized in Sydney in 1914, renamed *Barungra* a year later and torpedoed on 15 July 1918. The others were surrendered in 1919, *Tasmania* going to New Zealand Shipping Company and being scrapped at Rosyth in 1936, the same year that *Australia* was broken up in Osaka. *Java* sailed as Messageries Maritimes' *Min* until taken by the Germans at Bizerta in December 1942. Transferred to Italy as *Conegliano*, she was bombed and sunk off Olbia on 6 June 1943.

Pangani (1919, 5,735gt) was one of the seven-ship *Emir* class built for Deutsche Ost-Afrika Linie between 1911 and 1920 and the first of a pair built by Blohm & Voss, Hamburg, the others coming from Bremer Vulkan, Vegesack. Hull dimensions were 426 x 51ft and they were driven by quadruple-expansion machinery of 3,300ihp for eleven and a half knots, save for the second Bremer Vulkan delivery, *Urundi*, which had geared turbines. Their layout was unusual with a short forecastle and long quarter deck to which was added a raised bridge deck. War interrupted their intended service to East Africa and *Pangani* was surrendered to the UK Shipping Controller shortly after delivery and placed under Glen Line management. In 1921, she was sold to David Steamship Company, briefly holding the name *Cassio* before becoming part of the newly formed United Netherlands Navigation Company, which she served as *Nijkerk* until broken up in Holland in 1950. Sisters *Kagera* and *Rovuma* were ceded to France in reparation, becoming Compagnie Générale Transatlantique (CGT)'s *Indiana* and *Nevada* respectively. The former was used as a US war transport in World War II under Panamanian flag, reverting to CGT in 1945. She was sold to John Livanos & Sons in 1948 and converted into the emigrant ship *Derna*, being renamed *Assimina* a year later. The last survivor of her class, she was broken up in the UK in 1952, three years after *Urundi*, which had borne the names *Empire Thames* and briefly *Kalama*, had been demolished in Antwerp as *Valparaiso*.

The first motor cargo liners

Axel Axelson Johnson inherited his father's enthusiasm for the new diesel engine when he took over from him as head of Johnson Line in 1910. Early in 1912, he ordered two motorships for Rederi A/B Nordstjernan from Burmeister & Wain in order to improve performance in the Brazilian coffee trade. At about the same time, the East Asiatic Company of Denmark was taking delivery of *Selandia*, hailed as the world's first ocean-going motorship, but as she carried twenty-six passengers, Johnson's *Suecia* completed just ten months later could claim to be the first motor cargo liner. Moreover, her engine was positioned three-quarters of the way along her hull, a concept that would be taken up again in the 1920s and then more extensively in the late 1950s and beyond. After *Suecia's* sister, *Pedro Christophersen*, had completed trials in August 1913, Johnson ordered four similar ships, three of which were completed in 1914 and one in 1915. Four more followed between 1917 and 1919, the last two being sold to Rotterdam Lloyd (*Kedoe*) and Bergen Steamship Company (*Cometa*), and the series ended with the MAN-engined *Santos* from Kockums in 1925. Measuring some 3,730gt on dimensions of 365ft in length on a beam of 52ft, the initial pair had flush hulls, three masts and no discernible funnel, engine fumes being passed up a pipe on the mainmast. They were propelled by twin eight-cylinder Burmeister & Wain engines burning 7t of oil a day (comparable steamers needed five times as much coal) and developing 2,000bhp for a speed of ten to eleven knots. The 1914 quartet had six-cylinder engines and the 1917 vessel had more powerful units of 1,600ihp. Deadweight capacity was around 6,500t and all cargo handling was controlled by electric winches. Four of the class went on to survive World War II, three being sold to Hugo Stinnes Reederei and the lengthened and re-engined *Ellen Hugo Stinnes* (built as *Pacific**) lasted until 1980, latterly as the Panamanian *Castor*. (*World Ship Society*)

Shortly before the outbreak of World War I, Atlantic Transport Line commissioned three small cattle carriers, *Maryland*, *Mississippi** and *Missouri*, from Harland & Wolff, Govan for North Atlantic service. Their design featured a short bridge deck with three holds forward and two aft but their main interest lay in the choice of machinery. *Maryland* and *Missouri* had conventional quadruple-expansion engines driving a single screw but *Mississippi*, depicted laid up off Southend near the end of her days, was fitted with twin Burmeister & Wain diesels, each driving a screw, and was the first British motorship on the North Atlantic. The trio measured around 4,730gt on dimensions of 376 x 51ft, but *Mississippi's* cargo capacity was some 5 per cent greater at 416,747cu ft as a result of extra space that would otherwise have been taken up by coal bunkers. All three became casualties of the Great Depression and were broken up by P & W MacLellan at Bo'ness on the Firth of Forth in 1933.

Flushed with the success of its diesel-driven *Selandia* – a world first for ocean shipping completed in 1912 – Denmark's East Asiatic Company embarked on a programme of eleven-knot motor cargo liners starting with the 5,298gt sisters *Siam* and *Annam* delivered by Burmeister & Wain in 1913. Unlike the passenger carrying *Selandia* class, which had three masts and grey four-island hulls, the cargo ships had four masts and flush hulls painted black with a white line. Neither had funnels, engine exhausts in both instances being carried up masts, leading to their being referred to in the East as 'three (or four) sticks bamboo, no phut phut'. *Siam* was torpedoed off Monrovia in September 1942. Four sisters with the same dimensions of 410 x 55ft followed from Burmeister & Wain in 1914–15 but were fitted with twin six-cylinder four-stroke diesels instead of eight-cylinder units. Lead ship *Malakka* was wrecked on her maiden voyage off Mexico's west coast in December 1914 and *Tongking*, shown here in Fowey, was scrapped in Japan in 1938 after suffering fire damage off Penang. *Australien* was bombed at Palermo in 1942 when under German control and *Panama* capsized in the Atlantic in April 1945. A third, slightly longer (425ft), quartet led by *Columbia* followed between 1915 and 1919. All ten ships were employed on East Asiatic Company's extensive cargo services serving Bangkok and the Far East, Africa and Australia as well as the west coasts of the Americas via the West Indies. *Columbia* was torpedoed in August 1915 off Port Said and sisters *Peru* and *Chile* met similar fates in November 1941 and June 1942. *Asia* was scrapped in Japan in 1958 but *Annam* of the original pair outlived them all, becoming Polish Ocean Lines' *Romuald Traugutt* in 1955 and then an accommodation ship, not being broken up until 1972 in Bruges.

Oriental traders

Nederland Line had followed up its *Celebes* series (see page 30) in 1911–12 with the five-ship *Karimoen* class, which retained goalpost masts but had a greater array of kingposts, as well as being considerably larger at nearly 7,000gt on a registered length of 431 by 55ft beam. The next series comprised five 'R'-class ships, which were 29ft longer and 1ft greater in beam and, as with both preceding groups, was built in both British and Dutch shipyards. *Radja** and *Roepat* came from William Hamilton in 1913–14, the latter year also seeing *Riouw* completed by A McMillan, Dumbarton and *Rotti* and *Rondo* emerging from NSM, Amsterdam and Rotterdam Drydock respectively. Tonnage figures averaged 7,500gt and 10,400dwt and their three-cylinder reciprocating engines developed 5,200ihp for a respectable twelve and a half knots. Their conventional mast arrangement distinguished them from the *Karimoen* class and they also had a raised poop. To meet heavy postwar demand for passenger accommodation, *Riouw* was fitted with 187 second-class berths, in addition to her normal ten, between 1920 and 1924. The whole class became victims of the Great Depression and were broken up in 1933, the British-built ships in Japan and their Dutch counterparts in Italy.

Following its acquisition of Thomas & John Brocklebank's share of the Shire Line in 1911, the Royal Mail Steam Packet Company ordered a pair of ships from Workman, Clark & Company, Belfast for Shire's Far East service, which had been started by David Jenkins some fifty years earlier. The 9,426gt *Cardiganshire* and *Carnarvonshire** ranked amongst the finest cargo liners of their day when completed in 1913–14 and were capable of carrying 13,500t of cargo, including refrigerated produce. Overall length was 520ft on a beam of 62ft and they were originally fitted to carry up to 1,000 coolies or pilgrims in their 'tween-decks. Main machinery comprised two sets of triple-expansion engines developing 5,000ihp, which provided a speed of fourteen knots. The same builders were responsible for a smaller pair, *Carmarthenshire* and *Pembrokeshire* (7,823gt, 470ft bp), which each made maiden voyages to the River Plate in 1915 before switching to the Far East trade. These had only two pairs of kingposts at either end of the bridge deck and a single quadruple-expansion engine. The similar-sized *Brecknockshire*, with 2ft greater beam was captured and sunk by the German commerce raider *Möwe* on 15 February 1917, barely a month after entering service, some 490 miles east by north of Cape Frio. The lead ships of each pair were converted to the whale factory ships *Salvestria* and *Sourabaya* by Christian Salvesen in 1929 and became war losses in 1940 and 1942 respectively, whilst the remaining ships were broken up in 1936 at Osaka and Danzig.

CHAPTER

4

World War I

The outbreak of war in 1914 resulted in the removal from the seas of many German ships, which were either interned or seized in ports around the world. Those that made it back to Germany were effectively blockaded. Many shipowners were still taking delivery of ships ordered previously but as the war progressed, construction was increasingly delayed by shortages of materials. Nevertheless a few more early motor ships were built during this period, including some for British owners. In terms of design, a new development occurred in the United States when forward-thinking Luckenbach Line instigated the practice of housing the entire crew in a composite accommodation block amidships.

Germany's switch to unrestricted submarine warfare in 1917 changed the situation dramatically and merchant-shipping losses quickly began to mount, leading the British government to set up the office of the UK Shipping Controller to provide and maintain an effective supply of ships. New construction was standardised as far as possible and ships were built in series, many in foreign shipyards in North America, Hong Kong, China and Japan. Of these, only two fell into the cargo-liner category, notably the G-type refrigerated class. Following its entry into the war in 1917, the United States constructed several large emergency shipbuilding yards on green-field sites, including the hugely expensive Hog Island facility in the Delaware River, which was responsible for a standard series of cargo ships that would form the backbone of US liner services during the interwar period.

Tall-funnelled quintet

Unusually tall funnels 66ft in height distinguished Lamport & Holt's 7,200gt *Meissonier* class, four of which were delivered in 1914–15 by A McMillan & Son, Dumbarton (1) and Russell & Co, Port Glasgow (3), whilst *Marconi* was not completed by Harland & Wolff (launched at Govan), until 1917 due to war shortages. An otherwise well-balanced profile with short forecastle was somewhat hampered by a lack of sheer and they measured 440 x 56ft. Six holds were fully refrigerated for the carriage of frozen meat from Argentina. Propulsion was by means of twin four-cylinder quadruple-expansion engines giving a service speed of twelve and a half knots. The slightly smaller, single screw *Millais* (torpedoed as Blue Star's *Scottish Star* on 2nd February 1942) was completed by Harland & Wolff in September 1917 and on 3rd October *Memling* was sufficiently damaged by torpedo off Brest to be declared a constructive total loss. *Meissonier*, *Murillo* and *Moliere* were transferred to Nelson Line in 1929–30, passing to Royal Mail two years later and renamed *Nasina*, *Nalon* and *Nela* respectively. All five ships were chartered to Union-Castle Mail Steamship Company to lift seasonal fruit at various times between 1930 and 1937 and *Marconi* is shown here wearing that company's funnel colours. *Nalon* (ex-*Murillo*), was bombed and sunk west of Ireland on 6 November 1940 and *Marconi* was torpedoed on 21 May 1941 southeast of Cape Farewell. *Nasina* (ex-*Meissonier*) became SA Co-operativa di Navigazione Garibaldi's *Asmara* in 1935 and was torpedoed on 11 August 1943 by HMS *Unshaken* near Brindisi whilst acting as an Italian naval transport. Only *Nela*, the former *Moliere*, survived hostilities to be broken up by Van Heyghen Frères at Ghent in 1946.

Early British and Norwegian motor ships

Due to the enthusiasm of Lord Pirie, chairman of shipbuilder Harland & Wolff and also a director of Glen Line, the latter became the first British liner company to adopt the diesel engine wholeheartedly. Its first motor vessel, *Glenartney*, was acquired in 1915 from Elder Dempster for which she had been launched in Belfast as *Montezuma*. She was joined by sister *Glenamoy** in 1916 and both measured 7,263gt on a length of 436ft, being propelled at twelve knots by twin twelve-cylinder Burmeister & Wain diesels. *Glenartney* was torpedoed by *UC54* thirty miles northeast of Cape Bon on 6 February 1918 but her sister continued in service until 1936 when, with a worn-out engine, she was sold under the British government's 'Scrap and Build' scheme to Springwell Shipping and was broken up the following winter by Metal Industries at Rosyth.

The next ship built by Harland & Wolff for Glen Line was the 5,075gt *Glenavy*, which bore a passing resemblance to some of the new Scandinavian three-masted motorships. Her three-island-type hull incorporated three full decks whilst twin six-cylinder Burmeister & Wain engines provided a speed of ten and a half knots. In 1923, she was sold to Pacific Steam Navigation Company and renamed *Lagarto* (as shown). At the same time, her engine was adapted to the new airless injection system, which was rapidly becoming the norm. She served continuously on her owner's South American services up to the end of 1947, when engine trouble forced her to lay up at Birkenhead; she was scrapped at Troon the following year.

Fred Olsen & Company took delivery of Norway's first motorship, the 4,800gt *Brazil*, from Akers Mek Verksted, Oslo, in 1914. Built for South American service, she was joined by the 6,100gt *Bayard* in 1916 and in the same year Burmeister & Wain completed the even larger three-masted *George Washington*, shown here with World War I neutrality markings, for a new North Pacific service via the newly opened Panama Canal. She measured 461 × 56ft and was the first of a series of 9,500gt twin-screw vessels, *Theodore Roosevelt* following in 1920. The third and fourth units, *Knute Nelson* and *Benjamin Franklin* were completed by Odense Shipyard in 1926 and St Nazaire in 1927. Odense was also responsible for two improved versions with refrigerated capacity, *Abraham Lincoln* and *Laurits Swenson*, delivered in 1929–30. *George Washington* and *Theodore Roosevelt* were sold in 1934 and 1936, the former being renamed *Rabaul*; she was sunk by the German commerce raider *Atlantis* in May 1941, while the latter became the Norwegian *Helgoy*, the Polish *Mikolaj Rej* in 1950 and the Chinese *Nan Hai 148* in 1960, and was presumed scrapped about 1970. *Knute Nelson* saved 449 passengers and crew from the Donaldson liner *Athenia*, the first ship to be sunk in World War II but was seized by Germany in 1940 and mined and sunk off Obrestad in September 1944. The final pair survived the war and lasted until 1962 and 1963 respectively, *Abraham Lincoln* serving as the Finnish *Korsholma* from 1952.

Large British meat carriers

The offer of quick delivery dates plus a French government subsidy, led Federal Steam Navigation Company late in 1913 to order three refrigerated emigrant ships with 300 berths from Ateliers & Chantiers de France, Dunkirk for the Federal & Shire service to Australia operated jointly with Turnbull, Martin & Company. Due the outbreak of war, *Devon* (laid down as *Cornwall*) was the only one delivered to Federal, in 1915, her sisters having requisitioned by France. She measured 9,660gt and 11,300dwt on overall dimensions of 495 x 60ft and had a short forecastle and long bridge deck, incorporating No 3 hatch at its forward end, and was the first in the Federal fleet to have a cruiser stern. The four stump masts had tall, removable topmasts to enable passage up the Manchester Ship Canal. Twin triple-expansion engines developed 5,000ihp for thirteen knots. From Clyde shipyards, Federal ordered two replacements without passenger facilities and driven by twin geared turbines of 4,000shp for 14 knots. *Cumberland* was completed by Wm Hamilton in 1915 and *Westmoreland* (sic) by D & W Henderson in spring 1917. A few months later, on 6 July, *Cumberland* hit a mine laid by the German raider *Wolf* off Gabo Island, southeast Australia and was beached. After refloating, she sank near Eden, New South Wales on 12 August after a bulkhead collapsed. Meanwhile, the second of the French sisters, which had been launched as *Aberdeenshire*, had been completed in 1916 as Compagnie Générale Transatlantique's *La Perouse* and *Jacques Cartier* followed in 1918. *Devon* was sold to British India Steam Navigation Company in 1934 and became a cadet ship, but was sunk on 19 August 1941 by the raider *Komet* 200 miles southwest of the Galapagos. *Westmoreland*, having survived a torpedo hit in World War I and severe mine damage in the Liverpool approaches in January 1941, was sunk by *U566* with torpedo and gunfire, 240 miles north of Bermuda, on 1 June 1942. *Jacques Cartier* was renamed *Winnipeg* for Canadian service in 1929 and sold to Compagnie France Navigation in 1938, returning to CGT a year later when her new owner went bankrupt. Captured from Vichy France by the Dutch sloop *Van Kinsbergen* off Martinique in June 1941, she was managed for the British Ministry of War Transport first by Thomas & James Harrison and from 1942 by Canadian Pacific Steamships as *Winnipeg II*, but was torpedoed on 22 October by *U443* in North Atlantic convoy ON139. *La Perouse* became Blue Star's *Trojanstar* in 1924 and then *Trojan Star* five years later, outliving her sisters to be broken up in Blyth in 1955.

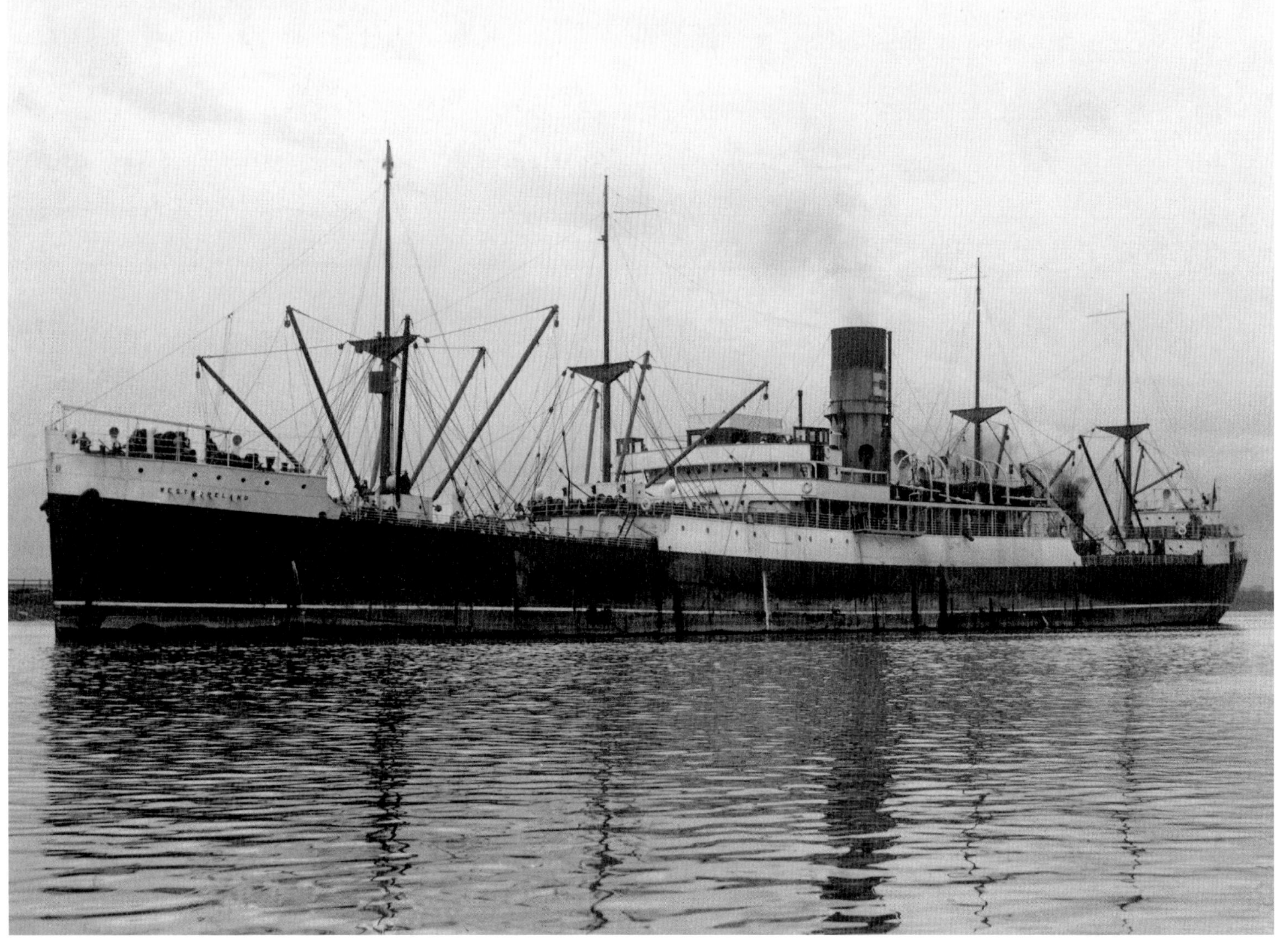

Federal Steam Navigation Company received a large single ship, *Northumberland*, from Swan, Hunter & Wigham Richardson, Wallsend, early in 1916. Shown here after the removal of her fore and jigger topmasts in 1935, she measured 11,559gt on overall dimensions of 530 x 63ft and had a capacity for 786,000 cu ft of cargo, about half of which was insulated in twelve chambers. Her basic layout was similar to *Devon*, but the forecastle was extended to the foremast. Two sets of double-reduction geared turbines gave her a service speed of fourteen knots. She served as a troopship in the latter part of World War I and her boilers were converted to oil-firing in 1926. She served as a cadet ship after *Devon* and was again employed for trooping duties during the early part of World War II, not being finally broken up until 1951 by Thomas W Ward at Inverkeithing after a useful thirty-five-year career.

Early Japanese cargo ships

Aided by government subsidies, the Japanese merchant marine expanded rapidly before World War I. Up to this time, leading company Nippon Yusen Kaisha had concentrated on the passenger business, relying on second-hand tonnage for its cargo needs. In 1913, however, it bought on the stocks two three-island cargo steamers under construction by Russell & Co, Port Glasgow, which were completed as *Tokushima Maru* and *Tottori Maru*. A third, 444ft-long version, *Tsushima Maru*, came from Port Glasgow, by which time Japanese naval architects had studied the earlier ships and come up with a very similar but even larger design of ship, six of which were built by Mitsubishi, Nagasaki and five by Kawasaki, Kobe. *Toyama Maru*, pictured here in the Suez Canal, was the second Mitsubishi delivery, in June 1915. Her hull measured 462ft overall by 58ft, giving tonnage figures of 7,386gt and 10,600dwt. Main machinery varied, some vessels having reciprocating engines and others steam turbines, but all were capable of twelve knots. One was lost in collision in February 1916, another became a war loss in 1918 and a further seven were lost in World War II. *Toyama Maru* was transferred to Nanyo Kisen Kaisha in 1935 and *Tokiwa Maru* was sold in 1939, leaving just *Toba Maru*, which was taken by the Nationalist Chinese in a damaged state in Keelung in June 1945, repaired and renamed *Tai Nan*. She became *Foo Yu* three years later and was finally broken up in Kaohsiung in 1958.

Advanced US Intercoastal cargo liners

The 8,151gt sisters *Edward Luckenbach* and *Julia Luckenbach* were delivered to Luckenbach Steamship Company in 1916–17 by Bethlehem Steel's Fore River Shipyard at Quincy. They had flush hulls with cruiser sterns and were the first freighters to house the entire crew in a composite two-deck superstructure amidships, a practice that would later be widely adopted. Measuring 456 x 57ft, they were followed in 1917–18 by the 468 x 56ft *F J Luckenbach*, *K I Luckenbach* and *Katrina Luckenbach*, whilst the similar *Walter A Luckenbach* was completed by Seattle Construction & Dry Dock Company in 1918 with six sets of posts and a single tall signal mast abaft a short funnel. A further quartet ordered from Sun Shipbuilding & Dry Dock Company, Chester – the first two intended as *M E Luckenbach* and *Jacob Luckenbach* – were delivered to the US Shipping Board in 1919 as *South Bend, Marica, Sol Navis* and *Edellyn*. They had two goalpost masts. Following service as troop transports, they were returned to Luckenbach between 1920 and 1923 and renamed *J L Luckenbach, Lilian –, Harry –* and *Dorothy Luckenbach** respectively. Finally, in 1919, the Quincy yard completed the 10,660gt/14,200dwt *Andrea F Luckenbach* and *Lewis Luckenbach* (527 oa x 68ft), which also had two goalpost masts and eight hatches. All but the first two ships had twin screws, motive power being geared steam turbines for speeds ranging from twelve and a half to fourteen knots. *Edward Luckenbach* was mined off the Florida Coast on 21 July 1939. Four were lost in 1943: *Andrea –*, torpedoed by *U221* on 10 March; *Harry –*, with all hands by *U91* a week later; *Lilian –*, through collision on the 27 March, and *Julia –*, also by collision, on 23 September. *Lewis –* and *Dorothy Luckenbach* were converted to the hospital ships *Louis A Milne* and *Ernestine Koranda* in 1944 and, after transfer to the USMC in 1946, were laid up and demolished on the US west coast at Portland and Oakland in 1957. *F J Luckenbach* became the barge *Comptroller* in 1947 and was broken up in 1951. Sisters *K I –* and *Katrina Luckenbach* were renamed *Stocksun* and *Stockstar* in 1951 and scrapped in Tokyo and Baltimore in 1954 and 1953 respectively. *J L Luckenbach* became the Panamanian *San Francisco* in 1948, then the Indonesian *Diponegoro* in 1951 and *Djakarta Raya* a year later. *Walter A Luckenbach* briefly held the name *A L Bisso*, before being sold to Turkey in 1950 and renamed *Mardin*. Re-engined in 1955 with reciprocating machinery taken from a corvette, she was finally scrapped in Bremerhaven in 1959, the same year that *Djakarta Raya* was demolished in Hong Kong. (*A Duncan*)

German wartime completions

In 1917, Bremer Vulkan delivered the first of five large *Friesland*-class vessels to Hamburg-America Line, none of which were destined to serve their owner. Measuring 10,965gt on dimensions of 521 x 64ft, they had three-island hulls with masts placed at either end of a long bridge deck. Two sets of triple-expansion engines provided a sea speed of twelve knots. All were ceded to Great Britain after World War I but *Rheinland* foundered en route. The rest became useful units of the Federal Steam Navigation Company fleet, sailing as *Hertford, Cumberland**, Huntingdon*, and *Norfolk* but all became victims of torpedo attack during World War II. *Cumberland* was the first to be lost, sinking eight miles from Inishtrahull on 24 August 1940, after being damaged during an attack on her convoy by *U57* the previous day. *Huntingdon*, and *Norfolk* were both sunk in the first half of 1941, the former in convoy 500 miles west of the Hebrides by *U96* on 24 February, and the latter by *U552* 150 miles northwest of Malin Head on 18 June. Finally *Hertford* succumbed to *U751* on 29 March 1942, 150 miles southwest of New Bedford, Massachusetts.

Federal Steam Navigation Company also received in 1919 the first of two slightly larger four-masters (10,982gt, 525 x 66ft), which had been delivered as *Vogtland* to Hamburg-America by J C Tecklenborg in 1916. She differed from *Friesland* in having a normal length bridge deck incorporating a very short hatch forward of a more composite accommodation block. Renamed *Cambridge*, she served her new owner throughout the interwar period but her luck ran out on 7 November 1940, when she foundered off Wilson's Promontory in the Bass Strait, after striking a mine laid by the raider *Pinguin*, formerly Hansa Line's *Kandelfels* (see page 80). *Vogtland*'s sister, *Kurland*, completed in 1920, was handed over to Dollar Steamship Company in 1921 and renamed *Robert Dollar*. She became *Chief Capilano** in 1928 and the Philippine *Don Jose* in 1937 but was bombed by Japanese aircraft whilst anchored off Corregidor on 2 January 1942 and beached. Refloated, she was taken to Hong Kong but was later bombed by US aircraft and broken up.

British wartime deliveries

Thos & Jno Brocklebank, which had been acquired by Cunard Line in 1911, first adopted the cruiser stern in *Maihar*, completed by Russell & Company, Port Glasgow, in June 1917. In other respects, however, she was a typical example of the three-island design favoured by the company, and is shown here transitting the Suez Canal in the 1950s after the removal of her main topmast. She measured 8,071gt on registered dimensions of 470 x 58ft and was driven at twelve knots by a triple-expansion engine. She was followed by sister *Mahsud*, whilst *Matheran* and *Malakand* came from the neighbouring Lithgow yard in 1918–19, the latter pair being lost in World War II. *Mahsud* had an eventful war, which ended when she was beached in Gibraltar Bay after being holed by an Italian human torpedo. Repaired in 1945, she was eventually sold to Greek breakers in 1956. Six years later, *Maihar* was sold to Liberia's Eastbound Tankers Corporation as *Capella* and was scrapped the following year in Hirao, Japan. Two larger pairs of sisters followed from the Clyde in 1920–21, *Mangalore* and *Mathura* from Charles Connell and *Manipur* and *Magdapur* from William Hamilton, which differed in having longer bridge decks with the superstructure split round the No 3 hatch and an extra hatch at the after end. The latter pair also had a long forecastle and poop. Too large for the Calcutta trade, they were laid up during the Depression years but, in 1935, in a most unusual move, they were shortened by 37.5 and 26.5ft respectively, in way of No 4 hold by Smith's Dock, Middlesbrough. Later Brocklebank ships, beginning with *Matra* in 1926, had the navigating bridge one deck higher and, apart from a shorter bridge deck ending before No 4 hatch, the same basic design was carried through to World War II.

In 1918, the Furness Withy Group took delivery of four large cargo ships for Prince Line's new westbound, round-the-world service. They were built in pairs, *Gaelic Prince** and *Celtic Prince* by Short Brothers, Sunderland, and *Gothic Prince* and *Slavic Prince* by Palmers, Jarrow. Their flush hulls were something of a rarity in British-built cargo liners and they could operate either as open or closed shelter-deckers, respective gross measurements being 6,506t and 8,655t. Propulsion was by quadruple-expansion engines giving twelve knots in service. They were replaced by more economical motor ships in 1926 and were sold to Hansa Line, becoming *Rheinfels*, *Schonfels*, *Sonnenfels* and *Rabenfels* respectively. In 1938, all four were sold on to Hamburg South America Line and later became war casualties. *Bahia Blanca* – the former *Celtic Prince* – foundered with all hands in January 1940 after hitting an iceberg in the Denmark Strait whilst attempting to re-supply a German cruiser. Four months later *Bahia Castillo* (ex-*Gaelic Prince*) hit a mine laid by HMS *Narwhal* off the Skaw on 1 May 1940, was towed to Kiel and broken up. *Bahia Laura* – the former *Slavic Prince* – was torpedoed by HMS *Trident* off the Lofoten Islands on 30 August 1941. Finally, *Bahia Camerones* (ex-*Gothic Prince*) was attacked by RN warships in January 1945 whilst repatriating German troops from Norway, beached and became a total loss.

World War I standard types

Japanese shipyards were responsible for a number of standard cargo-ship designs during World War I, the largest of which were the 'A' and 'T' types, suitable for the liner trades. Both had similar dimensions (445 x 58ft) to Nippon Yusen Kaisha's T-class ships (see page 47) but the former had both well decks filled in to form a shelter deck, which increased gross measurement to just under 8,200t. Five of these vessels were purchased by the UK Shipping Controller and sold on to British liner companies in 1919. *War Armour*, completed in 1918 by Asano Shipbuilding Company at Tsurumi, became Royal Mail's *Glamorganshire** until broken up in Holland in 1933. The others were sold off in 1919, *War Lance* and *War Sailor* to British India Steam Navigation Company as *Hatarana* and *Hatipara*, and *War Nymph* to Larrinaga Steamship Company as *Pilar de Larrinaga*. *War Helmet*, operated by Royal Mail on behalf of the Shipping Controller, was torpedoed by *UC75* in April 1918. (*A Duncan*)

Concerned at the heavy losses of refrigerated tonnage, the UK Shipping Controller placed orders with several British shipyards for a standard class of twenty-nine high-class insulated ships. Known as the 'G' type, they measured approximately 8,000gt on dimensions of 465ft oa by 59ft and their hull layout included a high forecastle and poop, the latter incorporating a heavy cruiser stern. Only *War Argus* was complete by the time the war ended and seven contracts were cancelled, but the remainder were divided into two groups, one having twin-screw reciprocating engines for thirteen and a half knots, and the other single-screw geared turbines giving fourteen knots. Completed to owners' requirements, they differed slightly in appearance. Six of the twin-screw versions were acquired by British India Steam Navigation Company in 1919, *Nardana** shown here on trials having been laid down as *War Sybil* by Barclay, Curle. In 1929, she was altered to accommodate thirty-nine cadets as one of the company's training ships but she was torpedoed by *U124* northeast of the Cape Verde Islands on 8 March 1941. Of the turbine ships, Port Line's *Port Curtis* and Koninklijke Hollandsche Lloyd's *Salland* had raked funnels and masts, whilst Nelson Line's *Highland Warrior* had her bridge mounted one deck higher than the others. Three were scrapped in the late 1930s and a further thirteen were lost during World War II. Of the surviving six, four were broken up in the UK in 1947–8 and *Salland* in Bruges in 1958, after sailing as *Panormitis* for the final two years. *Port Curtis* was sold in 1936 and passed through two ownerships before becoming the Soviet *Kronshtadt* after World War II. Some twenty years later, she went to Bulgaria as *Algeneb* and was finally scrapped in Bilbao in 1970 after a remarkable fifty-year career.

The United States' huge Hog Island emergency shipbuilding facility produced its first prefabricated 'standard ship', *Quistconck*, in December 1918, a month after the end of World War I. The facility was only just getting into its stride and went on to complete a further 122 ships by January 1921, 110 of which were 5,500gt, 7,500dwt 'Type A' 'tweendeckers, measuring 410ft oa by 46ft and fitted with 2,500shp oil-fired steam turbines for eight to ten knots. They had a three-island layout with a long bridge deck, vertical stem and counter stern and were totally devoid of sheer, which tended to give them a permanently hogged appearance, although their nickname 'Hog Islanders' was derived from their birthplace. They were quickly sold off with operating subsidies to US steamship lines and formed an invaluable part of America's interwar merchant fleet, some even being converted to passenger ships. Illustrated in Hamburg is *Conejos* (1920), which had a very short career, going missing in the Black Sea in December 1923 after leaving Poti. Fifty-eight of the class became casualties in World War II.

CHAPTER

5

Difficult Trading and the Rise of the Motorship

Most of Germany's surviving cargo liners were ceded to the Allies after the Armistice and trading conditions were generally good in the immediate postwar period. This situation proved to be short-lived, as surplus war-built tonnage flooded onto the market and the general economic situation deteriorated. Later widespread industrial unrest and rising prices culminated in the Wall Street crash of 1929.

In terms of ship design, accommodation for officers and crew was increasingly combined in a single midships structure and raked, soft-nosed stems began to appear together with the more widespread adoption of cruiser sterns. Towards the middle of the 1920s, a number of interesting ships began to appear with engine-rooms placed three quarters of the way aft, but the practice was short-lived and did not again come into fashion for another thirty years. A year or two later, the first special heavy-lift ships to be operated by liner companies began entering service, those of Hansa Line being early users of the new cutaway Maierform bow design aimed at lowering resistance.

On the propulsion front, the use of diesel engines gradually spread and a few more British liner companies, principally those engaged in the long-distance refrigerated trades, decided to make the switch from steam propulsion. Many of the more conservative owners, however, still hedged their bets and stuck to the tried and tested methods but even these were changing, as oil-fired steam turbines became more commonplace and existing plants began to be converted to burn oil instead of coal.

Note: An asterisk in a caption indicates the vessel shown in the photograph.

Meat carriers for the Argentine and Antipodes trades

To replace ageing tonnage, Royal Mail Steam Packet Co ordered four new 8,800gt meat carriers for its River Plate trade during World War I, *Navasota** and *Nagara* being delivered by Swan, Hunter & Wigham Richardson, Low Walker, in 1918 and *Nariva* and *Natia* by Alexander Stephen, Linthouse in 1920. They represented a marked advance on the company's previous tonnage with raised forecastle and long bridge deck extending forward of the bridge to incorporate Nos 2 and 3 hatches, whilst their 430 x 61ft hulls were the first in the fleet to have cruiser sterns. Twin four-cylinder, quadruple-expansion engines drove them at a steady thirteen to fourteen knots. All four were lost during World War II, lead ship *Navasota* (seen off Tilbury) being the first to go, torpedoed by *U47* (Otto Prien) 150 miles west of Bishop Rock on 5 December 1939. The others were also lost in the Atlantic: *Natia* by the raider *Thor* on 8 October 1940, *Nariva* was abandoned after being hit by *U600* and sunk by *U91* and finally *Nagara* was hit by *U404* on 29 March 1943 and sank six days later.

Between 1918 and 1923, sister companies Federal Steam Navigation Company and New Zealand Shipping Company took delivery of six advanced refrigerated meat carriers for the Antipodes trade. Palmers Shipbuilding & Iron Company was responsible for *Kent** and *Surrey*, Earle's Shipbuilding & Engineering Company for *Somerset* and *Tekoa*, Swan, Hunter & Wigham Richardson for *Middlesex* and William Hamilton & Company for *Turakina*. They were large ships averaging 8,600gt and 11,600dwt and had short forecastles and a long bridge deck incorporating three holds and a split superstructure. Dimensions were 460 x 63ft and propulsion by means of steam turbines geared to a single screw for a speed of around fourteen knots. *Tongariro* and the twin-screw motor ship *Limerick** completed by William Hamilton in 1925 for New Zealand Shipping Company and Union Steam Ship Company of New Zealand respectively, differed from the others in having a combined forecastle and bridge deck extending almost to the stern, which was of the cruiser type rather than the cruiser spoon of the earlier ships. Two slightly larger ships, the single-screw, 470ft *Hurunui* (originally intended for Federal Steam Navigation Company) and the twin-screw 495ft *Cornwall*, completed by Sir Raylton Dixon and Hamilton in 1920, also differed in having shorter bridge decks and the latter had a composite superstructure abaft No 3 hatch. Six became war losses, *Turakina* falling victim to the German raider *Orion* in the Tasman Sea in August 1940 after putting up a gallant fight. Of the four survivors, *Cornwall* was broken up at Briton Ferry in 1949, *Kent* at Blyth in 1955 and *Tongariro* in Hong Kong in 1960 after a final loaded voyage out as *Far East Trader*. *Tekoa* spent her final four years transporting whale products, firstly as Hector Whaling's *Enderby* and from 1960 as the Japanese *Kyokurei Maru*, before being scrapped in Japan in 1962.

US freighters with engines aft

Matson Lines pioneered the engines-aft passenger liner with *Lurline* in 1908 and five larger versions followed. In 1921, the concept was applied to two large cargo liners, *Manukai* and *Manulani**, which were specifically designed to transport fruit – mainly pineapples – from Hawaii to California. General cargo ships of this design were unusual; Holland's Koninklijke Paketvaart Maats. had built the 8,000dwt, twin-masted *Ombilin* in 1915 and Italian yards subsequently produced a number of 6,600dwt and 8,300dwt tramps, but the Matson pair were possibly unique in being fitted with four masts, together with a very tall funnel. Constructed by Moore Dry Dock, Oakland, they measured 9,550gt and 14,000dwt on a length of 480ft and were propelled at thirteen knots by steam turbines. In 1948, *Manukai* was sold to become the Panamanian *Sorol* and three years later went to Hong Kong owners as *St Vincent*. As such she suffered a machinery breakdown in 1952 and was broken up in Yokohama. Her sister became the Italian-owned but Panamanian-registered *Providencia* in 1949, her name being changed to *Previdance* in 1963, and she was scrapped at Split in 1967 after a remarkable forty-five-year career.

Turbine ships for the North Atlantic

The influence of the new Luckenbach (see page 48) ships was clearly to be seen in a series of five advanced 7,930gt cargo liners built for Furness Withy in 1922–3 by Furness Shipbuilding Company, Haverton Hill. Built on the straight-frame principle, they had no appreciable hull sheer, which gave them a permanently hogged look. They measured 450 x 58ft and were driven at fourteen knots by two sets of steam turbines. The lead ship, *Feliciana*, was soon renamed *London Mariner* to match the *London* prefix of subsequent ships, all being intended for the London–New York service. This proved unprofitable and their subsequent histories became varied. *London Merchant* was put on the North Pacific run in 1924 and three others were transferred to Prince Line in 1928 but all were laid-up during the Depression years. *London Importer*, the last in the series, was sold to the Admiralty in 1933, becoming the stores ship HMS *Reliant* and in 1935 the remainder were sold to Thos & Jas Harrison. All but one of these were lost during World War II, *Politician* being wrecked on Eriskay Island and gaining lasting notoriety as a result of Compton Mackenzie's novel *Whisky Galore*, which was based on the islanders' looting of her cargo of whisky. Survivor *Collegian* was broken up at Milford Haven in 1948, whilst *Reliant* was sold to Maltese owners in 1948 and converted to the cargo ship *Anthony G*. A year later she became *Firdausa* of Pakistan's East West Steamship Company and was not broken up until 1963 in Karachi. (*Laurence Dunn*)

The British & African Steam Navigation Company built four large steamers *Calgary, Cochrane, Calumet* and *Cariboo** for its Canadian service between 1921 and 1924. All products of John Brown & Company, Clydebank, they measured 7,206gt and 10,627dwt on dimensions of 440 x 59ft and were distinguished from earlier company ships by a long bridge deck incorporating hatches Nos 3 and 4, the former having a pair of kingposts unusually positioned half way between bridge and fidley. Two-deck ships, they had a cargo capacity of 464,000cu ft of grain and 18,000cu ft of refrigerated cargo in three chambers. They were driven by three sets of Curtiss steam turbines developing 2,500shp for eleven knots. *Cariboo* foundered in 1928 after striking rocks off East London whilst riding out a gale but her sisters passed into Elder Dempster ownership in May 1933, survived World War II and were converted to oil-burners in 1947. *Calumet* was the only one sold for further trading, becoming the Panamanian *Pacific Concord* in 1955 and the Hong Kong-registered *Oceanic Enterprise* a year later, being broken up at Mihara, Japan, in 1960. Her sisters were sold direct to British and Dutch breakers in 1957, *Calgary* being demolished by Thomas W Ward at Grays a year later.

Delivered by Van der Giessen & Zonen, Krimpen-aan-den-IJssel, in April 1921, *Burgerdijk* was the first of eight 6,850gt turbine-driven cargo liners for Holland-America Line's Canadian and US services. Three more came from Giessen, two from de Noord and one each from Boele's and Fijenoord. Their design featured a raised forecastle and split superstructure and their main machinery comprised twin double-reduction turbines developing 3,000shp, geared to a single screw for a service speed of just over twelve knots. *Blijdendijk* burned out in the Red Sea in March 1930 and four more were lost during World War II, the only survivor being *Blommersdijk*, pictured here in New York, which had been operated by the British Ministry of War Transport. In 1957, she was sold to Pietro Longobardo of Catania and as *Vivara* was broken up in Savona three years later. Two longer, 450ft versions, *Gaasterdijk* and *Grootedijk*, were completed by New Waterway Shipbuilding, Schiedam in 1922–3. In 1931 they were sold to United Netherlands Navigation Company, renamed *Gaasterkerk* and *Grootekerk* and rebuilt with lengthened Maierform bows. Both were torpedoed in World War II, the former by *U68* on 8 October 1942 in the Indian Ocean and the latter with all hands by *U123* on 24 February 1941 on a voyage from Swansea to Freetown. (*Roger Scozzafava*)

The final Harrison four-masters

The final deliveries in Thos & Jas Harrison's long series of large four-masted ships were slightly larger developments of the *Huntsman* quintet built between 1904 and 1912 by Charles Connell and D & W Henderson, two of which had become World War I losses. *Defender* was completed by Charles Connell in 1915, *Astronomer* followed from D & W Henderson two years later and finally Charles Connell delivered *Diplomat* and *Huntsman** in 1921. They had three-island hulls with a long bridge deck and averaged 8,300gt on a deadweight of around 12,000t. Dimensions were 482ft x 58ft and propulsion of the first two was by quadruple-expansion engines rated at 720nhp for a speed of thirteen knots. The final pair had three sets of double-reduction geared turbines rated at 871nhp but these turned out to be somewhat uneconomical in operation. *Huntsman* was captured in the South Atlantic by the German pocket battleship *Admiral Graf Spee* on 10 October 1939 and sunk two days later, her crew later being rescued by HMS *Cossack* from the supply ship *Altmark* in Jossingfjord. *Astronomer* was torpedoed by *U58* seventy-five miles north of Kinnaird Head on 1 June 1940 and *Diplomat* by *U104* off northwest Ireland on 27 November. *Defender*, which had survived a torpedo hit off Queenstown in July 1918 and later the huge ammunition explosion caused by a German air attack on Bari in December 1943, was finally broken up at Barrow in 1952 by Thomas W Ward.

Dutch East Indies sisters

Siantar and *Modjokerto* were built for Rotterdam Lloyd's eastern services by William Gray's Wear shipyard, Sunderland, in 1921. Measuring 8,439gt on dimensions of 433 x 57ft, they were single-screw vessels propelled by two sets of double-reduction geared steam turbines and could maintain eleven and a half knots in service. Between 1930 and 1934, *Modjokerto** was slowly converted to a motor ship by Wilton-Fijenoord in Rotterdam at the same time being given a Maierform bow and new squat funnel as depicted. Gross measurement was increased to 8,668t and length to 480ft, whilst new twin six-cylinder Sulzer diesels increased speed to fifteen and a half knots. *Siantar* was similarly modified by Rotterdam Drydock between 1932 and 1934. *Modjokerto* was torpedoed south of Tjilatjap on 1 March 1942 by the Japanese submarine *I54* and sunk with all hands by gunfire from the cruiser *Chikuma*. *Siantar* had left Tjilatjap a day earlier and was torpedoed two days after her sister by the submarine *I1* [*i one*] some 800 miles to the south en route to Australia.

Australian traders

The Commonwealth & Dominion Line was formed in January 1914 through an amalgamation of Corry, Milburn, Royden and Tyser. The new concern was acquired in 1916 by Cunard, which quickly renamed the fleet using Milburn's *Port* prefix, resulting in the line becoming known as Port Line. The first new construction consisted of three ships of the *Port Darwin* class, delivered by Workman Clark in 1918–19 and these were closely followed by ten similar ships with cruiser sterns, of which the 8,422gt *Port Adelaide**, the second of three from Hawthorn, Leslie, was the third to be delivered. Their design can be traced back to Tyser's *Niwaru* of 1902 but had the addition of a forecastle. Twin-screw propulsion was retained with reciprocating engines providing a useful fourteen knots in service. *Port Hardy*, the third Hawthorn, Leslie ship, delivered in 1923, was fitted to carry 650 emigrants and could be distinguished by her mast houses. Two of the class were wrecked before 1940 and seven more became war losses, leaving just four survivors, including *Port Darwin* and *Port Adelaide*, which were all broken up between 1949 and 1953. (*B Fielden*)

Ordered in 1920 by Australian Commonwealth Line, the 11,023gt refrigerated shelter-deckers *Fordsdale* and *Ferndale** were not delivered by Cockatoo Island Shipyard, Sydney, until 1924 and plans for two more sisters were abandoned. The largest Australian-built ships, they were designed to compete with the established lines in the Europe–Australia trade and featured a long forecastle with vertical stem and a cruiser stern. Their dimensions of 500ft oa on a beam of 63ft were the maximum for the Manchester Ship Canal, for which they were fitted with telescopic topmasts, short kingposts and a removable funnel top, but problems in the locks resulted in the idea being abandoned after just one voyage by *Fordsdale*. Twin-screw coal burners, their twin four-cylinder quadruple-expansion engines developed 11,000ihp for fifteen and a half knots. The ailing company was bought in 1928 by White Star Line, which a year later fitted extra refrigerated capacity in Nos 4 and 5 holds; however, the parent Kylsant group had overreached itself and collapsed in 1931. *Ferndale* was wrecked off Algeria in 1932 and a year later her sister passed to Shaw, Savill & Albion in which Furness Withy had purchased a one-third share (in 1936 Furness Withy purchased the remaining shares). She was sold to Hong Kong's Audax Shipping as *Ocean Neptune* in 1952 and passed through several more Eastern hands, eventually being scrapped as *Jui Yung* at Osaka in 1959 after thirty-five years' service.

A new generation of motor ships

Having experimented with several different motor-ship designs, Glen Line built four *Glenade*-class vessels of 6,682gt at Harland & Wolff's Govan yard in 1919–20 and these were followed in 1920 and 1922 by a further quartet built in pairs that were the largest motorships at the time. *Glenogle*, *Glenapp* (launched as *Glenfarne)*, *Glengarry* and *Glenbeg** measured 9,500gt on dimensions of 486 x 62ft and adhered to a three-island design with two decks and an awning deck. Six hatches were served by twenty-four derricks, including two heavy derricks, and they were propelled at twelve and a half knots by twin eight-cylinder Harland–Burmeister & Wain diesels developing 5,500bhp. *Glenshiel*, a fifth ship delivered by Harland & Wolff, Belfast, in 1924, differed in having the bridge and superstructure combined abaft the No 3 hatch. So successful was the *Glenogle* design that the Royal Mail Steam Packet Company built three similar ships: *Lochkatrine* by John Brown in 1922, *Lochgoil* by Harland & Wolff, Govan, in 1922 and *Lochmonar* by Harland & Wolff, Belfast, in 1924 whilst Holland-America Line received a further pair, *Dinteldijk* and *Drechtdijk*, from Belfast in 1922–3. In 1929, the five Glen ships were fitted with superchargers, raising their speed to fourteen knots. *Glengarry* was renamed *Glenstrae* in 1939 and *Glenshiel* was torpedoed east of the Maldive Islands on 2 April 1942. The four original sisters were transferred to Ocean Steam Ship Company in 1949 and traded as *Deucalion*, *Dardanus*, *Dolius* and *Dymas* respectively, until broken up in the UK between 1952 and 1957.

The British India Steam Navigation Company introduced diesel propulsion with its passenger ship *Domala* of 1921 and the names of all its subsequent motor ships began with the letter D. Its first motor cargo liner was *Durenda*, a cargo version of *Domala,* completed by Robert Duncan, Glasgow, in 1922, but the first to be specifically designed as such was the 5,952gt *Dalgoma** delivered by Alexander Stephen, Linthouse, in 1923 for the India trade. A twin-screw, three-island vessel, her hull dimensions were 430 x 54ft and her main propulsion comprised two four-cylinder Sulzer diesels, developing 3,600bhp for a service speed of eleven to twelve knots. The company returned to steam propulsion for subsequent cargo series and did not employ diesels again until the Doxford-engined *Orna* and *Ozarda* of 1938–40. Having come through World War II unscathed, *Dalgoma* survived a temporary grounding off Fremantle in June 1945 after dragging her anchor in a storm, and finally arrived in Ghent for scrapping in December 1946.

Norwegian shipowner Wilh. Wilhelmsen first adopted diesel propulsion with the three-masted *America* in 1921. She was followed in 1922 by three 5,655gt Burmeister & Wain-built motor ships of the *Teneriffa* class, which continued the theme of three masts and a flush hull but with the addition of a small funnel. They measured 435 x 55ft and had two six-cylinder Burmeister & Wain oil engines developing 3,100bhp for a service speed of eleven and a half knots. *Teneriffa* was bombed in the Bristol Channel on 26 February 1941 and *Tennessee*, having sailed as Olav Ringdal's *Vigrid* since 1937, was torpedoed by *U371* south-southeast of Cape Farewell on 26 June in the same year. *Thalatta** became a constructive total loss in April 1949 after grounding in the Maldives and was broken up in Bombay. Eight ships with raised forecastles followed between 1922 and 1924, the latter year seeing the delivery by the Odense Shipyard of the 5,798gt *Tourcoing*, which, with the addition of a raised poop and more extensive array of derrick posts, set a pattern that was to serve the company well over the next thirty years.

American-Hawaiian Line's twin-screw *Californian* and *Missourian** were unusual in being US motorships. Built at Chester, Pennsylvania, by the Merchant Shipbuilding Corporation in 1922, they had the following main particulars: 7,899gt; 11,450dwt; length oa 462ft, beam 60ft, and were driven at twelve knots by twin six-cylinder Cramp-Burmeister & Wain engines. They saw initial service on the North Atlantic before settling down on their intended US inter-coastal route. In 1940, they were members of a batch of ninety US ships sold to the British Ministry of War Transport and were placed under Runciman Shipping Company management. *Californian* became *Empire Kite* then *Empire Seal*, before being torpedoed in the western North Atlantic in February 1942. *Missourian* served as *Empire Swan* and from 1942 as the Belgian-owned *Belgian Freighter*. Bought by her managers, Compagnie Maritime Belge, in 1946 and renamed *Capitaine Potié*, she was sold to Compagnia Genovese d'Armamento in 1948 and converted to the emigrant carrier *Genova*. In the winter of 1954–5, she was again refitted to carry more than 1,000 emigrants and was renamed *Flaminia*, sailing to Australia under the Cogedar Line banner. Following a Zim Line charter for Mediterranean service in the winter of 1961–2, she was was sold to Saudi Arabian owners in 1964 and renamed *King Abdelaziz* for the pilgrim trade. After striking a reef off Jeddah in March 1965, she was repaired in Italy but was sold for demolition in Kaohsiung after forty-eight years of service.

Round-the-world services

Under the Bank Line title, Andrew Weir & Company ran a complex web of worldwide services in the cross trades. After World War I, Bank Line's chairman, Lord Inverforth, took the unprecedented step of ordering a series of eighteen twin-screw motorships from Harland & Wolff, Govan, the first of which, *Inverbank**, was delivered in May 1924 and the last, *Springbank*, in the same month two years later. They had flush hulls and featured a split superstructure, prominent houses abreast the foremast and two pairs of tall kingposts, the after set mounted close to the stern. Measuring around 5,150gt on dimensions of 420 x 54ft, they were propelled by twin six-cylinder Harland-Burmeister & Wain diesels for a service speed of twelve knots. *Clydebank* and *Speybank* were taken up in 1939 and converted into an auxiliary AA ship and fighter catapult ship respectively, the former being scuttled off Normandy to form part of the Mulberry Harbour. *Speybank* was captured by the German raider *Atlantis* on 31 January 1941, taken to Bordeaux and converted to the auxiliary minelayer *Doggerbank* She later became a blockade runner but was mistakenly torpedoed by *U43* on 3 March 1943 about 1,000 miles west of the Canary Islands. Six more were sunk but of the remainder, the majority were broken up in the Far East in 1959–60, *Forresbank* having stranded on the African coast in November 1958 following an engine-room explosion. *Inverbank* went to La Spezia breakers in 1959 a year after becoming the Italian *La Liguria*. (*World Ship Society*)

Having failed to find a British yard that could match the quote from German shipbuilders, the Furness Withy Group reluctantly placed an order with Deutsche Werft, Hamburg for five new motorships for Prince Line's round-the-world service operated by Rio Cape Line. *Javanese Prince* was the first to be completed, in January 1926, her sisters following later the same year. Distinctive ships, they had a short raised forecastle and an unusual mast arrangement consisting of foremast, twin tall posts and a second mast without topmast forward of the superstructure, with mainmast and a second pair of posts right aft. Note also the unusually large ventilators, necessary for the long periods spent in the tropics. Measurement was 6,734gt with dimensions of 458ft oa x 60ft; a service speed of fifteen knots was assured by twin sixteen-cylinder AEG diesels driving twin screws. Two further ships were subsequently delivered by Blythswood Shipbuilding Company in 1929, *Cingalese Prince* and *Siamese Prince* being identified by an extra pair of posts abaft the accommodation. All bar *Malayan Prince*, the second German delivery, seen here transitting the Suez Canal, were lost to torpedo attack during World War II and she survived until broken up by T W Ward at Inverkeithing in 1950.

Engines three-quarters aft

The three-quarters aft design pioneered by Johnson Line in 1912 re-emerged in 1922–3 with two unusual motor cargo liners completed by Deutsche Werft in Hamburg for local shipowner Deutsche D G Kosmos, which had run a liner service to the west coast of South America since 1872 and the west coast of North America from 1901. The 4,454gt *Isis** and *Osiris* measured 376 x 52ft and were propelled by twin six-cylinder AEG diesels but their layout was quite unique, with the accommodation block incorporating a diminutive funnel and machinery placed well aft whilst retaining the traditional German feature of a short well between forecastle and long combined bridge and poop deck. Kosmos merged with Hugo Stinnes early in 1926 and in November of that year was acquired by Hamburg-America Line. *Isis*, illustrated here in Kosmos colours, foundered in a severe storm off Land's End on 8 November 1936 just a few months after her sister had been sold to Hamburg South America Line and renamed *Babitonga*. She was used as a supply ship in World War II and was scuttled by her crew off St Paul's Rocks in the mid-Atlantic on 21 June 1941 to avoid capture by the cruiser HMS *London*.

Amongst the earliest British cargo ships with engines in the three-quarter aft position were the 3,908gt motor ships *Sycamore* and *Tramore* built by Furness Shipbuilding Company in 1923–4 for Furness Withy's Johnston Line. Two larger examples were the 5,122gt *Silverlarch** and *Silverpine* completed by Swan, Hunter in 1924 for the New York-based Kerr Steamship Company and managed by Thompson Brothers. The featured a split superstructure and measured 417 x 55ft whilst twin Doxford diesels enabled them to maintain a service speed of thirteen knots. They were employed on Kerr's new westbound round-the-world service sailing alternatively with Prince Line ships, and this became registered as the Silver Line in November 1925. Both sisters were re-engined in 1936 but *Silverpine* was torpedoed 450 miles west of Malin Head on 5 December 1940. The surviving sister was sold to Finland in 1947 becoming *Bore VIII* and was scrapped at Hendrik-Ido-Ambacht in 1958.

Yet another variation on the three-quarters-aft theme appeared in 1928 when James Chambers & Company took delivery of two motor vessels for its Lancashire Shipping Company, which operated a round-the-world service in competition with Silver and Prince Lines. Built at Birkenhead by Cammell Laird & Company, the 5,853gt sisters *Greystoke Castle* and *Muncaster Castle* had an overall length of 440ft with the bridge deck extended to the foremast, whilst all three masts were fitted with topmasts, unlike the Silver ships. Their speed, however, was similar, provided by twin six-cylinder engines. *Muncaster Castle*, depicted loading china clay in Fowey, possibly on her initial voyage, was torpedoed by *U68* in the South Atlantic on 30 March 1942. *Greystoke Castle* was sold to Elder Dempster in September 1943, along with two of Chambers & Company's conventional-looking motor ships. As *Freetown*, she traded to West Africa until August 1958, when she was sold to Hamburg shipbreakers Eisen & Metall AG.

One of Alfred Holt's first motorships, *Tantalus* (1923, 7,777gt), had her funnel placed aft of amidships, but *Alcinous*, completed by Scotts' in 1925 and her two Caledon-built sisters, *Stentor* and *Phrontis*, echoed the Silver Line design, but with the addition of a long raised bridge deck and short poop, all three islands being slightly longer in the Caledon pair. Other differences included a greater array of posts and derricks and, despite being motor ships, tall, steamship-type funnels. At around 430ft long on a gross tonnage of 6,635, they could carry some 520,000cu ft of cargo and were driven by twin eight-cylinder Burmeister & Wain engines, producing a total of 4,800bhp for a sea speed of fourteen knots. Only *Stentor*, which became a war loss, operated under the British flag, her sisters being managed by Holt's Dutch subsidiary N S M 'Oceaan'. Of these, *Alcinous* was transferred to Ocean Steamship Company in 1950, trading as *Phemius* until broken up in Hong Kong in 1957, whilst the following year *Phrontis* briefly flew the Saudi Arabian flag as *Ryad* before following her sister to Hong Kong, where she is depicted with green funnel and grey hull awaiting the breakers torch.

Standard Norwegian motor ships

In 1927, Deutsche Werft completed the 6,732gt *Taronga* and *Talleyrand*, first of a dozen fourteen-and-a-half knot 'standard' cargo liners ships, which were amongst the most advanced of their day and suitable for employment on any of Wilh. Wilhelmsen's main liner services. Deutsche Werke, Kiel, delivered four sisters in 1929, Kockums, Malmö, a further quartet in 1929–30, with the final pair coming from Burmeister & Wain in 1930. Five of the class were given *Tai* prefixes and an extra pair of posts on the forecastle, as shown in this trials view of *Tai Shan*, for service on the Barber Steamship Company/Chambers US east coast–Far East service, which Wilhelmsen had joined in 1927. Hull dimensions were 461 x 61ft and they were propelled by twin eight-cylinder Burmeister & Wain diesels developing around 7,000bhp. *Taronga* became a constructive total loss after catching fire and being beached on Perim Island in the Red Sea in January 1933 and was replaced a year later by a namesake with a Maierform bow. Four of the twelve became war losses: *Tudor* was torpedoed by *U48* northwest of Cape Finisterre in June 1940; *Triton* was torpedoed by *U566* northeast of the Azores in August 1942; *Thermopylae* was scuttled after being bombed south of Crete in a Malta-bound convoy in January 1942, and *Tai Ping* and *Templar* were seized by the Germans in Oslo in 1940 and used as the mine destruction vessels *Sperrbrecher 14* and *– 17*. The former was scuttled in the Gironde but the latter survived and, with the remaining ships, lasted until the early 1960s. *Tai Shan* was scrapped in Mihara in 1960. Four were sold for further trading in 1961–2: *Templar*, *Tai Yang* and *Tai Ping Yang* to Achilles Frangistas as *Katerina*, *Mousse* and *Sophia* respectively, and *Troja* to Karageorgis as *Ioanna*, which went for scrap in La Spezia late in 1966 following an engine-room explosion and fire in the Red Sea on 20 March. The final three ships were broken up in 1970 and 1972 at Shanghai and Fener.

North Pacific traders

Furness Withy first used oil engines in the Doxford-built *Pacific Commerce* (ex-*Dominion Miller*), *Pacific Shipper* and *Pacific Trader* built between 1922 and 1924 for west coast of North America service. Their success led to the ordering of seven improved motorships: *Pacific Reliance*, *Pacific Enterprise*, *Pacific Pioneer** and *Pacific Exporter* from Blythswood Shipbuilding, Glasgow, in 1927–8, *Pacific President* and *Pacific Grove* from Deutsche Werke, Kiel, (as late war reparations) in 1928 and finally *Pacific Ranger* from Burmeister & Wain, Copenhagen in 1929. The German-built ships measured 7,115gt and 470 x 61ft, compared with 6,735gt and 455 x 60ft for the rest. Their hold arrangement reflected the reverse of the first-generation motor ships with three holds placed forward of the machinery and two aft, whilst propulsion was either by twin six-cylinder or twin eight-cylinder diesels for a speed of around thirteen knots. Five of the class succumbed to torpedo attack in World war II: *Pacific Reliance* to *U29* in March, *Ranger* to *U59* in October and President to *U43* in December 1940, *Pioneer* to *U132* in July 1942 and *Grove* to *U563* in April 1943. Of the survivors, *Pacific Enterprise* stranded on Point Arena, California in September 1949 and was abandoned. This left only *Pacific Exporter*, which two years later became Costa Line's *Giacomo C*. She finally arrived in Savona for demolition in 1958.

Cross traders between the Americas

Norway's A/S Ivarans Rederi first entered the liner trade in 1925 through co-operation with New York-based Garcia & Diaz, which operated ageing steamships between the east coasts of the United States and South America under the Linea Sud Americana title. Ivarans' three new motorships, *Primero*, *Secundo* and *Tercero*, constructed in 1925–6 by Burmeister & Wain, provided a considerable boost to the service and in 1928 they were rechristened *Sud Argentino*, *Sud Uruguayo* and *Sud Cubano* to bring the names into line with a second trio of larger ships, *Sud Atlantico*, *Sud Pacifico* and *Sud Africano*, delivered by B&W in 1928 and registered to the new joint company A/S Linea Sud Americana. These measured 4,640gt on dimensions of 397ft oa x 54ft and their layout was unusual with flush hulls and four masts, the inner two being placed hard up against the fore and aft ends of the split superstructure. Twin B&W diesels developing 3,200bhp gave a speed of eleven knots. Two much larger and faster twin-funnelled cargo-passenger ships, *Sud Americano* and *Sud Expreso*, were completed at Kiel in 1929 but failed to maintain designed speed and were returned to their builders in 1931, eventually becoming Norddeutscher Lloyd's *Elbe* and *Weser* (see page 80). Due to the economic crisis, the arrangement with Garcia & Diaz was wound up and *Sud Atlantico*, *Sud Pacifico* and *Sud Africano* were transferred to Ivarans' ownership and renamed *Argentino*, *Uruguayo* and *Paraguayo**, sailing from 1932 in a new joint service with Moore & McCormack, whose colours they wore, with the three earlier ships which, having reverted to their original names, were quickly switched to tramping duties due to poor trading conditions. The association with Moore & McCormack ended in 1938 and the *Argentino* trio sailed under the Ivaran Lines banner from 1939 as *Buenos Aires*, *Montevideo* and *Santos*. They were requisitioned as British war transports in 1941 and sailed in North Atlantic convoys, *Santos* being lost in August 1943 after being rammed by the torpedoed Liberty ship *Theodore Dwight Weld*. The surviving pair passed to Finland's Gustaf B Thordén in 1952 and 1953 becoming *Marita Thordén* and *Greta Thordén*. The latter was scrapped in Hong Kong in 1959 and the former in Helsinki in 1968 after spending her last eight years as the grain storage hulk *Merivakka*.

New refrigerated motorships

In 1925, Houlder Brothers introduced *Upwey Grange*, the first of a new type of refrigerated ship and its first motorship, to the River Plate trade. Her design featured a long forecastle separated by a short well at No 2 hatch from a very long bridge deck, which extended from foremast to mainmast and incorporated hatches Nos 3, 4 and 5, the middle hatch of which was trunked through a forward extension of the promenade deck. Built at Govan by the Fairfield Shipbuilding & Engineering Company, she measured 9,130gt on an overall length of 451ft and a beam of 62.5ft. Her insulated capacity of 500,000cu ft was the largest yet, despite being confined to the four holds forward of the machinery space to lessen the amount of piping needed; extra tween-deck space was provided for hanging chilled carcasses. Main propulsion comprised twin twelve-cylinder Burmeister & Wain diesels for a service speed of fourteen knots with one knot in reserve. The 9,500gt sisters *Dunster Grange* and *El Argentino** delivered in 1927 and 1929 were 2ft broader and had shorter funnels but otherwise were similar in design. The even larger 464ft oa, 10,160gt *Beacon Grange* was received from Hawthorn, Leslie in 1938; she had her well-deck enclosed. Meat carriers became prime targets in World War II and only *Dunster Grange* survived the conflict, passing first to Finnish owners as *Vaasa* in 1951 and then to Japan in 1958 as the crab factory *Krayo Maru*. She ended her days at Aioi in 1974, having sailed for the final eleven years as *Yoko Maru*.

Port Line introduced the first motorships to the UK–Australia service in 1925, *Port Dunedin* and *Port Hobart* being completed by Workman, Clark, Belfast and Swan, Hunter & Wigham Richardson on the Tyne. Designed by H G Dearden, they had a gross measurement of around 7,460t on overall dimensions of 495 x 60ft and differed from the earlier 'Port' ships in having a split superstructure around No 3 hatch. Twin four-cylinder opposed-piston Doxford diesels gave a speed of fourteen knots. *Port Hobart* was sunk by the pocket battleship *Admiral Scheer* in the Sombrero Channel on 4 November 1940 but Port *Dunedin* survived the conflict to be broken up in Genoa in 1962. They were followed in 1927–8 by the five-ship *Port Fremantle* class, of which just the first ship came from Workman, Clark, the rest being built by Swan, Hunter. These were some 7ft longer and 3ft beamier and had slightly shorter funnels, accentuated by a taller pair of cowl-topped kingposts serving No 3 hatch, as seen in this Cape Town view of *Port Huon*. *Port Fairy* brought the first chilled beef cargoes from Australia and New Zealand in the late 1930s and was not broken up until 1965, after a single voyage to Hong Kong as the Greek *Taishikan*. Three modified versions led by *Port Chalmers* in 1933, which measured 489 (507 oa) x 65ft, carried their boats one deck higher and had an additional hatch served by a second set of kingposts abaft the superstructure. *Port Chalmers* was the only ship to survive the famous 'Pedestal' Malta convoy unscathed and went to Kaohsiung breakers in 1965. (*A Duncan*)

Blue Star Line received four large meat carriers in 1926–7, *Stuartstar** and *Africstar* from Palmer's, Newcastle, and *Rodneystar* and *Napierstar* (launched as *Raleighstar*) from Lithgows on the Clyde. They were three-island ships of around 11,500gt with a cruiser stern and a towering bridge structure at the forward end of a long bridge deck. Insulated capacity was 461,000cu ft in eighteen chambers and main machinery comprised four single-reduction steam turbines driving two shafts for a service speed of fourteen knots. The *star* part of their names was separated into a suffix in 1929. In 1935, the appearance of *Stuart Star* and *Rodney Star** was completely altered when their well decks were plated over (see inset photo). Following collision with the White Star liner *Laurentic* off the Mersey Bar in August 1935, *Napier Star* was repaired on the Tyne and at the same time her well decks were enclosed and a new Maierform bow with raised forecastle added, increasing length by 24ft. The lead ship was wrecked at Hood Point Light near East London on 20 November 1937 and the others became war losses. *Napier Star* was torpedoed by *U100* (Schepke) 300 miles southwest of Ireland on 18 December 1940, *Afric Star* fell victim to the raider *Kormoran* northeast of Brazil on 29 January 1941 and *Rodney Star* to *U105* 420 miles west of Freetown on 16 May.

Following Port Line's introduction of motorships to the Australian trade in 1925, Shaw, Savill & Albion cancelled an order for two seventeen-knot, 20,000gt passenger liners, substituting in their place four refrigerated motorships for its Australasian services, two from Swan, Hunter & Wigham Richardson on the Tyne and two from Fairfield Shipbuilding & Engineering Company on Clydeside. *Karamea*, the first of the latter, entered service in February 1928 and sisters *Zealandic**, *Taranaki* and *Coptic* were all in service by July. Designed for a mix of frozen meat and general cargo, they set a company pattern that was to last until the 1960s. They were the last of the company's ships to have counter sterns. Main dimensions were 483 x 64ft on a gross tonnage of around 8,500t and their hulls incorporated a short forecastle and a long bridge deck with bridge and superstructure split by No 3 hatch. Twin six-cylinder Sulzer diesels developed 7,500bhp for a sea speed of fifteen knots when new. *Zealandic*, the second Tyne-built ship, was lost with all hands to torpedo attack by *U106* in January 1941 soon after leaving Liverpool, but her sisters remained in commercial service until the 1960s, *Coptic* being the last to go for demolition in Antwerp in 1965. (*B Fielden*)

Completed by Palmer's, Newcastle in April 1930, the 11,449gt *Tuscan Star* was the second of two large refrigerated ships delivered to Blue Star Line. Unlike the turbine-driven *Sultan Star* (12,306 gt), delivered two months earlier by Cammell Laird, Birkenhead, she was the company's first motor vessel and was fitted with twin eight-cylinder Sulzers giving a speed of around fifteen knots. Whereas the earlier ship had a long combined forecastle and bridge deck extending to the mainmast, *Tuscan Star* had a short well at No 2 hatch, but both had vertical stems and outward sloping cruiser sterns. Her dimensions were 471 x 68ft, slightly smaller than *Sultan Star*'s 486 x 70ft. Neither of these powerful-looking ships survived World War II. *Sultan Star* was torpedoed by *U48* off Land's End on 14 February 1940 and *Tuscan Star* by *U109*, some 450 miles west of Freetown on 6 September 1942 whilst homeward bound from Santos.

The New Zealand Shipping Company also switched to oil engines in a handsome new design of refrigerated cargo liner in 1930. *Otaio** was built at Barrow by Vickers-Armstrongs, whilst sisters *Opawa* and *Orari* came from Alexander Stephen's Linthouse yard in 1931. Two-deck ships with a part third deck forward, they measured 10,048gt and around 13,000dwt and had hull dimensions of 490ft oa x 67ft. Their three-island design featured a long forecastle and poop, coupled with a very long bridge deck incorporating Nos 3 and 4 hatches on either side of a composite superstructure block. Propulsion was by means of twin eight-cylinder Doxford diesels developing 9,390bhp for a service speed of around sixteen knots. *Orari* survived a torpedo attack 450 miles west of Ireland in May 1940 and managed to reach the Clyde, drawing 41ft aft. Following three months' repair by her builders, she returned to service and her luck held when she survived a Malta convoy in June 1942, despite receiving mine damage. In the meantime her two consorts had been sunk, *Otaio* torpedoed by *U558* in August 1941 and *Opawa* by *U106* in February 1942. *Orari*'s postwar commercial service for the New Zealand Shipping Company ended in July 1958, but she traded on to the River Plate for a further thirteen years as *Capo Bianco* for Genoa-based Andrea Zanchi, until broken up at Savona in 1971.

Turbine steamers for Canada

In 1927, the Canadian Pacific Railway took delivery from William Denny & Brothers, Dumbarton, of *Beaverburn**, the first of five outstanding 10,000gt cargo liners, which were notable for their four goalpost masts. Two pairs of sisters followed in 1928 from Barclay, Curle & Co, Whiteinch, and Armstrong, Whitworth & Co, Low Walker. They were designed by Denny for North Atlantic service under the management of Canadian Pacific Steamships and sailed between London and North Continental ports and the St Lawrence in summer and St John, New Brunswick in winter. Deadweight tonnage was around 12,800 on overall dimensions of 521 x 62ft. Their ice-strengthened hulls incorporated a short raised forecastle, a central accommodation block and cruiser stern. Although diesels were rapidly gaining in popularity, the company opted for steam propulsion and six sets of Parsons steam turbines developed 8,000shp and which drove twin screws through single-reduction gearing for a speed of fourteen knots. Steam was supplied in the Tyne-built pair by manually fired Babcock & Wilcox water-tube boilers, but the others were given Yarrow units with Erith-Roe mechanical stokers, a first in British vessels. Sadly all these fine vessels were lost during World War II, *Beaverburn* and *Beaverdale* to submarine attack and *Beaverbrae* to enemy aircraft in 1940–1. *Beaverford* distinguished herself, however, in an uneven confrontation with the pocket battleship *Admiral Scheer* following the sinking of the armed merchant cruiser HMS *Jervis Bay*, before herself being sunk on 5 November 1940. The surviving *Beaverhill*, which had been fitted with accommodation for 138 passengers, was lost through stranding on Hillyards Reef near St John, New Brunswick on 24 November 1944.

German fleet renewals

Hansa Line built an unusual-looking series of four ships in 1925: *Schwarzenfels* at Deutsche Werke, Kiel, *Weissenfels** at J C Tecklenborg, Wesermünde, *Neuenfels* at A G Weser, Bremen, and *Altenfels* at Vulcan Werke, Hamburg. Gross measurement averaged around 8,000t on a deadweight of 11,200t and dimensions were 469 x 60ft. *Braunfels* and *Rotenfels*, delivered by A G Weser in 1927, were similar but a few feet longer. All six vessels were propelled at around twelve knots by twin six-cylinder MAN diesels, those of the first quartet being four-stroke single-acting units, whilst the latter pair had two-stroke units, that of *Rotenfels* being double-acting. Their hulls had three long islands with only short wells at Nos 2 and 4 hatches. *Schwarzenfels* became Deutsche Lufthansa's aircraft support and catapult ship *Schwabenland* in 1933 and survived a torpedo attack by HM submarine *Terrapin* off Bergen in March 1944 when under naval control. She became a war prize and was scuttled in the Skagerrak on the last day of 1946 with a cargo of gas bombs. Her three sisters were all war losses and *Braunfels*, interned at Mormugao on the outbreak of World War II, was scuttled in March 1943 to avoid being seized by Portugal but was later raised and broken up in Goa. *Rotenfels* had the longest career, surviving the war to become a British prize. She traded as *Alcyone Hope* from 1947 and a year later was re-engined with a nine-cylinder Sulzer unit. In 1954, she became, in quick succession, the Bahamas-registered *Sterling Valour* and the *Pioneer Merchant* of Hong Kong and was finally scrapped in Kaohsiung in 1966, after trading for the last four years as the Panamanian *Segamat*.

The first major series of cargo liners to be built for Norddeutscher Lloyd's Far East and Australian services after World War I commenced with the 7,625gt sisters *Aller** and *Main* from Bremer Vulkan in 1927. They measured 527 x 63ft and their triple-expansion engines developed 6,400ihp for fourteen knots in service. Over the next two years, ten more 'River'-class ships followed from four other German yards, all being distinguished by short forecastles and four lofty masts. Although outwardly similar in appearance, dimensions varied and *Trave, Saale* and *Havel* of 1928 were thirteen-and-three-quarter knot motorships, which lacked the small hatch and posts immediately forward of the funnel. The final pair, *Isar* and *Donau*, had curved Maierform bows and measured just over 9,000gt. In 1938 the three motorships – *Trave, Saale* and *Havel* – were lengthened and re-engined for sixteen and a half knots, being renamed *Regensburg, Marburg* and *Coburg* respectively, but they became war losses along with all but three of the steamers. *Aller* was one of the survivors, being bought by Portugal in 1943 and serving as Companhia Colonial's *Sofala* until broken up in Spain in 1975. The others were *Lahn*, which was sold to Lloyd Argentino in 1940 becoming *San Martin* and in 1942 Flota Mercante del Estado's *Rio Parana*. She passed to Empresa Lineas Maritimas Argentinas in 1943, serving for a while as a pilot station in the Plate estuary and was not broken up until 1975. *Isar* transported iron ore from Narvik to Germany during World War II and was towed to the UK in a damaged state from Moss in 1945. After repair she re-entered service in 1947 as J A Billmeir & Company's *Stanroyal* and five years later was sold to Turkey, bearing the names *Haran* and in 1959 *Necip*, before being demolished at Halic in 1965.

Hamburg-America Line's answer to Nordeutscher Lloyd's 'River' class were its six *Neumark*-class vessels, which were designed for Far East trade and were the last in the company to have counter sterns. Both the lead ship and the final unit, *Kurmark*, were completed by Howaldtswerke, Kiel in 1929–30 whilst the remainder came from four separate shipyards in 1930. With a short forecastle and three holds either side of the accommodation block, they measured 477ft oa on a beam of 63ft, which gave an average 7,360gt on a deadweight of 7,550t. Four sets of single-reduction geared turbines, built between 1923 and 1926, drove a single screw for a speed of fourteen to fifteen knots. Early in World War II, Blohm & Voss converted *Neumark** and *Kurmark* into the commerce raiders *Widder* and *Orion*, which between them were responsible for capturing or sinking sixteen Allied ships, whilst mines from the latter accounted for a further four off New Zealand, including the Union Steam Ship Company of New Zealand's passenger ship *Niagara*. *Orion* was sunk by Russian aircraft off Swinemünde in April 1945 whilst acting as a gunnery training ship but *Widder* survived to become the Greek *Ulysses* and then Unterweser Reederei's *Fechenheim* before stranding near Bergen in 1955. Of the rest, *Uckermark* (Blohm & Voss) was scuttled at Massawa in 1941 but *Bitterfeld* (Krupp), *Nordmark* (Flensburg) and *Stassfurt* (Bremer Vulkan) were seized by Holland in the East Indies in 1940 and renamed *Mariso, Mandalika* and *Langkoeas* respectively. All had succumbed to Axis torpedo attack by 1943.

Heavy-lift ships

Specialist heavy-lift ships were pioneered by the Norwegian naval captain Christen Smith in 1924. These were operated as tramps but their success attracted the attention of a number of liner companies including Germany's Hansa Line, which was often called upon to carry heavy equipment to India. In 1929, the Deschimag shipyard in Bremen completed the 7,457gt *Lichtenfels*, the first of four heavy-lift ships, which was followed by sisters *Freienfels*, *Geierfels* and *Uhenfels* in 1929–31. Their 506 x 62ft hulls had a raised forecastle and they were amongst the first large ships to have a curved Maierform stem, claimed to reduce skin friction and ease water flow, whilst their cruiser sterns were also of a novel sloping design. The foremast mounted a 120t derrick (not yet fitted in this trial view of *Freienfels*), serving a long No 2 hatch. The uncluttered foredeck permitted the stowage of heavy deck cargoes, whilst the pillar-less holds were fitted with special rails for the carriage of rolling stock. Propulsion was by means of a three-cylinder triple-expansion engine assisted by a low-pressure exhaust turbine giving around thirteen knots. Hansa lost its entire fleet during World War II, *Freienfels* being mined along with sister *Geierfels* off Leghorn in 1940, just six days before Christmas. *Uhenfels* was captured by the destroyer HMS *Hereward* off Freetown in November 1939 and renamed *Empire Ability* under Elder Dempster management but was lost to torpedo attack by *U69* off the Canaries in June the following year. *Lichtenfels* was scuttled in Massawa in April 1941 and the wreck broken up in 1950.

Delivered to Ellerman Hall by Barclay, Curle in 1930, at 5,787gt, the one-off *City of Barcelona* was Ellerman Hall's first specially designed heavy-lift ship. She had an overall length of 444ft on a beam of 58ft and her hull incorporated a short, high forecastle and a counter stern – a feature abandoned by the group for its large cargo liners since before World War I. A triple-expansion engine gave a speed of twelve knots. Her foremast was strengthened with four thick supporting struts enabling it to carry a 130t derrick serving No 2 hold. Depicted here in the Little Bitter Lake in the Suez Canal with mandatory searchlight slung over her bow, she had the distinction of having the heaviest lift capability under the Red Ensign, until broken up in Antwerp in the summer of 1958 after a long and uneventful career.

Between 1927 and 1930, Elder Dempster Lines renewed its cargo fleet with five 3,790gt *Dunkwa*-class ships and eight 4,025gt 'Explorer'-class ships beginning with *Henry Stanley* in 1929. This ship had a fifth hatch just forward of the funnel raising overall length from 367ft to 382ft but both classes had a small kingpost on the poop which supported a derrick for handling surf boats. The final 'Explorer' ship *Mary Kingsley**, delivered by Ardrossan Drydock & Shipbuilders to the African Steamship Company in late 1930, differed in being specially adapted to carry heavy cargoes. Her masts were repositioned to the breaks of the forecastle and poop and two new short heavy masts mounting 100t derricks were fitted at either end of the superstructure. In addition, special guides were fitted for the carriage of locomotives and rolling stock for Nigerian Railways. As with the rest of the class, she was driven by an eight-cylinder Burmeister & Wain diesel giving a speed of around fourteen knots. Laid up briefly at Dartmouth during the Depression, she was transferred to Elder Dempster in 1935 and apart from an incident that September, when a railway engine broke loose in heavy weather off the Scilly Isles, and later engine problems, she had an exemplary career and was broken up by Thomas W Ward at Preston in 1954. (*B Fielden*)

North American traders

Sweden's Rederi A/B Transatlantic was established in 1904, its first service to Cape Town starting later that year. This was extended to Australia three years later and a North Pacific service was also inaugurated. The Gothenburg-based company had adopted the diesel engine in 1918 and its *Yngaren* and *Eknaren* were the first to be powered by Doxford oil engines. In 1928, it received two motor cargo liners from Götaverken A/B, the 5,800gt *Mirrabooka* and *Parrakoola*, to serve the cross trade from the west coast of North America to Australia. Their clean lines set a pattern for many subsequent Scandinavian motor ships and they originally had accommodation for around twenty passengers. Deadweight measurement was 9,244t on dimensions of 457 x 57ft and twin diesels provided a speed of around fourteen knots. After thirty years' service, *Mirrabooka* became in turn *Dieter Nielsen* in 1958, Sten Olsson's *Birgit* in 1960, the Panamanian *Gitte* in 1963 and was scrapped in Nagoya in 1965. Her sister passed to Olof Wallenius as *Otello* in 1958 and was sold to Bulgaria in 1965, first as *Rubin* and then Navigation Maritime Bulgare's *Dobri Chintulov* in 1970, eventually being demolished at Split in 1973.

Lloyd Royal Belge built three new cargo liners for its Antwerp–New York service in 1929, just one year before its fleet – which included the large German war reparations *Mercier* and *Carlier* – was acquired by Compagnie Belge Maritime du Congo, the new group being restyled Compagnie Maritime Belge (CMB). The three new cargo liners were the 5,859gt *Emile Francqui* and *Jean Jadot* (shown in original livery) from Flensburger Schiffsbau, and *Henri Jaspar* from Rotterdam Drydock. Their hulls had a slightly raked bow, a short forecastle and long poop culminating in a rather bulbous cruiser stern, whilst the bridge was split from the rest of the midships superstructure by No 4 hatch. Deadweight measurement was 9,300t on dimensions of 460 x 57ft; they were driven at thirteen knots by quadruple-expansion machinery. *Emile Francqui* was torpedoed by *U664* on 16 September 1942 and her German-built sister, *Jean Jadot*, by *U453* on 20 January 1943. *Henri Jaspar* survived hostilities and was sold in 1953, becoming *Trade Winds* and then *Transcarib*, until broken up in Tokyo in 1960.

The economic outlook was gloomy when Compagnie Générale Transatlantique took delivery of its first purpose-built series of cargo liners for its North Pacific service. Starting with *San Antonio*, the 6,000gt *San* ships were all built at Belfast by Harland & Wolff between 1930 and 1933 and were twin-screw flush deckers with six holds, No 3 being placed between bridge and funnel. They measured 431 by 57ft and were driven at fourteen knots by twin four-cylinder triple-expansion engines of 5,000ihp, only the final ship *San Pedro* having an additional low-pressure exhaust turbine. All bar *San Jose* fell into German hands in 1942, *San Antonio, San Diego* and *San Francisco* succumbing to Allied air attack the following year. The rest survived the war and later had their boat decks extended across No 3 hatch. They were sold in 1953–4 to Hong Kong owners Wheelock, Marden, *San Mateo** stranding as *San Mardeno* almost immediately. *San Jose* (as *San Rolando*) and *San Pedro* lasted until broken up in 1957 in Hong Kong and 1960 in Osaka respectively, the latter successively under the names *Uranus*, *Anto* and *Eastwind*.

New motorships for eastern routes

In the mid-1920s, Rotterdam Lloyd ordered a series of advanced 9,500dwt motor cargo liners, which could also serve the annual Hadj pilgrim trade from the Dutch East Indies to Jeddah. Starting with *Kota Inten* in 1928, three each were built by Kon. Maats. De Schelde, Flushing, and NV Maats. Fijenoord, Rotterdam, and single ships by NV Wilton's Maschinefabriek & Scheepswerf, Rotterdam and Nederlandsche Scheepsbouw Maats, Amsterdam. They averaged 7,300gt on dimensions of 450 x 61ft and they adhered to a three-island design with a long bridge deck and split superstructure. Appearances differed; some had goalpost masts and *Kota Agoeng** and *Kota Nopan* had shorter funnels, whilst *Kota Pinang*'s funnel was the dummy taken from the company's liner *Patria* during a refit. Propulsion was either by twin single-acting Sulzers or seven-cylinder double-acting MAN diesels, developing around 5,200bhp for fourteen knots. As built, they could accommodate just over twenty first-class passengers and 2,000 pilgrims on deck, hence the large number of boats. *Kota Pinang* was captured during the German invasion at Rotterdam in May 1940 and became a German reconnaissance ship but was sunk by the cruiser HMS *Kenya* 750 miles west of Cape Ortegal, Azores, on 3 October 1941. *Kota Radja* was bombed by the invading Japanese in Sourabaya on 24 February 1942, burned and was later sunk by the Dutch minelayer *Krakatau*. Meanwhile, *Kota Nopan* had been captured by the raider *Komet* near the Galapagos Islands in August 1941 and taken to Bordeaux, where she was converted to the supply ship *Karin* and then *Passau*, before being sent to Japan as a blockade-runner. She was scuttled on the return voyage some 650 miles off Brazil's Cape Natal on 2 February 1943 when approached by US warships. *Kota Tjandi* was torpedoed off Freetown while on Ministry of War Transport charter some three months later on 30 April by *U515*. *Kota Baroe* and *Kota Agoeng*, which had sailed as US troopers during World War II, were broken up with the two other surviving ships in Hong Kong in 1958.

Nederland Line followed up its four *Poelau*-class passenger/cargo ships of 1928–9 with a series of seven smaller but similar looking 'T'-class cargo liners beginning with *Talisse* in 1930. She and *Tanimbar* were built in the UK by Caledon Shipbuilding & Engineering, Dundee, and *Tarakan* by NV Maats. Fijenoord, Rotterdam, the remainder coming from Nederlandsche Scheepsbouw Maats., Amsterdam, in 1930–1. They measured 8,168gt and 10,275dwt on dimensions of 469 x 62ft and were originally fitted to carry up to 2,000 pilgrims during the annual six week Hadj season. Main machinery was an eight-cylinder, two-stroke, single-acting Sulzer diesel, developing just over 7,000bhp for a service speed of fourteen and a half knots, but the final delivery, *Tajandoen*, was the first ship to have a double-acting Sulzer with an output of 7,600bhp for fifteen knots. Provision was made for the carriage of palm oil and other liquid cargoes in deep tanks. During the Depression years, every bit of extra revenue helped, and *Tarakan* was used for cheap six-day summer cruises to the Norwegian fjords for up to 540 young people in 1935, 1936 and 1939. She and *Talisse* also carried 100 passengers for a while after World War II. *Tajandoen*, was the first war loss, being torpedoed by *U47* forty miles north of Ushant on 7 December 1939 and *Tanimbar* suffered a similar fate south of Sardinia at the hand of Italian torpedo bombers on 14 June 1942 while in a Malta-bound convoy. The remainder, including *Tabian*, shown here in Singapore, returned to commercial service and were demolished by Eastern breakers during 1960–62.

Despite the depressed economic situation at the time, Blue Funnel Line took delivery of five twin-screw motorships for its Far East and round-the-world services between 1929 and 1931. *Agamemnon**, the first to be completed, was a product of Workman, Clark, Belfast and she was followed by *Deucalion* from Hawthorn, Leslie, *Menestheus* and *Memnon* from Caledon Shipbuilding & Engineering, Dundee, and *Ajax* from the company yard of Scotts' Shipbuilding & Engineering, Greenock. They measured 7,829gt on dimensions of 478ft oa x 59ft and were driven at fourteen knots by twin eight-cylinder turbo-charged Burmeister & Wain engines developing 6,600bhp. War intervened after less than a decade in service and in 1940, *Agamemnon* and *Menestheus* were taken up by the Royal Navy for minelaying and minesweeping duties respectively. In 1943, both vessels were converted to Pacific Fleet recreation ships with Nos 3 and 4 hatches decked over and a second dummy funnel added. Amenities included a cinema/theatre, brewery and swimming pool. *Memnon* was torpedoed by *U106* on 11 March 1941, northeast of the Cape Verde Islands and *Deucalion* was bombed and torpedoed by Italian aircraft on 12 August 1941 whilst in a Malta-bound convoy near Galita Island. The recreation ships re-entered commercial service in 1946 and 1948 but in April 1953 *Menestheus* was abandoned following an engine-room explosion and fire, towed to Long Beach and broken up. *Ajax* was transferred to sister company Glen Line as *Glenlochy* during 1957 and 1958, taking the name *Sarpedon* on her return and was scrapped in 1962, a year before *Agamemnon* followed her to Hong Kong breakers.

Delivered by the Nakskov Shipyard in 1930, *India* was the last and largest of the Danish East Asiatic Company's four-masted cargo ships. At 9,549gt and just under 13,450dwt, she measured 470 x 64ft and differed from preceding ships in having a long raised bridge deck and only four holds, albeit served by six hatches. Her exceptionally large No 2 lower hold accounted for more than a third of her total cargo capacity. Her twin eight-cylinder Burmeister & Wain diesels had two more cylinders than the company's preceding motor cargo liners and developed 5,500bhp for a speed of thirteen and a half knots. Accommodation was provided for sixteen passengers. Apart from the war years when she was laid up in Denmark, her commercial service, during which she suffered a number of fires, was split equally between the Pacific and Far East routes and she is depicted here in Singapore two years before she went to Hong Kong breakers in 1962.

CHAPTER

6

Depression and Renaissance

The 1930s began in a sombre mood when the slump created by the Wall Street crash in 1929 turned into the Great Depression. Trade levels tumbled, leading to the inevitable laying up of many ships. Only a handful of liner companies managed to keep all their ships trading, and the collapse of the Kylsant shipping group, which had overreached itself, sent shockwaves through the industry. Meanwhile, rising nationalism enabled the Japanese economy to recover more quickly than other nations, largely due to a process of remilitarisation. This provided a welcome boost to the domestic shipbuilding industry, which set about upgrading both the naval and merchant fleets. As the economic situation eased and normal trading began to resume, a new breed of large 'Empire Food Ships' was built to service the UK's need for meat and dairy produce from Australia and New Zealand. The late-1930s saw elements of streamlining being introduced, in particular rounded bridge fronts, whilst on the propulsion front, the increased output and reliability of diesel engines resulted in some ships requiring only a single engine and screw in place of the more traditional twinned outfit.

Note: An asterisk in a caption indicates the vessel shown in the photograph.

New Japanese motorships

Japanese liner companies began to adopt diesel propulsion in the late 1920s, in Osaka Shosen Kisen (OSK)'s case with its *Santos Maru* and *Buenos Aires Maru* classes of cargo/passenger ships. Shortly after delivery of the last of these in 1930, Mitsubishi's Nagasaki shipyard completed in some secrecy the 8,357gt *Kinai Maru*, the first of six advanced 10,100dwt diesel cargo liners, which set the pattern for more than fifty similar fast vessels built with the help of government subsidy during the 1930s. She measured 445 x 60.5ft and had a raised forecastle with vertical stem and cruiser stern, propulsion being by twin six-cylinder Sulzer diesels producing 7,200bhp for a service speed of more than sixteen knots (eighteen and a half knots on trial). *Tokai Maru*, *Sanyo Maru* and *Hokuriku Maru* followed in 1930 and *Nankai Maru* and *Hokkai Maru**, which had new Mitsubishi engines, in 1933. All six were employed on the express Japan–New York (via Panama) service, *Kinai Maru* cutting ten days off the thirty-five-day Prince Line record on her maiden voyage. World War II cut short their careers and the same fate befell two modernised versions, the seventeen-knot *Tozan Maru* and *Kyushu Maru* (8,684gt), built in 1938 with curved, raked stems and four goalpost masts. Their dimensions were similar to Nippon Yusen Kaisha (NYK)'s *Akagi Maru* class but twin Mitsubishi diesels developing 9,600bhp gave trial speeds of just under twenty knots. During World War II, many of these fast ships were taken up by the Imperial Japanese Navy as transports, though *Sanyo Maru* (1930) was initially a seaplane tender. All were sunk, six by US submarines and two by Allied bombers, including *Hokkai Maru*, the last to be lost, off Sourabaya, in August 1945.

Nippon Yusen Kaisha was quick to follow Osaka Shosen Kisen's example and built six 7,140gt, fifteen-knot motorships for its own New York service in 1934–5: *Noto Maru*, *Noshiro Maru* and *Nojima Maru* from Mitsubishi's Nagasaki yard, *Nagara Maru* and *Narutu Maru* from Yokohama Dock and *Nako Maru* from Uraga Dock. They were unusual for high-class Japanese liner tonnage in being three-island ships with a long bridge deck incorporating Nos 3 and 4 hatches. Their mast arrangement differed slightly from *Kinai Maru*, a third goalpost mast replacing conventional kingposts immediately forward of the bridge as shown in this view of *Nagara Maru*. A single seven-cylinder Sulzer diesel of 6,700bhp gave a trial speed of eighteen and a half knots. Their introduction cut the Yokohama–New York voyage time from thirty-six to twenty-eight days. All succumbed to Allied action between November 1942 and November 1944. Five similar but slightly longer (459ft) *Akagi Maru*-class ships followed from Mitsubishi during 1936–38. These lacked the goalpost abutting the bridge, whilst their Mitsubishi engine had an extra cylinder for a total output of 8,000bhp producing a trial speed of around nineteen knots. Nippon Yusen Kaisha's final prewar cargo liners were the twin-screw *Sakito Maru* class (1939–40, 7,180gt). Seven of these were built by Mitsubishi at Nagasaki (the first four) and Yokohama between 1939 and 1940 for the company's eastbound round-the-world and Los Angeles–Panama–New York services. These differed in having just a short forecastle on a hull measuring 508ft oa x 62ft and were equipped with a 50t jumbo derrick on the foremast. Twin Mitsubishi or MAN diesels developed 9,600bhp for a trial speed of just under twenty knots. Not a single ship from all three classes survived World War II.

In the early 1930s, Mitsui & Company availed itself of government subsidies to expand its traditional tramping operation into the liner trades. It entered the Japan–New York run via Panama in 1932 with *Shikisan Maru*, followed by the diesel-powered 7,623gt *Azumasan Maru* and *Amagisan Maru* in 1933, which marginally bettered Osaka Shosa Kisen's *Kinai Maru* class (see page 74) in terms of speed. These were followed by five 477 x 62ft ships that were 1,000t larger: *Aobasan Maru* and *Asosan Maru* in 1935 and *Arimasan Maru**, *Asakasan Maru* and *Atsutasan Maru* in 1937. An even larger pair, *Awajisan Maru* and *Ayatosan Maru* measuring 9,790gt on dimensions of 483 x 64ft, were delivered in 1939. Speed was around the sixteen-to-eighteen-knot range, supplied by single diesels. From 1935, Mitsui changed its hull colours from black with 'MITSUI LINE' in large white letters to an attractive pale green, the funnel being silver grey with three white rings. All but *Arimasan Maru* became war losses between December 1941 and December 1944, and she owed her survival to having served as a hospital ship in the latter stages of the conflict. She became part of the merged Mitsui-OSK Lines in 1962 and was sold four years later, becoming *Katsuragawa Maru* then *Chokyu Maru* in 1968, finally going for scrap at Etajima in 1970.

The now all-but-forgotten Kokusai Kisen Kaisha was another leading Japanese liner company on the main New York and Europe trade routes in the 1930s, its funnel colours being black with a large white 'A' on a red band between two narrow white bands. Following two fifteen-knot *Katsuragi Maru*-class ships delivered in 1931, it received seven similar but slightly larger ships measuring approximately 8,500gt (9,200–9,500dwt) between 1933 and 1936 from Harima, Uraga Dock and Kawasaki. All were diesel-driven with speeds of around sixteen and a half knots and their hulls incorporated a short forecastle and six holds along with two masts and three sets of prominent goalposts. The latter were replaced by normal posts in subsequent ships, those in front of the bridge and right aft being dropped altogether. The same basic design was continued in 1938, albeit with the bridge placed one deck higher, in the 509ft oa *Kinka Maru** and *Kinryu Maru* from Kawasaki. All were lost to US aircraft and submarines during the Pacific war, *Kinka Maru* being bombed on 13 November 1944.

Four masts and Maierform bows

Maierform bows were adopted by United Netherlands Navigation Company for an unusual pair of motorships for its Australian service. *Aagtekerk** and *Almkerk* were delivered by Nederlandsche Scheepsbouw Maats., Amsterdam, in the first half of 1934 and shared a unique profile with three short hull islands, four very tall masts and a compact superstructure topped by a diminutive funnel. Their measurements were 6,811gt and 9,114dwt with hull dimensions of 460 x 60ft. Two six-cylinder Stork diesels with a total output of 8,300bhp ensured a fifteen-and-a-half-knot service speed. In May 1940, they were transferred to Phs van Ommeren management from London but sadly both became war losses, *Almkerk* being torpedoed by *U106* about 180 miles south of the Cape Verde Islands on 16 March 1941 and her sister succumbing to German air attack north of Tobruk while in a Malta-bound convoy on 14 June 1942.

Empire Food Ships

Federal Steam Navigation Company's *Durham* and *Dorset** were developments of sister company New Zealand Shipping Company's *Otaio* class with a different mast arrangement and both well decks filled in to give a flush hull. The final ships from Workman, Clark's Belfast yard, they were delivered in 1934 and measured 10,902gt and 13,370dwt on dimensions of 513ft oa by just less than 67ft. Twin Sulzer diesels developed 11,000bhp for a service speed of sixteen knots. *Durham* was fitted out as a cadet ship for the combined fleet, having accommodation and classrooms for forty persons. Both ships remained in commercial service on the outbreak of war but were taken up for Malta convoy work. *Durham* was holed by a mine in August 1941 and, whilst awaiting repairs in Gibraltar Bay, was struck in No 6 hold by an Italian limpet mine and had to be beached. Refloated four months later, she was patched up and finally left in tow early the following September for permanent repairs in the UK. Her sister was lost on 13 August in an aircraft-launched torpedo attack during the famous Pedestal convoy. *Durham* was finally broken up in Kaohsiung in 1966, having made the outward voyage as *Rion* under the Panamanian flag.

Shaw, Savill improved on its *Zealandic* design with five larger and faster 'W'-class ships built by Harland & Wolff in two groups: *Waiwera* and *Waipawa* at Belfast and *Wairangi** at Govan in 1934–5 and *Waimarama* and *Waiotira* in Belfast in 1938–9. The first group ships measured 10,782gt (12,320dwt) and the others 11,092gt (13,000dwt) due to having a raised poop and all had cruiser sterns. Hull dimensions were 535ft oa x 70ft and the earlier trio could easily maintain sixteen knots with their twin ten-cylinder single-acting Burmeister & Wain diesels of 12,000bhp, whilst the later pair were about a knot faster with two six-cylinder double-acting engines developing 13,500bhp. Insulated capacity ranged between 500,000 and 600,000cu ft, equating to more than 150,000 carcasses. The inbound *Waiotira* was torpedoed by *U95* 160 miles northwest of Rockall on Boxing Day 1940 and *Waiwera* by *U754* in the North Atlantic on 29 June 1942. On 13 August of the same year, both *Wairangi* and *Waimarama* were sunk close to Malta in the famous Pedestal convoy. Only *Waipawa*, which had taken part in the Sicily and Italy landings, survived the war and she was sold to Greece in 1968 for a one-way voyage to Kaohsiung breakers as *Aramis*. (*B Fielden*)

The doctrine of Imperial Preference (which involved the taxation of goods imported from non-Empire countries) resulting from the 1932 Ottawa Conference had an adverse effect on British liner companies involved in the River Plate meat trade. To counteract this, Blue Star Line switched its refrigerated shipping operations to the Australasian trade, where initially it only had loading rights for return cargoes, and in 1933 ordered eight specially designed seventeen-knot motorships of around 600,000cu ft capacity, five from Harland & Wolff, Belfast and three from Cammell, Laird & Company, Birkenhead. *Imperial Star**, the first to be completed in Belfast in January 1935, had a raised forecastle and long bridge deck and her distinctive profile with single mast and funnel earned her the nickname 'the big tug' on the Australian waterfront. She and sister *New Zealand Star*, which followed two months later, measured 12,427gt on dimensions of 543ft oa x 70ft and had twin four-stroke single-acting ten-cylinder Burmeister & Wain engines. Subsequent deliveries, *Australia Star*, *Empire Star* and *Sydney Star* from Belfast and *Dunedin Star*, *Melbourne Star* and *Brisbane Star* from Birkenhead differed in having a raised poop and no boat-deck extension over No 3 hold, whilst their engines were two-stroke double-acting six-cylinder units. A further two ships, *Auckland Star* and *Wellington Star* had been completed in Belfast by 1939 and *Adelaide Star*, destined never to sail for Blue Star, was under construction by Burmeister & Wain in Copenhagen. In August 1942 *Brisbane Star* and *Melbourne Star* survived the famous Pedestal convoy to resupply Malta but seven sisters were lost during the war, *Dunedin Star* through stranding off South Africa. The final ships adhering to this design, a new *Imperial Star* and *Melbourne Star* completed by Harland & Wolff, Govan, in 1948, were appreciably longer at 572ft oa and were fitted with more powerful eight-cylinder engines developing 16,000bhp. (*B Fielden*)

Laid down for the New Zealand Shipping Company but delivered to P&O and managed by Federal Steam Navigation Company, whose colours they originally bore, *Essex* and *Sussex* of 1936–7 were amongst the finest long-distance cargo liners of their day. Continuing the flush-hull design introduced by *Durham* (see page 76), but considerably larger at 11,063gt, they had their masts positioned one hatch nearer the superstructure in addition to six pairs of kingposts, which became a feature of both Federal and New Zealand Shipping Company's postwar tonnage. A more pointed cruiser stern helped to increase overall length to 551ft on a beam of just more than 70ft. A third sister, *Suffolk*, was delivered to Federal in 1939 and all were products of John Brown's famous Clydebank yard. Capacity was 535,000cu ft refrigerated and more than 20,000cu ft general in No 1 hold and the tween deck, whilst one 50t and twenty 10t derricks were provided for cargo handling. Twin five-cylinder Doxford opposed-piston diesels with an output of 13,250bhp enabled them to maintain up to eighteen knots if required. *Essex* was bombed in Malta in January 1941 and subsequent hits left her lying partially submerged for two years; however, she was towed back to the UK in August 1943 and rebuilt. *Sussex* also had an interesting war, surviving magnetic mine and bomb hits and just escaping from Singapore before it fell to the Japanese. In 1946–7, P&O took back *Essex* and *Sussex* for its Australian service and renamed them *Paringa* and *Palana* (depicted here in the Suez Canal). The latter spent more than eighteen months at Sydney's Cockatoo Dock undergoing repairs after striking a submerged reef off Mackay early in 1951. In 1954, she reverted to Federal management as *Cambridge*, her sister *Paringa* becoming *Norfolk* under New Zealand Shipping Company management a year later. Both arrived in Japan, at Yokosuka and Sakai respectively, for demolition in 1962. *Suffolk* was scrapped six years later in Kaohsiung.

To compete with some of the fast new tonnage introduced by its rivals in the Australasian trade, Port Line took delivery of the 9,687gt *Port Jackson* from Swan, Hunter's Wallsend yard in 1937. Her three-island hull, which incorporated a long forecastle and extra long bridge deck, marked a major shift in company design and set the pattern for eight subsequent ships. Measuring 521ft oa x 68ft, she could maintain a steady sixteen knots from her twin four-cylinder Doxford diesels, which delivered 11,500bhp. As with many other cargo liners, her passenger accommodation was doubled to twenty-four during World War II, which she survived unscathed apart from a brief brush with a U-boat that scored two shell hits. Her postwar career was relatively uneventful, apart from a serious collision in the River Elbe with Scindia Line's *Jalavikram* in March 1959, which necessitated her being beached. Following repairs, she continued in service until 1967 when she was sold and renamed *Legation* for a single voyage to Japanese breakers in Kure.

Scandinavian motorships

Following the delivery of three *Axel Johnson*-class liners for its North Pacific service in the latter half of the 1920s, Johnson Line began planning a series of cargo liners that would eventually number twenty-one by the time the last was delivered in 1948 and which would incorporate a number of important innovations. The initial group of nine 7,000dwt open shelter-deckers, led by *Argentina* and illustrated here by *Chile* (1937) in the Scheldt, were built by Götaverken, Gothenburg, between 1935 and 1940. They followed the basic design of the *Axel Johnson* trio, which had broken from the earlier funnel-less designs, but had a longer forecastle and berths for just twelve instead of fifty passengers. Twin eight-cylinder Burmeister & Wain engines of 6,800bhp gave a speed of around fifteen knots. Two modified groups with double the passenger accommodation (twenty-four) and more powerful engines were ordered during World War II. Eight 7,700dwt ships came from Götaverken, the third of which, *Suecia* (1944), was the first large ship to be fitted with controllable pitch propellers fabricated by the Johnson Group's KaMeWa subsidiary company. The final four 7,900dwt ships, led by *La Plata*, were built by Kockums and were the first European-built cargo liners with welded hulls. Despite Sweden's neutrality in the conflict, three of the first group became war losses; *Venezuela* was torpedoed by *U123* in the North Atlantic in 1941, *Argentina* was mined in the North Sea in 1942 and *Brasil* in the Skagerrak in January 1943 whilst preceding her sister, *Ecuador*, in convoy with the tanker *Svea Jarl*, which was also lost. The others were mainly employed in the North Pacific trade or used on safe-conduct voyages. Two were later wrecked, *Colombia* outside Örnsköldsvik, Gulf of Bothnia, on 24 November 1954 and *Ecuador* on Terschelling Island on 29 February 1956. *Nordstjernan*, *Uruguay* and *Chile* – which had been repaired after sinking following a fire in Copenhagen in 1959 – were sold in 1968 and scrapped in Taiwan a year later as *Frances*, *Lily* and *Vakis*, respectively. *Peru*, the last to survive, was demolished in Shanghai in 1971, having become *Maco Venture* the previous year.

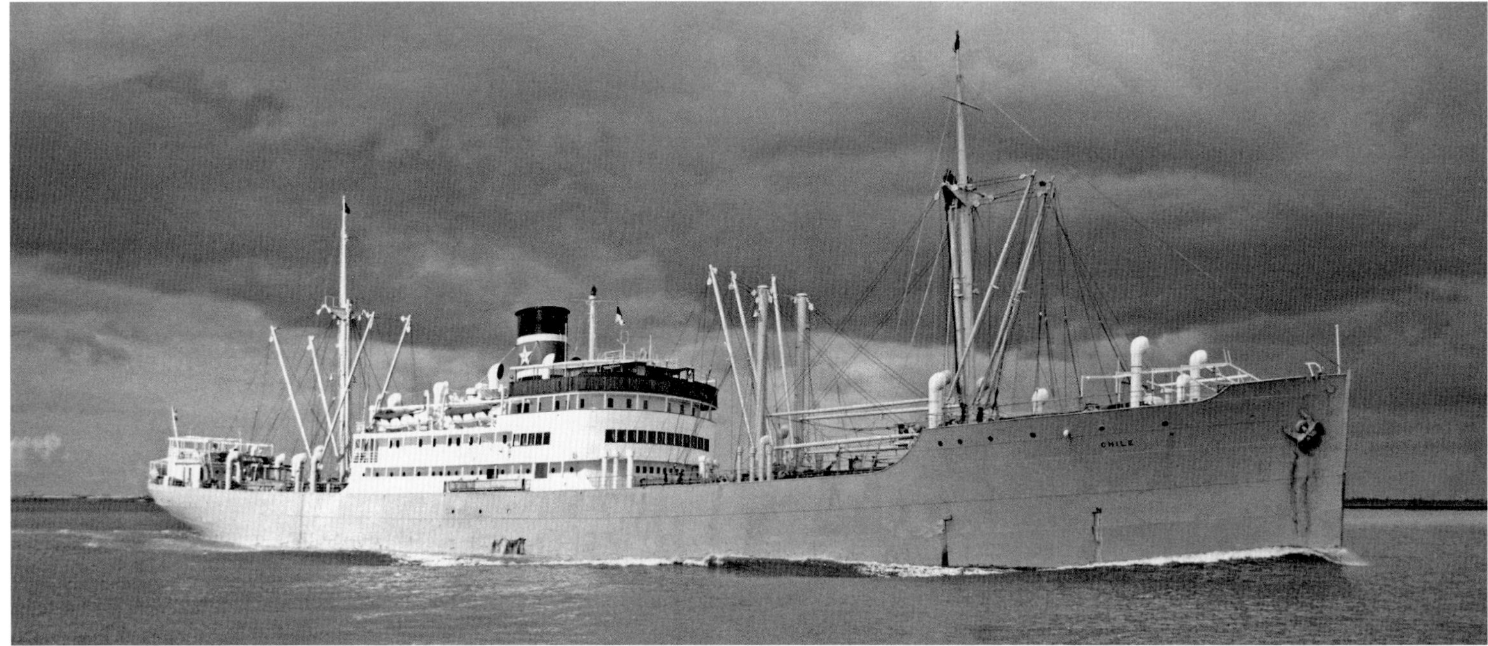

Knut Knutsen OAS of Haugesund, whose black funnels carried two red bands (as opposed to Wilh. Wilhelmsen's two blue bands), ran services from northwest Europe to the Pacific coasts of North and South America and later from the North Pacific to Western Australia via the Far East and Singapore Strait. An early advocate of motor ships, some of which had three masts, the company embarked on a fine series of new ships with *Martin Bakke* completed by Götaverken, Gothenburg, in 1936. She measured 5,484gt and 8,500dwt on dimensions of 453 x 59 feet and she was propelled at fifteen knots by a five-cylinder Burmeister & Wain diesel developing 5,750bhp. *Elisabeth Bakke*, which followed a year later, and three further sisters *Sofie Bakke, Margrethe Bakke* and *Ida Bakke**, completed in 1938, had six-cylinder engines giving sixteen knots. Subsequent ships had a long forecastle, increasing length by some 22ft and gross tonnage to 5,868, and could maintain sixteen and three quarter knots with a seven-cylinder Burmeister & Wain diesel producing 8,000bhp. *Sofie Bakke* (replacing her namesake lost in collision off Peterhead on 4 August 1940), *Knut Bakke* and *Olaf Bakke* were all delivered in 1945 and *Anna Bakke* and *Gjertrud Bakke* completed the ten-ship series in 1950. Two were wrecked, *Olaf Bakke* off Buenaventura in October 1959 and *Martin Bakke* in the Scheldt in November 1963, but the others had successful careers and lasted until the 1970s. *Margrethe Bakke* was the last to be demolished, in Split, in 1977 as the Cypriot *Iokasti*.

Danish tramp and tanker owner A P Møller first entered the liner business under the Mærsk Line banner in 1928 with a regular service from US east and west coast ports to Japan and the Far East. Initially, it was maintained by three-masted motor tramps but between 1930 and 1932 two pairs of cargo liners adhering to roughly the same design were completed by Møller's own shipyard at Odense. The 5,038gt twin-screw *Gertrude Mærsk* and *Nils Mærsk* were completed in 1930–1 and the 5,476gt *Peter Mærsk* and *Anna Mærsk*, which had single 5,500bhp machinery for fifteen knots, were delivered in 1932. The 6,271gt *Nora Mærsk* completed in 1934 had a cruiser stern. A serious fire in her copra cargo in Zamboanga two years later led to her sale to Kawasaki Kisen Kabushiki Kaisha. Repaired, she re-entered service as *Terukawa Maru* but was torpedoed by the US submarine *Skate* in December 1943. An even larger pair, the 6,576gt *Grete Mærsk** and *Marchen Mærsk* were completed by Bremer Vulkan in 1937 with Maierform bows. Twin five-cylinder MAN diesels provide a sea speed of sixteen knots. The final prewar delivery was *Laura Mærsk*, which had a conventional bow and an extra kingpost on the forecastle. Mærsk ships were taken over by the US Navy during World War II, *Grete* and *Marchen* becoming the troop transports *Pennant* and *Perida*, respectively, in 1941. They reverted to their original names after the war. *Grete Mærsk* became the Japanese *Zuiyo Maru* in 1953 and was scrapped at Mihara in 1965. Her sister went to Polish Ocean Lines as *Przyjazn Narodow* in 1951 and was demolished at Whampoa in 1972, a year after *Laura Mærsk*, which had undergone several name and ownership changes since 1963.

German developments

In 1934, Norddeutscher Lloyd purchased two interesting ships with a controversial history using Depression emergency aid. Originally delivered by Deutsche Werft, Kiel, in 1929 as *Sud Expreso* and *Sud Americano* for Ivarans Rederi's New York–east coast of South America service, they were twin-funnelled motorships with accommodation for thirty passengers. Although intended to have a speed of eighteen knots (which was reached on trials), they failed to live up to their owner's expectations and were returned to the builders. Taken over by the state, they were briefly chartered to Blue Star Line for Pacific coast service, adopting that company's colours and being renamed *Wenatchee Star* and *Yakima Star*. Returned to Germany in 1933 and 1934, the former briefly held the name *Holstein* before Norddeutscher Lloyd rebuilt them with a new fore body with raked stem and a single large funnel, at the same time renaming them *Elbe* and *Weser* (shown here on trials). New engines provided a service speed of seventeen knots and passenger complement was reduced to seventeen. Revised tonnage measurements were 9,179gt (10,350dwt), and overall dimensions were 510ft x 61ft. Their new careers were brief, *Elbe* being sunk as a naval blockade runner on 6 June 1941 some 900 miles northwest of the Cape Verde Islands by aircraft from HMS *Eagle* during the *Bismark* operation. *Weser* was captured off Manzanillo on 25 September 1940 by the auxiliary cruiser HMCS *Prince Robert* whilst trying to take supplies to the raider *Orion* (ex-Hapag's *Kurmark*) in the Marshall Islands. Taken to Esquimault in British Columbia, she was renamed *Vancouver Island* by the Canadian authorities in November but was torpedoed by *U558* on 15 October 1941 some 750 miles southwest of Fastnet Rock and lost with all hands.

Hansa Line followed up its *Lichtenfels* heavy-lift series with four ordinary cargo liners from the same builder, A G Weser. Lead ship *Ehrenfels* was completed in 1935, followed by *Reichenfels** and *Kandelfels* a year later and *Kybfels* in 1937. They were three-island ships with a long raised forecastle and bridge deck extending to the mainmast and measured 7,752gt and 10,250dwt on dimensions of 485 x 61ft. Propulsion was by two six-cylinder MAN diesels developing 7,600bhp and geared to a single screw for sixteen knots. Two slightly longer versions, the 7,862gt *Goldenfels* and *Hohenfels*, were built by Bremen Vulkan in 1937–8. Early in World War II, *Kandelfels* and *Goldenfels* were converted into heavy auxiliary cruisers by Deschimag. The former, as *Pinguin*, had both well-decks filled and the latter, as *Atlantis*, just the forward well whilst a second dummy funnel was added. They became the most successful of the German World War II surface commerce raiders, sinking or capturing twenty-eight (136,642gt) and twenty-two ships (123,265gt) respectively, until 1941 when *Pinguin* was sunk by HMS *Cornwall* in May and *Atlantis* was scuttled in November when surprised by HMS *Devonshire*. The only ship to survive the war was *Hohenfels*, which became the Dutch *Ridderkerk* in 1947 and was scrapped in Hong Kong in 1962.

Following the Depression, Germany's Hamburg-America Line began to experiment with different propulsion systems. The 6,737gt *Wuppertal* was a one-off cargo liner measuring 497ft oa x 61ft and was built by Deutsche Werft, Hamburg, for the company's Australian service in 1936. She was the first ship to have diesel-electric machinery using AC transmission, comprising three seven-cylinder MAN engines with a total output of 7,800bhp connected to three Brown-Boveri generators and a single shaft. This allowed an average speed of fifteen knots to be maintained on the fully loaded return voyage, only twelve to thirteen knots being required for the part-loaded outward journey. Diesel-electric propulsion was used in several subsequent Hapag passenger and passenger/cargo ships, including *Steiermark* (8,736gt/12,305dwt), which was completed by Krupp in 1938. She later became the successful commerce raider *Kormoran*, responsible for sinking the cruiser HMAS *Sydney* with all hands off Western Australia on 20 November 1941 before herself being scuttled and abandoned in a sinking state. *Wuppertal* was seized by the Dutch at Padang in May 1940 and was operated by the Dutch government as *Noesaniwi* in the closed shelter-deck condition, which raised her tonnage to 8,241gt. After the war she was transferred to Rotterdam Lloyd and renamed *Kertosono*, as shown, and was eventually broken up in Kure, Japan, in 1961.

Further UK deliveries

The 6,210gt *Inventor**, completed in Glasgow in 1935 by D & W Henderson, was the largest Thos & Jas Harrison ship since *Huntsman* (see page 55), last of the four-masters, and its first to have a cruiser stern. With a deadweight tonnage of 9,294, she measured 453 x 56ft but was still conservatively powered by a three-cylinder reciprocating engine for a modest twelve and a half knots. Three sisters, *Explorer*, *Tribesman* and *Strategist*, followed and then a further quartet led by *Scientist*, which had low-pressure Bauer-Wach exhaust turbines added, raising speed by two knots. The final versions of the class, beginning with *Settler* in 1939, were fifteen-and-a-half knot ships with double-reduction LP exhaust turbines. The post-war *Craftsman* trio of 1947–8 were similar but marginally larger than the *Settler* group and had shorter funnels. The three contemporary *Herdsman*-class motor ships powered by Doxford diesels had thicker funnels and a higher bridge. *Tribesman* was sunk by the pocket battleship *Admiral Scheer* 200 miles southwest of the Cape Verde Islands on 1 December 1940. *Explorer* and *Strategist* were scrapped in Hong Kong in 1959 and 1963 respectively and *Inventor* was demolished in Ghent by Van Heyghen Frères in 1960.

In the mid-1930s, Clan Line Steamers embarked on a large fleet rebuilding programme that eventually comprised more than twenty-five ships built over a decade, all products of Greenock Dockyard save one which came from William Denny & Brothers. They were the first twin-screw ships built for Clan Line and the first to have long forecastles but retained the split superstructure of previous tonnage. Sturdy in appearance, they could be divided into several groups commencing in 1936 with the refrigerated *Clan Macarthur*, *Perthshire* and *Clan Macaulay* which measured 10,448t on an overall length of 498ft. *Clan Cameron* of 1937 was the first of a large group of shorter ships (485ft–488ft oa) which enabled them to enter the Calcutta dock system. Later ships of this type had an extra accommodation deck beneath the funnel and when finally delivered to Clan in 1946 following wartime service as the midget submarine depot ship HMS *Bonaventure*, *Clan Davidson* could be distinguished by a long bridge deck and shorter raked funnel. All these ships were propelled by two three-cylinder reciprocating engines exhausting into a low-pressure turbine with an output of around 8,300shp for a speed of fifteen to sixteen knots. The final group comprised more large refrigerated ships: *Clan Macdonald* (1939), seen leaving Sydney in 1965, and *Clan Macdougall* (1944), which were motorships and the turbine-driven *Lanarkshire* (1940). These measured 505ft oa and had an extra hold abaft the engine casing. The reciprocating-engined 500ft *Clan Urquhart* (1943) was similar. Many of these fine ships were lost during World War II, three of them whilst trying to re-supply Malta. *Clan Macdonald* turned out to have the longest career of all, being in her thirty-first year when broken up in Shanghai in 1970.

Elder Dempster switched to a compact superstructure with the 5,353gt *Sobo**, delivered by Scotts' Shipbuilding & Engineering, Greenock, in 1936. A sister, *Swedru*, followed a year later and *Seaforth* from Caledon, Dundee, in 1939, all destined for West African service. Two further deliveries from Scotts' in 1939, *Sansu* and *Sangara*, had funnels placed further aft. Although similar in length at 379ft to the *Dunkwa* class, they had a raked stem and cruiser stern and two-deck superstructures. *Sobo* was used as an assault ship at the North African landings in 1942 and was broken up in Ghent in 1963. *Swedru* was bombed by long-range Focke-Wulf Kondors and sunk by convoy escorts on 16 April 1941, 150 miles off Ireland's Achill Head. *Seaforth* was lost with all hands after being torpedoed by *U103* on 18 February 1941, 350 miles west of the Isle of Lewis. *Sansu* and *Sangara* survived the war and were broken up at Preston by Thomas W Ward in 1961 and 1960 respectively.

Lamport & Holt caused a stir with the combined bridge and funnel – the latter containing the wireless room – of its 7,783gt *Delius**, the first of seven similar ships built by Harland & Wolff, Belfast, between 1937 and 1945. They only carried general cargo and shared the same hull dimensions of 456ft oa x 62ft and the same six-cylinder Burmeister & Wain diesels giving an economical twelve to thirteen knots; however, their appearances differed. The first three – *Delius, Delane* and *Devis* – were as shown, *Defoe* (1940) and *Debrett* (1942) had wider funnels extending to the front of the bridge. *Devis* and *Defoe* became war losses, the former to torpedo from *U593* off Derna, Sicily, in September 1943 and the latter through explosion southwest of Rockall a year earlier. They were replaced in 1944–5 by new ships bearing the same names, which had extra kingposts forward and aft of the superstructure, whilst *Defoe* also had a long bridge deck extending to the masts. *Devis* was propelled by the first Harland & Wolff double-acting opposed-piston diesel. During 1954–55, the remaining ships were transferred for varying periods to Blue Star Line for Pacific coast service, taking on Blue Star names and, excepting *Devis*, being fitted with refrigerated space. In 1961, *Delius* and *Delane* made one-way voyages to breakers in Japan and Hong Kong as the Panamanian *Kettara VII* and – *VI*. *Devis* was scrapped in La Spezia in 1962 and *Debrett* in Osaka three years later after a single voyage as *Ambasciata*. Finally, *Defoe*, which had become *Argolis Star* in 1966, was scrapped in Shanghai in 1970.
(*B Fielden*)

The twin-screw *Lochavon*, delivered by Harland & Wolff, Belfast in 1938, was Royal Mail Line's first new cargo ship for its main River Plate service since the N class of 1918–20 (see page 52). Her design incorporated a forecastle and long bridge deck with No 3 hatch separating the bridge and funnel, as well as a typical Belfast outward-sloping cruiser stern. Measuring 9,205gt on overall dimensions of 498 x 66ft, she was driven at sixteen knots by twin twelve-cylinder Burmeister & Wain engines. Cargo capacity was 530,000cu ft (grain) and she mounted a heavy derrick on the forward side of her mainmast. Her life was tragically short, being torpedoed 200 miles west of Bishop Rock, Scilly Isles in October 1939, barely a month after war was declared. The war precluded the building of any sisters, but in 1947 Harland & Wolff completed the broadly similar *Loch Avon* and *Loch Garth*, which had their boat deck extended across No 3 hatch. Other differences included additional pairs of kingposts abaft the bridge and right aft, as well as cruiser spoon sterns. They were propelled by three double-reduction turbines geared to a single screw, giving sixteen knots in service on their North Pacific run, a speed which could be comfortably bettered when required. *Loch Avon* was sold in 1967 to the Singapore arm of C Y Tung and renamed *Hongkong Observer*, going to Taiwan breakers in 1971, three years after her sister.

Following its acquisition of the ailing Glen Line in 1935 from the wreckage of the collapsed Kylsant Group, Alfred Holt ordered eight advanced twin-screw cargo liners from yards in the UK, Holland, Denmark and Hong Kong to ensure prompt delivery. Designed by Alfred Holt's naval architect Harry Flett, the 9,784gt *Glenearn* class introduced a look that was to become an instantly recognisable Holt trademark for the next eighteen years. This consisted of a three-island design with a long bridge deck incorporating Nos 3 and 4 hatches either side of the main accommodation block, topped by the traditional upright funnel. Measuring 507ft oa x 66ft, they were fitted with a comprehensive array of kingposts and were driven by twin six-cylinder Burmeister & Wain diesels developing a total of 12,000bhp for a sea speed of eighteen knots. Only *Glenearn*, *Glenroy** and *Denbighshire* had been delivered by the outbreak of World War II, but the first two, along with *Glengyle*, performed valuable work as naval transports and later as infantry landing ships. *Breconshire* and *Glenorchy** were sunk in Malta convoys, whilst *Glengarry* was seized in Copenhagen and completed as *Meersburg*, becoming a submarine depot ship and later the minelaying training ship *Hansa*. She survived hostilities and was reconstructed along with her remaining sisters, which were phased into Far East service during 1947–9, the two losses being made good by a new *Breconshire*, laid down for Holt but completed as the escort carrier HMS *Activity*, and the transferred *Priam*, which became *Glenorchy* in 1948. These were some 6ft longer and lacked the conspicuous ventilators around the funnel. Until the early 1960s, these eight ships, backed up by a ninth chartered in from Holt to make up for increasing port delays, provided a fortnightly express service that fully lived up to prewar expectations. The introduction of new, faster ships and increasing problems with their engines hastened their end and all had gone to Far East breakers by 1971, four having briefly assumed Holt livery and names.

Prewar Low Countries tonnage

In 1937, Compagnie Maritime Belge turned to Denmark's Nakskov Shipyard for an improved twelve-passenger version of the *Emile Francqui*-class ships on its New York service. Named after the recently deceased managing director of the company, the 5,965gt *Alex van Opstal* was a handsome-looking vessel with a short raised forecastle mounting two prominent kingposts and a long raised poop carrying the mainmast at its forward end. The long accommodation block incorporated a trunked No 4 hatch abaft a high bridge with a rounded front. Main dimensions were 455ft oa x 58ft. Sadly, she became an early war casualty, succumbing to a mine near the Shambles light vessel whilst proceding to a contraband inspection area in Weymouth Bay. Three similar ships were ordered from John Cockerill SA, Hoboken, in 1940, with just one completed during hostilities as *Kanonier* for German account. She survived and was renamed *Alex van Opstal* (2) but her two sisters, *Armand Grisar* and *Gouverneur Galopin*, which were launched as *Grenadier* and *Musketier*, differed slightly in having no teak bridge and cabs whilst the forward kingposts had conventional tops. More importantly, they were converted to carry ninety passengers to cope with extra demand on the Congo service. All were sold to Yugoslavia in 1959, becoming *Bled*, *Bovec* and *Bohinj* respectively, the first two being scrapped in La Spezia and Whampoa in 1970 and *Bohinj* at Split two years later.

Depicted in Singapore, *Bantam* was the third unit in the four-ship *Weltevreden* class of 9,245gt cargo liners, which were built in pairs in 1937 and 1939 by P Smit Jnr, Rotterdam, and De Schelde, Flushing, for Rotterdam Lloyd's Far East services. The earlier ships originally had a tonnage opening in the long forecastle but all were three-deck ships with the superstructure split around No 3 hatch. Cargo capacity was around 12,000dwt on dimensions of 515ft oa x 62ft. Twin eight-cylinder Krupp diesels in the first pair and Sulzers in the second pair drove twin screws for sixteen knots in service. The first three served as US troop transports during World War II and *Bantam* sailed in a Malta aviation-fuel supply convoy in November 1942. Their boats were reduced to one either side on gravity davits when they returned to commercial service in 1945–6. *Weltevreden* was scrapped in Bruges in 1963, *Brastagi* was lost on Caldeira Island, Mozambique, in October 1947 and *Japara* and *Bantam* were sold in the mid-1960s to Eastern owners as *Celebes Mariner* and *Pearl Glory/Millstar* respectively, eventually being scrapped in Kaohsiung in 1969 and Shanghai in 1971 respectively.

Particularly tall kingposts and an old-fashioned counter stern distinguished the Kon. Paketvaart Maats. *Straat Soenda** and *Straat Malakka*, which were completed by Van der Giessen in 1938–9 for the Bangkok–Africa run. Built as either open or closed shelter deckers, they measured 8,300gt and 8,622 dwt as closed shelter deckers on dimensions of 476 x 62ft. Their twin screws were driven by two eight-cylinder Werkspoor diesels for a service speed of sixteen and a half knots. Their original passenger complement of seventeen was reduced to twelve after World War II, during which conflict *Straat Soenda* was chartered to the British Ministry of War Transport. In 1947, both ships were transferred to Koninklijke Java-China-Paketvaart Lijnen, which they served for twenty years before being sold to Pacific International Lines of Singapore. Renamed *Kota Selatan* and *Kota Timur*, the former was wrecked off the Kenyan coast near Pemba Island in May 1971 and her sister was broken up in Shanghai two years later.

Delivered to Nederland Line by A G Weser, Bremen, just three months before the outbreak of World War II, *Java** was the first of a new class and the only one to be built outside the Netherlands. Measuring 9,250gt (11,927dwt) on dimensions of 495 x 63ft, she had a long bridge deck and was the first in the fleet to have a cruiser stern. Main machinery comprised twin seven-cylinder MAN oil engines with a total output of 8,000bhp geared to a single screw and giving a service speed of sixteen knots. Sisters *Sumatra* and *Celebes* were completed by Nederlandsche Scheepsbouw Maats., Amsterdam, as naval supply ships for the occupying Germans and did not enter Nederland Line service until 1945–6. *Sumatra* had a twelve-cylinder Werkspoor diesel and *Celebes*, which initially carried eighteen passengers, an eight-cylinder Stork unit. *Borneo* and *Bali*, also Werkspoor driven, by De Schelde and Rotterdam Drydock, were scuttled by the retreating Germans in 1944 and were not completed until December 1947. *Java* was scrapped in Hong Kong in 1963 and *Sumatra* in Kaohsiung in 1968 but the others went for further trading, *Celebes* to Peru as *Paracas* in 1966, and *Borneo* to Cyprus as *Azalea* in 1969, being broken up three years later in Shanghai. *Paracas* was involved in a serious collision with the tanker *Texaco Caribbean* in the English Channel on 11 January 1971. The latter exploded, broke in two and sank and the next day the wreck was hit by Hamburg-America's *Brandenburg* which also sank. Some five weeks later the Greek *Niki* foundered after striking the submerged wrecks and the overall loss of fifty-one lives from the three incidents resulted in the setting up of the Dover Strait Traffic Separation Scheme. *Paracas* returned to service following repairs in Hamburg and eventually went to Taiwan breakers in Kaohsiung in 1974, *Bali*, which had become *Luck Three* in 1971, following in 1979.

New Italian cargo liners

Italian shipbuilders were noted for some fine passenger ships but it was not until the eve of World War II that some notable new cargo-liner tonnage was ordered, all part of the nationalistic policy of the Mussolini government. C R dell'Adriatico, Monfalcone, was responsible for six 10,350dwt ships for a proposed eastbound round-the-world service for Soc. Italiana d'Armamento, Fiume (Sidarma Line). They are illustrated here by *Andrea Gritti* (1943) the sole survivor of hostilities, latterly under Ellerman Hall management following the Italian surrender. They measured 471 x 61ft and were driven by a six-cylinder double-acting Fiat diesel developing a maximum of 8,000bhp for a service speed of around sixteen knots. The final ship was delivered to N S M 'Oceaan' as *Jason* – the first 'Blue Funnel' to have a cruiser stern – but she only flew the Dutch flag for a single day on trials, before being taken over by the Italians and reverting to her original name of *Sebastiano Veniero*. She was torpedoed by HMS *Torbay* on 15 December 1941 near Navarino Bay, was beached and abandoned.

A second ship of the same name delivered in 1944 sailed as the German navy's *Kapitan Diederichsen* until attacked by the French destroyer *Le Fantasque* off Premuda near Isto in February 1944, later sinking whilst being towed towards Pola. Following an interesting career as an Axis blockade runner under Hapag management, lead ship *Pietro Orseolo* (1939) was finally caught and sunk by British aircraft in Concarneau Bay in April 1943.

Five *Fabio Filzi*-class cargo liners ordered by Lloyd Triestino from C R dell'Adriatico, Monfalcone, did not enter service until after war was declared and were quickly taken up as military transports to serve Italian forces in North Africa. Tonnage figures were 6,386gt (9,000dwt) on dimensions of 464 x 62ft and they were driven at sixteen knots by a Fiat diesel. The first four were lost to torpedo attack, the lead ship and *Carlo del Greco* by HMS *Upright* when in convoy off Taranto on 13 December 1941, *Gino Allegri* by HMS *Taku* and HMS *Proteus* on 31 May 1942 and *Reginaldo Giuliani* by aircraft 125 miles off Benghazi on 5 June 1942. The fifth ship, *Mario Roselli*, pictured on trials in wartime livery, was delivered to Italia Line in 1942. She survived a torpedo hit by British aircraft in June 1942 but was seized by the Germans at Corfu in September and sunk by US aircraft the following month. Raised early in 1951, she was towed to Monfalcone for repair and finally entered commercial service in 1952 as Società di Navigazione Italnavi's *Alpe*. In 1969 she was sold to Costa and a year later to Uruguayan owners, being finally scrapped at Blyth in 1972. After the war, Spanish shipyards completed several ships to a very similar design. Known as the *Monasterio* class, two of the early deliveries had their superstructure extended aft to enable passengers to be carried, whilst the others were redesigned as passenger ships.

A third group of Italian cargo liners ordered before World War II comprised the four-ship *Nino Bixio* class built for Genoa-based Soc. Anon. Cooperativa di Nav. Garibaldi by Ansaldo, Sestri Ponente in 1940–2. They were stylish-looking ships and were designed for their owner's service to East Africa. As built they had distinctive cowl tops to their funnels and comfortable accommodation for twelve passengers. Their main hull dimensions were 472 x 61ft giving a deadweight measurement of around 9,000. They were propelled by seven-cylinder double-acting Fiat diesels developing 6,000bhp for fifteen to sixteen knots. The final delivery, *Risolino Pilo*, was sunk fifty miles south of Pantellaria in August 1942 in a combined aircraft and submarine attack; the others were also severely damaged. For example, *Agostino Bertani* (launched as *Carlo Pisacane*) was sunk by aircraft at Tripoli on 15 January 1943 but was raised and rebuilt after the war. She bore the name *Anacapri* during 1950–52 but was wrecked at Tsamkong in February 1968 and scrapped at Vado Ligure. *Nino Bixio* is shown here entering Venice in 1967, three years before she went for demolition in La Spezia. *Luciana Manara* (1942) became *Giuseppe Canepa* in 1953, then Polish Ocean Lines' *Malgorzata Fornalska* in 1955. In 1965, she was sold to the People's Republic of China and renamed *Chong Ming* then *Hong Qi 144* in 1971 and finally *Hang Xiu 2* in 1991. She was deleted from the Register in 1992 after a fifty-year career.

CHAPTER

7

The US Maritime Commission Shipbuilding Programme and World War II Construction

Under the Merchant Marine Act of 1936, the United States set up a Maritime Commission to rebuild its merchant fleet, which consisted largely of ageing and uncompetitive World War I emergency tonnage. The first of the new cargo-liner types were just beginning to be delivered when Europe was again plunged into war. Production continued, but after the United States entered the war in December 1941 following the Japanese attack on Pearl Harbor, both existing and new ships were increasingly taken up for military use, many of them being completed as auxiliary aircraft carriers or troop transports.

Lessons learned during World War I were applied with vigour when it came to emergency shipbuilding and, of the two principal cargo-ship types, the best known and most numerous were the 'Liberty' ships built to a prewar UK tramp-ship design. Prefabrication and welding allowed unskilled workers to construct the ships in remarkably little time and, in all, 2,751 were built. However, as the war progressed, it became clear that a faster type of ship was needed, one better able to evade U-boat attack and that would be suitable for postwar employment with US steamship companies. The result was the 'Victory' ship, which began to appear late in the war but with more than 500 eventually being completed, represented by far the largest class of cargo liners ever built.

In the UK, a number of fine cargo liners had been lost whilst trying to resupply beleaguered Malta and many more had fallen victim elsewhere to air, surface and submarine attack. Although the British wartime shipbuilding programme was largely taken up by naval construction, time was found for a few Empire-type fast cargo ships, as well as a number of private contracts, some of which were based on existing designs.

Note: An asterisk in a caption indicates the vessel shown in the photograph.

The C2 type

Completed by Sun Shipbuilding, Chester, Pennsylvania, in June 1939, *Donald McKay* was the first freighter to emerge under the USMC's ambitious fleet replacement programme. One of six C2-type fifteen-knot motorships ordered by Moore McCormack Lines, she measured 6,200gt and 8,656dwt on dimensions of 459ft oa x 63ft and her hull incorporated three holds forward and two aft, with a short bridge deck and half-height forecastle and poop. All six were taken up as naval stores ships in 1940–41 and named after stars. In 1947, *Arcturus*, *Alcyone* and *Betelgeuse* (the former *Mormachawk*, *Mormacgull* and *Mormaclark*) were acquired by Sweden's Johnson Line for its new Persian Gulf–Far East service and the prefix *Star* was added to their names. *Star Alcyone*, shown here in Singapore in 1959, was broken up in Kaohsiung in 1969, *Star Arcturus* at Tadotsu in 1971 and *Star Betelgeuse* also in Kaohsiung a year later. Lead ship *Donald McKay* became the US Navy stores ship *Polaris* during World War II and after a brief break during 1946–8 was recommissioned and served in the Korean War, remaining active until 1957. Assigned to the National Defense Reserve Fleet at Suisun Bay, she was finally scrapped at Oakland in 1974.

Modified C2 types

An interesting modification of the Maritime Commission's C2-S design was adopted for six 7,100gt ships for Seas Shipping Company's Robin Line service from New York and Baltimore to South Africa. Built by Bethlehem Steel at Sparrows Point in 1941, *Robin Locksley*, – *Doncaster*, – *Kettering*, – *Sherwood*, – *Tuxford* and – *Wentley* measured just under 487ft oa x 61ft and their hulls, which lacked sheer, incorporated a long forecastle. The provision of a particularly large funnel mounted on a semi-streamlined superstructure gave them a powerful appearance.
A service speed of around sixteen knots was provided by twin steam turbines geared to a single screw. During World War II, *Robin Doncaster* briefly flew the Red Ensign as *Empire Curlew* during 1941–2, while *Robin Kettering* served as the US attack transport *Alhena*. All were sold to Isbrandtsen Lines in 1957, *Robin Doncaster*, – *Kettering*, – *Tuxford* and – *Wentley* being renamed *Flying Gull*, – *Hawk*, – *Endeavor and* – *Fish* respectively; the latter is depicted here off Singapore in 1959. *Flying Gull* was broken up at Bilbao in 1968 and the rest in Kaohsiung during 1970–72.

Later versions of the C2s designated C2-S-B1, of which seventy-one were completed at Oakland by Moore Dry Dock Company between January 1943 and June 1945, are perhaps best remembered by those operated by United States Lines on its postwar transatlantic and transpacific services, where their economic operation resulted in careers lasting into the container age. They had a modified superstructure with a projecting mid-portion of the bridge front, the funnels mounted farther forward than in the motor ships and they carried their boats two decks higher. The heavy tapered kingposts, which doubled as hold vents, were also distinctive, together with the short, mushroom-topped posts above the bridge. Gross tonnage was just under 8,000 and they were propelled by two steam turbines at fifteen and a half knots, although *Challenge* averaged 16.8 knots on an Atlantic crossing in 1939. Pictured here is *American Flyer*, completed by Moore Dry Dock Company, Oakland, in 1945 as *Water Witch*. Renamed in 1947, she became *Flyer* in 1965 and was broken up at Portland, Oregon in 1976. United States Lines also operated ten full-scantling versions (C2-S-AJ1) built by North Carolina Shipbuilding Corporation in 1945–6, and which could be identified by a single mast in place of the forward goalpost, conventional kingposts and a thinner funnel.

C3 types

American Export Lines and the US Maritime Commission co-operated in 1938 to design the first of the larger C3-type vessels, the C3-S-A3 or *Exporter* class, named after the first of eight ships to be completed by Bethlehem Steel's Quincy yard in September 1939. A second group of ten ships, identical save for slightly wider funnels, followed from the builder's Sparrows Point facility between 1943 and 1946. Impressive-looking ships, they measured 6,724gt on dimensions of 473 x 66ft and were amongst the last cargo liners to have counter sterns, seen to advantage in this Suez Canal view of *Executor* (1945). Particular attention was paid to humidity and temperature control in all six holds to safeguard perishable cargoes. A speed of sixteen and a half knots was maintained by a single 8,800shp steam turbine. War service apart, they were mainly employed in the US east coast–Mediterranean trade and, following the acquisition of American Export by Isbrandtsen in 1960, assumed the latter's funnel colours of yellow with a black top over a white band. *Executor* became Grace Line's *Santa Ines* in 1975 and was broken up at Terminal Island, Los Angeles, in 1976. Four similar but smaller *Exceller*-class ships had single masts in place of posts on the foredeck and shorter funnels. Designed to serve the lesser Mediterranean ports, they were completed by Bath Iron Works in 1941–2.

The largest of the initial USMC freighter designs was the C3, many of which were completed as World War II escort carriers or naval auxiliaries. Impressive ships with a short raised forecastle and elegant sheer line, they came in two versions, the C3-S-A1 at just over 8,000gt and the A2 type. All thirty-eight of the A1 version were completed as escort carriers and all bar one came from the Seattle-Tacoma Shipbuilding Corporation, Tacoma, the single ship being completed by Ingalls, Pascagoula, which was also responsible for fifty-eight out of a total of 94 A2s. Postwar, the C3s saw widespread deployment in both US and Allied liner fleets, in which their speed of sixteen and a half knots (lead ship *Sea Fox* achieved nineteen and a half knots on trials in 1940) supplied by twin steam turbines of 9,000shp placed them amongst the foremost tonnage of the day. They measured 492 x 70ft and their mast arrangement varied, particularly in the placing of the goalposts, whilst others had no posts on the forecastle. *Exchequer*, first of a batch of ten ships from Ingalls, delivered to American Export Lines in October 1940 was the first US-built ship with a welded hull. Shown here at San Pedro is *President Johnson*, which operated on American President Lines' transpacific services for twenty years until sold in 1968 to Waterman Steamship Corporation, which she served for a further six years before being broken up in Kaohsiung. She had been launched as *Sea Carp* by Western Pipe & Steel Company, San Francisco, in January 1943 but was completed as the attack transport USS *Clay* (APA 39) and saw extensive war service in the Pacific.

The C1 type

Lykes Lines' flush-decked *Joseph Lykes*, completed by Federal Shipbuilding & Engineering, Kearny, in November 1940, was the first of the C1 design, which, at a length of 412ft, was the smallest of the USMC designs. The class eventually numbered 173 ships, which were divided into open- or closed-shelter deckers and designated C1-A and C1-B respectively. The latter group, starting with *Cape Alava* in April 1941 and including sister ship *John Lykes* (1941), which had a thirty-one-year career, could be identified by a full-length combined bridge and boat deck, whereas the bridge deck of the A-type was set in half way along its length to allow for a small lower boat deck. Mast arrangements varied, most of the Bs having an extra set of posts in front of the bridge and a single mast instead of twin posts between Nos 2 and 3 hatches. Gross tonnages averaged 5,028 and 6,750 respectively, on dimensions of 412ft (C1-A), 418ft (C1-B) x 60ft. Propulsion was by single screw driven by either two steam turbines or twin six-cylinder diesels for a service speed of around fourteen knots.

The C4 type

The C4 type was the largest and fastest of the US Maritime Commission designs. Evolving from a 1941 engines-aft design for American-Hawaiian Lines, fifty-five of these distinctive ships were built by Kaiser Company's west coast yards at Richmond and Vancouver, whilst a further twenty came from Sun Shipbuilding, Chester, from January 1944 onwards. Some were completed as troop ships, others as hospital ships, but after the war a number were converted back into cargo carriers. Their hull design was unusual, with a long forecastle and poop; the forecastle carried a small bridge house and the poop had a large box-like superstructure on which was placed a small cowl-topped funnel. Of the seven hatches, two were placed on the forecastle, four in the well deck and one aft. They measured 10,709gt and around 14,000dwt on dimensions of 522ft oa x 72ft. A seventeen-knot service speed was provided by twin turbines developing 9,000shp and geared to a single screw. Pictured here is *Keystone State*, which was completed by Sun Shipbuilding in 1945 as the C4-S-B5 *Marine Flyer* for the US War Shipping Administration. Purchased by States Marine Lines in 1955, she was broken up at Kaohsiung in 1972.

US emergency tonnage – the 'Victory' ship

The 'Victory' ships were designed by Bethlehem Steel's Quincy Yard and the first to be completed was *United Victory* in February 1944 by Oregon Shipbuilding Corporation, Portland. They came in two main groups, the VC2-S-AP2 with 6,000shp turbines for fifteen knots, of which 272 were completed, whilst the 141 AP3s had more powerful 8,500shp units giving seventeen knots. In addition, the 'Victory' hull was used for one experimental, diesel-powered AP4 and 117 AP5 attack transports. With their long forecastle, three stump masts with wide crosstrees and tall upright funnel, the Victories were instantly recognisable and became a regular feature of postwar liner trades, where the simple but efficient layout gained widespread acclaim. Tonnages averaged 7,600gt and 10,600dwt on dimensions of 455ft oa x 62ft. Illustrated in Gatun Lake, Panama Canal, in February 1969, a few months before being broken up in Kaohsiung, is North East Shipping Corporation's *St Joan*, which had passed through several hands including American-Hawaiian Steamship Company and Matson Navigation Company since being completed as the AP2 *Adrian Victory* by Oregon Shipbuilding Corporation, Portland, in 1945. Few cargo liners survive today but the Victory design will live on, because three are currently preserved in working order in the USA: *American Victory* in Tampa, Florida, *Lane Victory* in San Pedro, California and *Red Oak Victory* in Richmond, California.

UK emergency tonnage – the fast Empire type

The 'Standard Fast' Empire-type cargo liners were the equivalent of the World War I G-type cargo liners but were designed for general rather than refrigerated cargo. Capable of maintaining fifteen knots, they were suitable for postwar employment and fourteen were completed by six different yards between 1943 and 1946, commencing with *Empire Chieftain* from Furness Shipbuilding Company, Haverton Hill in October 1943. Measuring 9,777gt on dimensions of 497ft oa x 64ft, their general layout placed them on a par with the US-built C3s (see page 90) and the majority were powered by steam turbines, just three being motor vessels, distinguished by their shorter funnels. Designed to carry up to thirty-six passengers, a wartime measure later reduced to twelve or removed altogether, they served with a number of liner companies after the war – Union-Castle Line's *Good Hope Castle* shown here being a typical example – and often changed hands several times. An even larger number of similar ships were completed after the war, incorporating owners' individual requirements, perhaps the most distinctive being Canadian Pacific Steamship Company's *Beaverdell* quartet with four goalpost masts. (*A Duncan*)

UK private contracts

Ordered from Harland & Wolff, Belfast, by Royal Mail Lines before World War II, the 5,400gt *Pardo* was the forerunner of a class of eight sister ships, the last, *Pilcomayo*, being completed in 1945. They were general-purpose cargo carriers measuring 450ft oa x 61ft and had six-cylinder diesels that gave a speed of around fifteen knots. Two were sunk during the war, *Pampas* being bombed in Malta in March 1942 and *Palma* torpedoed in the Indian Ocean by a Japanese submarine in 1944. *Parramatta* was renamed *Pampas* in honour of her lost sister and acted as a headquarters Infantry Landing Ship during the Normandy invasion, later becoming HMS *Persimmon* for similar duties in the Far East. Harland & Wolff also completed the similar but slightly larger (466ft oa x 63ft) *Samanco* and *Sarmiento* in 1943 and 1945 for the Pacific Steam Navigation Company. The same design with boats raised one deck higher was used for four subsequent ships ending with *Salamanca* in 1948.

Amongst the private contracts was one for a pair of large meat carriers for Royal Mail Lines to replace the loss of its steamers *Natia* and *Navasota*. Delivered by Harland & Wolff in 1942–3, *Deseado* and *Darro** differed in being motorships and having their bridge deck positioned one hold further aft. Somewhat larger at 9,641gt on dimensions of 470ft oa x 65ft, they had four decks and were driven at fourteen knots by twin six-cylinder double-acting Burmeister & Wain diesels. The loss of the remaining two 'N'-class ships early in 1943 led to the building of a second pair, *Drina* and *Durango*, which had identical hull dimensions but lacked the forward well-deck and had bridge and accommodation split round No 3 hatch. They were built specifically for the chilled meat trade from the River Plate but later carried frozen meat and general cargo. They were also fitted with gas-tight fruit compartments, which were particularly useful when they served on Royal Mail's Pacific coast route. All four retained their austere war-built appearance until broken up in 1967–8, *Deseado* in Hamburg and the rest in Kaohsiung; *Drina* and *Durango* had sailed under Shaw, Savill & Albion colours as *Romanic* and *Ruthenic* from the mid-1960s.

Delivered by J L Thompson & Sons, Sunderland, to Prince Line in 1943, the 9,485gt *Chinese Prince* was another wartime new-build for private ownership. Overall measurements were 490 x 63ft and her design incorporated forecastle and poop with a trunked hatch abaft the bridge. What made her distinctive was her two-step superstructure, which became something of a Furness Group trademark and was used in a number of postwar ships built between 1948 and 1958 (see page 101). Propulsion was by twin four-cylinder Doxford diesels developing 6,800bhp for fifteen knots. Thompson & Sons delivered a sister, *Silveroak**, to Silver Line in 1944 and later that year the slightly smaller *Javanese Prince* (8,879gt, 482ft oa x 62ft) was completed by Blythswood Shipbuilding, Glasgow for Rio Cape Line. Due to Admiralty restrictions, she had just a single six-cylinder Doxford engine. *Chinese Prince* was bare-boat chartered to Shaw, Savill & Albion as *Nordic* for thirteen years in 1950 and was broken up at Hirao, Japan, in 1964. *Silveroak* ran as *Port Stephens* on charter to Port Line during 1955–6 before becoming Ben Line's *Benvannoch*. Ben also took *Javanese Prince*, which was renamed *Benlarig* in 1961 and both went to Eastern breakers in Kaohsiung and Hong Kong respectively in 1969.

Yet another private contract secured British India Steam Navigation Company's *Canara**, the first of thirteen 'C'-class ships, which became familiar workhorses on the line's main routes to India, Australia and East Africa after World War II. They were built in two groups, the first comprising two pairs in 1942 and 1944 and the second comprising nine ships delivered between 1949 and 1952, all by Barclay, Curle & Company, save four of the latter which came from Swan, Hunter & Wigham Richardson. Barclay, Curle was also responsible for sisters *Cannanore* and *Coromandel*, which were delivered to P&O in 1949 and the broadly similar twin screw *Socotra*, which was built for P&O in 1943. Gross tonnage ranged between 7,000 and 7,250 (7,500 in respect of the 1950-built *Chindwara* and *Chantala*, which initially carried thirty cadets, later fifty-two) and deadweight around 9,800. Hull dimensions were 485ft oa x 63ft and they were driven at fourteen to fifteen knots by a six-cylinder Doxford opposed-piston diesel developing 6,800bhp. After useful careers of around a quarter of a century, disposal began in 1969 and by 1973 just three remained to be transferred to the new P&O General Cargo Division. Only *Chakdina* lasted long enough to receive a *Strath* name (*Strathlairg*) in 1975, being demolished in Kaohsiung two years later.

CHAPTER

8

Postwar Reconstruction

The postwar period was dominated by the need to replace losses and most companies embarked on a process that would continue well into the next decade. Neutral countries such as Sweden had been able to plan ahead and consequently were in a better position to produce advanced new ships soon after the war. On the other hand, Germany and Japan had lost most of their cargo-liner tonnage during the conflict and even the few which had survived were ceded to the victorious Allies. Their shipyards had also largely been destroyed, but once Allied restrictions had been lifted, both countries lost no time in re-establishing their industries and their revitalised yards began to turn out many fine cargo liners, initially for domestic owners and then increasingly for export to other countries.

In terms of design, welded hulls became more commonplace and new steel, folding hatch covers began to replace traditional hatch boards. Advances in diesel engine design with better reliability and increased output reduced the need for twin-screw plants in high-powered ships. Speeds in general began to increase, seventeen knots becoming quite common and some ships achieving considerably more, notably two Swedish series' in the late 1940s and the United States' heavily subsidised 'Mariner' class in the early 1950s. The latter were propelled by steam turbines, a form of propulsion still popular in the UK and Germany, and they were the only cargo ships of note built in the United States during this period, because it still had a surplus of war-built tonnage. In cargo-handling terms, limited use began to be made of hydraulic deck cranes in place of the traditional derricks and a new type of heavy-lift mast developed by Stülckenwerft and Hansa Line made its first appearance in one of the latter's ships.

Note: An asterisk in a caption indicates the vessel shown in the photograph.

Ordered in 1943 but not completed until after World War II, the 8,366gt *Mongolia*, seen here at Aden, marked the start of an extensive new building programme for Denmark's East Asiatic Company that would eventually number seventeen ships in three distinct series, seven M-type, five Ps, starting with *Panama* in 1950, and finally eight S-type, commencing with *Songkhla* in 1953. *Mongolia* and *Manchuria* were delivered by Burmeister & Wain, Copenhagen, in 1945 and the other five by Nakskov Skibsværft A/S between 1945 and 1951. They measured 474ft oa x 61ft; each of the succeeding classes was in turn 7ft longer and 1ft greater in beam. All followed the same basic layout of short forecastle and poop with three holds forward and two aft of the machinery. There were minor differences in promenade deck windows and the final M-type ships, *Mombasa* and *Magdala* carried their boats one deck higher and were fitted with two cranes in place of posts at the aft end of the superstructure, this development being continued in the later series. They were propelled by six-cylinder Burmeister & Wain engines rated at 6,700bhp for fifteen knots and operated mainly to India. They were sold between 1969 and 1972, *Malaya* and *Magdala* lasting longest in Chinese hands as *Jing Hai 3* and *Zhan Dou 11*, the latter possibly until 1990. Of the P class, *Poona* was broken up in 1971 following a fire in Copenhagen and the rest were sold to Far Eastern owners in 1972–3; *Panama, Patagonia* and *Pretoria* went to Chinese subsidiary Yick Fung as *Celebes Sea, Caribbean Sea* and *Bering Sea*, the former transferring to the Chinese flag as *Hong Qi 102* in 1975 and being the last to be broken up, in 1983. The S class had turbo-charged engines for seventeen knots in service and all but *Sibonga* had three bipod masts. Between 1966 and 1968, most of them were given insulated space for Pacific services and in addition the final three deliveries, *Simba, Sargodha* and *Sinaloa* had their No 2 holds altered to carry containers.

Seized German Ships

During World War II, Germany ordered several large cargo liners from yards in occupied countries; however, construction was delayed and they were seized after the Armistice. A particularly fine trio, designed for Norddeutscher Lloyd (NDL) and launched by John Cockerill SA at Hoboken as *Coburg, Marburg* and *Regensburg*, were eventually completed in 1946–7 for the Belgian government, which then chartered them to Compagnie Maritime Belge for its New York service. Renamed *Stavelot, Houffalize** and *Bastogne* after towns in the Ardennes region, they could be described as improved versions of NDL's River class (see page 67) and were notable as the last examples of a long line of German-designed, four-masted ships. Tonnage figures were 8,000gt and 11,000dwt on overall dimensions of 546 x 64ft, but their machinery layout was unusual, comprising three six-cylinder Sulzer diesels, each driving a screw with a combined output of 10,000bhp for eighteen knots. In 1955, they were sold to NDL – the owner for which they were originally intended – and re-christened *Rothenstein, Reifenstein* and *Ravenstein* respectively, being employed thereafter in both the Far East and Australian trades. *Ravenstein* had her funnel heightened and is shown here in Singapore in 1960. Re-engined in 1961–2 with three five-cylinder MAN units developing a total of 12,000bhp, they were sold in 1971 to the Cyprus-based Olistim Navigation Company, which dropped the last four letters of their names. *Ravens* was broken up in Karachi in 1978 and *Reifens* and *Rothens* in Kaohsiung in 1978 and 1979 respectively.

The German government ordered several cargo liners from shipyards in occupied countries during World War II, including the 545ft oa, 12,400dwt *Brandenburg* from Burmeister & Wain, which eventually emerged in 1947 as *Kambodia* for Denmark's East Asiatic Company. Three similar but slightly smaller ships were constructed in France in 1942, two from Chantier & Ateliers de St Nazaire and one from Ateliers et Chantiers de la Loire, Nantes. Construction was seriously delayed and it was not until 1949 that the first two were completed as *Washington** and *Wyoming* for Compagnie Générale Transatlantique's North Pacific service; sister *Winnipeg* followed a year later. Measuring 8,696gt and 10,195dwt on dimensions of 516 x 64ft, they were driven at seventeen knots by twin eight-cylinder diesels. In 1959, they were transferred to North Atlantic service following the delivery of the new *Magellan* class (see page 130) and two years later *Wyoming* was sold to Japan and converted to the fish-processing ship *Seifu Maru*. *Washington* went to Singapore in 1968 as Guan Guan Shipping's *Golden Summer* and was broken up at Hsinkiang in 1974, the same year that the former *Wyoming* met a similar fate in Kaohsiung. *Winnipeg* became the Greek *Lambros L* in 1975 but was laid up near Piræus in early 1978 following a fire and was eventually demolished in Turkey in 1982. A fourth sister was laid down as *Vancouver* by the Arsenal de la Marine, Brest, but emerged in 1950 as *Mékong* for Compagnie des Messageries Maritimes, which, prior to World War II, had operated a mix of World War I standard types and surrendered German tonnage. She differed from the Compagnie Générale Transatlantique ships in having a raised bridge deck and a different mast arrangement and was followed by two sisters *Meinam* and *Peï-Ho*.

A Canadian trio

Canada's first postwar construction comprised three modern motor vessels for Canadian National Steamships, which operated a Bermuda–British West Indies–British Guiana service from Montreal in summer and Halifax in winter. The 6,745gt *Canadian Cruiser*, *Canadian Constructor** and *Canadian Challenger* were delivered respectively by Canadian Vickers, Montreal, in 1946, and by Burrard Dry Dock, Vancouver and Davie Shipbuilding & Repairing Company, Lauzon in 1947. With a tonnage of 7,500dwt, they measured 436ft oa by 59ft and had 370,000cu ft available for general cargo and 16,000cu ft for refrigerated space for the carriage of fruit. They were powered by four-cylinder Doxford diesels, the largest yet built in Canada, developing 6000bhp, which provided a sea speed of sixteen and a half knots. In 1958, *Canadian Cruiser* and *Canadian Challenger* were sold to Cuba and renamed *Ciudad de Detroit* and *Ciudad de la Habana*, the former becoming *Manuel Ascunce* in 1962, the same year that *Canadian Constructor* joined them as *Conrado Benitez*. *Ciudad de la Habana* was sold to Hellenic Lines in 1967, becoming *Italia*, and was scrapped in Kaohsiung in 1980. *Conrado Benitez* was hulked at the end of 1980 and later sunk as a target. *Manuel Ascunce* was demolished at Cartagena de Indias in 1982.

An unusual Brazilian series

Immediately after World War II, the state-owned Lloyd Brasileiro placed orders for a remarkable series of twenty 5,400gt cargo liners, fourteen with Ingalls Shipbuilding, Pascagoula, and six with Canadian Vickers, Montreal. *Loide America* and *Loide Canada* – launched as *Canadaloide*, a proposed form of nomenclature that was dropped after the fourth Canadian launch – were the first to be completed by each yard in the summer of 1947 and all had been delivered by November 1948. They measured 444ft oa x 59ft on deadweight tonnage of 7,800dwt and their design, which lacked sheer, incorporated a long forecastle and was notable for the substitution of a tapered pipe in place of a conventional funnel. Although officially designated the 'Nations of America' class, they were referred to locally as the 'Bombs'. The placing of the mainmast and after posts closer than usual to the superstructure resulted in an exceptionally long, clear afterdeck. Mast arrangements varied, *Loide Brasil** carrying her mainmast on a goalpost, whilst others mounted the main topmast on their diminutive exhaust. Main propulsion consisted of two General Electric steam turbines geared to a single screw for sixteen to seventeen knots. After forming the mainstay of Lloyd Brasileiro's cargo operations throughout the 1950s and early 1960s, they were finally replaced by new, twenty-knot ships and were broken up within six months of each other in 1969 and 1970, fifteen at four different locations in Spain and five in Italy at La Spezia. (*John G Callis*)

Fast Swedish types

Sweden's ever-innovative Johnson Line surprised the austere, postwar shipping world in 1947 with the introduction of *Seattle**, the first of seven striking-looking, twin-screw ships for its North Pacific service. Kockums Mekaniska Verksteds shipyard in Malmö was responsible for the construction of the lead ship and *Golden Gate* and *Los Angeles* in 1948, *Lions Gate* in 1950 and finally *California* and *Canada* in 1953. *Silver Gate* and *Portland* were delivered by Howaldtswerke, Kiel, in 1952. Their clean profile was enhanced by a complete absence of derrick posts, cargo being handled entirely by an outfit of ten 3t and four 5t Asea electric cranes. High speed was another feature, nineteen and a half knots in service being provided by twin seven-cylinder MAN diesels totalling 14,400bhp, all but the first two deliveries having controllable pitch propellers. Their hulls, which incorporated a long forecastle, were almost fully welded and measured 500 x 64ft. Meticulously maintained, they were fitted with MacGregor steel hatch covers and converted to burn heavy fuel oil in the mid-1960s. *Seattle* was the first to be sold, becoming the Singaporean *Timur Venture* in 1971. The following year *Golden Gate* and *Los Angeles* were briefly renamed *Anhwei* and *Gele*, before demolition in Kaohsiung and Burriana, respectively. *Portland* also went to Kaohsiung in 1973 as the Panamanian *Five Lakes*. *Lions Gate* was converted into a livestock carrier in Singapore by A/S Uglands Rederi and sold to Lebanese owners as *Farid Fares*. She caught fire 200 miles south of Adelaide on 27 March 1980 and sank three days later, along with her cargo of 40,000 sheep. The remaining three ships were sold to Singapore in 1977 and, as *United Vulcan*, – *Vitality* and – *Vision* were demolished in Kaohsiung in 1979.

Rederiaktiebolaget Transatlantic also introduced fast ships in 1947 starting with the 6,749gt *Nimbus*, first of four more conventional vessels from Götaverken A/B, Gothenburg, for its Australian service. The vessels were of similar power and speed to Johnson's *Seattle* class (see above) but were fitted with conventional cargo gear. *Stratus* followed in 1948 and the larger *Cirrus** and *Cumulus* in 1950, which had an extra hold aft, giving an overall measurement some 32ft longer at 526ft, whilst beam was also 4ft greater at 66ft. In 1965, *Cumulus* was rebuilt by Rheinstahl Nordseewerke and her masts and kingposts were replaced by two single and two twin cranes. *Stratus* and *Nimbus* were sold to Panamanian owners in 1971–2, becoming *Anne of Cleves* and *Char Hwa* respectively, both eventually going to Kaohsiung breakers, the former in 1977 and the latter as *Panaf Star* in 1973. *Cirrus* and *Cumulus* went to Greek owners as *Kastor* and *Elenos* in 1976 and were demolished at Gadani Beach and Bombay, respectively, in 1982 and 1981. (*John G Callis*)

A fast Dutch pair

The twin-screw *Annenkerk* and *Arendskerk** built by Wilton-Fijenoord, Rotterdam, and Nederlandsche Scheepsbouw Maats., Amsterdam, in 1947–8, were United Netherlands Shipping Company's first postwar deliveries. Designed for Australian service, they were reasonably large ships at just over 8,000gt and 11,250dwt and had an overall length of 523ft on a beam of 63ft. Their layout featured a short forecastle and poop and a split superstructure but their machinery outfit differed, *Annenkerk* having a pair of five-cylinder MAN diesels and her sister twin seven-cylinder Stork units, each delivering around 11,000bhp for a service speed of seventeen and a half knots. Both became part of the Koninklijke Nedlloyd fleet in July 1970 and *Annenkerk* was sold a year later for demolition in Shanghai. The same year saw her sister briefly become the Panamanian *Salomague* before disposal to Karachi shipbreakers in 1972. Two similar but smaller replacements for war losses *Aagtekerk* and *Almkerk* (see page 76) were originally planned to resurrect their names but were completed as *Heemskerk* and *Hoogkerk* by Nederlandsche Scheepsbouw Maats. in 1949. Identified by taller kingposts and a larger sloping-topped funnel, they measured 479 x 61ft and were driven at sixteen knots by a single six-cylinder Stork engine. They passed to Ignazio Messina in 1969 and 1968 respectively and traded as *Albertoemme* and *Rossellaemme* for a further ten years each until broken up in La Spezia.

UK fleet renewals

The 7,639gt *Calchas**, delivered by Harland & Wolff, Belfast, in January 1947, marked the start of Blue Funnel's major postwar fleet replacement programme, which would eventually number twenty-seven ships. Her design emulated that of the prewar *Glenearn* class (see page 83) but dimensionally she was smaller at 487ft oa x 62ft, whilst her single eight-cylinder Burmeister & Wain diesel developed less than half the power at 6,800bhp, giving a service speed of fifteen knots. *Calchas* was followed by five more Mark A ships: *Anchises* (the class name ship, renamed *Alcinous* in 1973), *Aeneas* and *Achilles* from Caledon, Dundee and *Anchises* and *Astyanax* from Scotts' Shipbuilding & Engineering Company. Beginning with *Clytoneus* in 1948, the next batch of six A2s were fitted with 'tweendeck accommodation and extra boats for Blue Funnel's traditional seasonal pilgrim trade from Asia to Jeddah, but this was removed after entry into service in 1959 of the large specialist pilgrim carrier *Gunung Djati*. *Bellerophon*, completed by Caledon Shipbuilding & Engineering Company in October 1950, headed the next batch of five Mark 3s. The Mark 4 quartet was led by *Adrastus* and *Eumaeus* in December 1953. Returning to the Mark As, three were temporarily transferred to Glen Line, *Achilles* as *Radnorshire* between 1949 and 1963, after which she was renamed *Asphalion*, followed by six years on loan to N S M 'Oceaan' as *Polyphemus* from 1966. *Calchas* transferred to Glen Line as *Glenfinlas* and *Astyanax* as *Glenfruin* between 1957 and 1962. *Agapenor* was trapped in the Suez Canal by the Six Day War in June 1967 and, after her release in 1975, became the Greek-owned *Nikos*. She was scrapped at Gadani Beach in 1981, having outlived the other Mark As, which had all gone to Kaohsiung breakers between 1972 and 1979, *Calchas* following a fire at Port Kelang in July 1973 and *Asphalion* (as *Gulf Anchor*) in 1979.

The series underwent more significant change with the Mark 5 versions *Demodocus*, *Diomed* and *Dolius*, completed by Vickers-Armstrongs, Newcastle, in 1955–6. These 7,968gt ships were some 5ft longer with finer hull lines and were fitted with more powerful six-cylinder Burmeister & Wain engines with an output of 8,000bhp giving an extra knot of speed. The teak-sheathed bridge of the earlier ships was dropped and the second pair of boats was moved to a deckhouse abaft No 4 hatch. The final batch of the series consisted of three Mark 6s, *Antenor**, *Achilles* and *Ajax*, which were very similar apart from minor differences in island lengths. The Mark 5s and *Antenor* were transferred to Glen Line as *Glenroy*, *Glenbeg*, *Glenfruin* and *Glenlochy* between 1970 and 1972 when the Mark 6s were renamed *Dymas*, *Dardanus* and *Deucalion*. *Dolius* was sold to Chinese front company Nan Yang Shipping, Macao, in November 1972 and the rest followed in 1973, their new names being *Hungsia*, *Kaising*, *Hungmien*, *Kaiyun*, *Kiago* and *Kailock*. *Hungmien* and *Hungsia* were transferred to China in 1977 and 1979 and renamed *Hong Qi 119* and *Hong Qi 137*. *Hong Qi 137* was broken up in China in 1982, while *Hong Qi 119* became *Zhan Dou 51* in 1984 and was deleted from the register in 1992. The remaining ships were broken up in 1982–3.

Built by J L Thompson & Sons, Sunderland, for Silver Line's eastbound round-the-world service via South Africa in 1948, the 7,242gt (10,750dwt) *Silverplane* and *Silverbriar** were notable as the last cargo liners to have two funnels in the traditional fore and aft position, the forward funnel being a dummy. Their hulls measured 503ft oa x 65ft and incorporated a long forecastle and short poop, whilst cargo capacity amounted to 762,880cu ft (grain). A speed of sixteen knots was maintained by three sets of Parsons steam turbines developing 8,800shp and driving a single shaft through double-reduction gearing. In 1951, Silver Line withdrew from liner operations to concentrate on tramping and these two fine ships were bought by Cunard and renamed *Alsatia* and *Andria* for North Atlantic cargo service. In 1963, they were replaced by new tonnage and sold to China Union Lines of Taiwan, which employed them in its service to New York via Panama as *Union Freedom* and *Union Faith*. The latter was lost as a result of a fire in New Orleans following a collision on 6 April 1969, while the former was broken up in Kaohsiung in 1977.

P&O's 9,080gt, twin-screw *Soudan* and *Somali** were in the vanguard of British postwar high-speed liner tonnage and could maintain an easy eighteen knots in service. Built for their owner's Far East service by Barclay, Curle & Company in 1948, they were larger versions of the 1943 *Socotra* design with a short forecastle and long superstructure incorporating No 3 hatch. They had a capacity of 10,750dwt on dimensions of 525ft oa x 67ft. No 3 hold was fully refrigerated and the cargo-handling outfit consisted of eighteen derricks and a similar number of electric winches, two of which had auxiliary barrels for operating an additional 50t jumbo on the foremast. Main propulsion comprised twin six-cylinder Doxford diesels developing 13,600bhp. *Soudan*, which could be identified by a large ventilator post on her forecastle, went to Taiwan breakers in 1970, some two years before her sister, which had become the Greek Cypriot-owned *Happyland* in 1969. Four 523ft single-screw turbine-driven versions with taller funnels were also built: *Surat* and *Shillong* by Vickers-Armstrongs' Naval Yard, Walker-on-Tyne in 1948–9 and 2ft broader *Singapore* and *Sunda* by John Brown & Company in 1951–2. *Shillong* sank in the Gulf of Suez on 22 October 1957 following collision with the tanker *Purfina Congo*. *Singapore* was renamed *Comorin* in 1964 and given the Strath livery of white hull and yellow funnel. The three remaining ships were renamed *Pando Head*, *Pando Cove* and *Pando Strait* in 1968; four years later *Pando Cove* was broken up in Bilbao and the others at Inverkeithing.

The second group of ships in Frank C Strick & Company's postwar reconstruction programme began with the 8,409gt *Armanistan*, which was completed by the favoured yard John Readhead & Son, South Shields, in April 1949. She was followed by two sisters, *Goulistan* and *Muristan*, in 1950 and all three adhered to a three-island layout with the bridge deck extended forward to incorporate No 3 hatch in a throwback to some of the company's early twentieth-century ships (see *Gorjistan*, page 29). Although comparatively slow when compared to other ships on long distance services, their fourteen knots was an improvement on Strick's earlier *Nigaristan* class, and the company's postwar shift to a grey hull livery coupled with the white paint carried down to weather-deck level gave them an impressive appearance. A rather pretentious touch was the stowage of the anchors in large recesses, a practice more normally found in fast passenger tonnage. The original short funnels were later lengthened and *Muristan* at one stage sported a Thornycroft-type top as shown. Deadweight was 10,880t on overall dimensions of 512 x 62ft and main propulsion was by means of a three-cylinder triple-expansion engine coupled with a double-reduction low-pressure turbine. Machinery damage forced *Goulistan* to an early demise in 1962 at the hands of breakers in Bremerhaven. Three years later, *Armanistan* was sold to Liberian-registered owners and renamed *Conway* before passing to Greek ownership in 1967 as *Mitera Maria*. A third change came in 1971, when she hoisted the Somali flag as *Marbella* but an engine-room fire at Karachi on 13 February 1963 ended her career and she was scrapped at nearby Gadani Beach early the following year. A third sister, *Muristan*, also went to Greece, becoming *Atlas Trader* in 1966 and then the Liberian *Yaling* in 1970, being broken up in Kaohsiung two years later.

The general layout of the war-built *Silveroak* (see page 94), in particular the two-level superstructure, was continued in a number of ships in Furness Withy Group's postwar reconstruction programme, beginning in 1948 with *Pacific Fortune* and *Pacific Unity*, which as their names imply were intended for the west coast of North America service. These were followed by the handsome sisters *Cingalese Prince** and *Eastern Prince* completed by Vickers-Armstrongs' High Walker yard in 1950 for Prince Line's westbound round-the-world service. *Cingalese Prince* is depicted passing Kabrit in the Suez Canal. Two more Furness ships, *Pacific Reliance* and *Pacific Northwest*, appeared between 1951 and 1954, followed by *Pacific Envoy* and *Pacific Stronghold* in 1958, the latter pair being distinguished by a single tall mast above the bridge in place of twin masts in the earlier deliveries. In 1960, *Cingalese Prince* and *Eastern Prince*, were transferred to sister company Shaw, Savill & Albion and renamed *Gallic* and *Bardic* respectively, the former reverting to her original name two years later. In 1964, both were sold to Bibby Line, becoming *Gloucestershire* and *Staffordshire* and they looked particularly good in Bibby colours. *Gloucestershire* changed hands again in 1971 and as *Cresco* was broken up at Whampoa in 1972, a year after her sister had been demolished in Hong Kong.

The Ellerman Group's immediate postwar reconstruction programme comprised several classes of cargo liner. They were all turbine-driven, save for the distinctive *City of Johannesburg* (1947), the intended fifth unit of the *City of New York* quartet, which was completed with diesels for comparison purposes. The largest class numerically was the ten-ship *City of Oxford* class, built in six UK yards to ensure delivery within an eighteen-month period from the end of 1948. They were of around 7,600gt with a corresponding deadweight of 10,800t and were 480ft oa x 62ft. Three Parsons turbines geared to a single screw developed 7,200shp for a speed of just over fifteen knots. The lowering of the white paint to main-deck level, an Ellerman trademark, made these ships appear more substantial than their size would suggest. They were employed on Ellerman's worldwide services and group chairman Sir John Ellerman would sometimes use one of them, with a hand-picked crew, for his private natural-history expeditions. Pictured in Singapore is the Swan, Hunter-built *City of Coventry*, one of six of the class sold in 1967. She became the Liberian flag *Ingrid* and two years later the Taiwanese *Annie*, before being scrapped in Kaohsiung in 1970. The other five went to Greece and two of these were later lost. *City of Manchester* also went to Greece in 1971 and *City of Birmingham* was broken up. The surviving pair, *City of Oxford* and *City of Leeds* (previously *City of Ottawa*), were sold in 1976, the lead ship being the last to be broken up, as *Union Arabia*, in 1978.

Radically different from its *City of Oxford* class, Ellerman's *City of Brisbane* was the first of two large turbine steamers built for the Australian service. Originally ordered as *City of Ripon*, she was completed by Cammell Laird at Birkenhead in 1951 and was followed a year later by *City of Winchester* from William Denny & Brothers. They were registered to Ellerman & Bucknall and measured 10,594gt and 13,249dwt on overall dimensions of 568 x 71ft. Their design incorporated a long forecastle and short poop; however, the single mast and generally low profile, coupled with a massive funnel, gave them a unique appearance. Cargo capacity amounted to 545,538cu ft (bale), whilst an additional 162,535cu ft was insulated for the carriage of refrigerated cargo. Three sets of double-reduction geared turbines developed 14,300shp and drove a single screw for a service speed of seventeen and a half knots. Many cargo liners at this time still had large crews and these ships were no exception, with a total complement of ninety-seven persons. Faced with increasing competition from new container services, Ellerman agreed to pool its Far East services with Ben Line in 1970 and the two ships were transferred to the latter company and renamed *Bencairn* and *Benvannoch*. This final phase of their careers lasted for another five years before they were broken up in Kaohsiung.

New French design

In 1947, Compagnie Générale Transatlantique embarked on a new building programme comprising three groups of cargo ships, the 4,310gt *La Hague* class for Caribbean service, the 6,079gt *Caraibe* class for North Atlantic service and a series of larger ships for the Mexican Gulf and South America west coast services. Delivery of the latter began in 1949 with the 6,916gt *Cavelier de la Salle* and *Le Moyne d'Iberville** from Forges et Chantiers de la Gironde, Bordeaux. They were distinguished by a large, three-deck superstructure with open alleyways and had a deadweight capacity of 9,210 on dimensions of 467 x 62ft. Propulsion machinery was a ten-cylinder Sulzer diesel providing a service speed of sixteen knots. Both were sold to Liberian-registered Adriatic Maritime Company in 1968 and were renamed *Cavalier of Athens* and *Garden City*. The latter was lost a year later, after colliding with the Polish bulker *Zaglebie Dabrowskie* northeast of the Dover Strait; her sister was broken up in Kaohsiung in 1971. Two similar pairs of ships, which differed in having the lower superstructure deck extended around No 3 hatch, followed in 1950–1. First came the 476ft *Chili* and *Pérou* from Burmeister & Wain, Copenhagen, the latter being sold on the stocks to Messageries Maritimes and renamed *Indus*. Then came the 482ft *Equateur* and a replacement *Pérou* from Forges et Chantiers de la Gironde, which were distinguished by a more streamlined funnel. *Indus* was scrapped in Savona in 1973 after a final voyage as *Encicla*, but the Compagnie Générale Transatlantique ships were sold in 1966–7 to Chilean owners as *Graciosa*, *Piura* and *Lima*. *Graciosa* was scrapped in China in 1977 after seven years as *Golden Tower*. *Piura* and *Lima* were sold on in 1974 becoming *Eleistria VI* and *Amy* (later *Nena*) respectively, eventually going to Kaohsiung breakers in 1979.

Large insulated ships for Australia and New Zealand trade

Federal Steam Navigation Company and New Zealand Shipping Company lost just more than half their combined fleet during World War II, but had already started to replace some of these during the conflict with the 10,000gt, turbine-driven *Papanui* class, which eventually numbered five units. Postwar reconstruction started in earnest in 1947 with the delivery of *Norfolk*, the first of eight larger vessels (11,270gt/14,350dwt) that were developments of the prewar *Essex* design (see page 77). *Norfolk*, *Haparangi*, *Cumberland*, *Sussex** and *Hinakura* were products of John Brown & Company's Clydebank yard, *Huntingdon* was delivered by A Stephen & Sons and *Hertford* and *Hurunui* by Vickers-Armstrongs. The last two Brown ships, completed in 1949, differed in having their boats slung from gravity davits. Overall length was 561ft on a beam of 70ft and they could maintain a steady sixteen to seventeen knots in service by means of twin six-cylinder Doxford diesels developing 12,800bhp. In 1953, the fleet split was balanced at four apiece when *Norfolk* was transferred to New Zealand Shipping Company as *Hauraki* but she re-adopted Federal colours in 1966 along with the other NZS ships. Seven years later, all eight were transferred to the new P&O General Cargo Division but never looked happy in the latter's new blue funnel livery with white P&O lettering. Their days were numbered, however, and after useful lives of more than twenty-five years, all but *Hertford* went direct to Far Eastern breakers. The latter became the Greek-Cypriot *Thia Despina* in 1976 but was declared a constructive total loss and laid up in Piræus in 1977 after grounding off Port Said on 9 July. Purchased by other Cypriot interests in 1978, she was renamed *Georghios Frangakis* and was finally scrapped at Aliaga in 1985.

Port Line's new flagship *Port Brisbane**, delivered by Swan, Hunter & Wigham Richardson in February 1949, was designed to be distinctive and she certainly achieved this in the postwar austerity years with her single mast, streamlined bridge front and tapered funnel set on a sloping bridge roof. These features were all echoed to a lesser extent in subsequent Port Line tonnage. Her dimensions of 559ft oa x 70ft were similar to the more conventional *Port Napier*, which was delivered by the same yard in 1947, but the new ship's forecastle and bridge deck were considerably longer and she had no poop. All of her 560,000cu ft of insulated space was lined with aluminium, a process partially pioneered in the *Port Napier*, and she was the first Port Line ship to have a 5t electric deck crane serving Nos 4 and 5 holds. Sister *Port Auckland*, delivered two months later by R & W Hawthorn, Leslie & Company, Hebburn, was distinguished by a slightly larger funnel with rounded top and a different sequence of bridge-deck windows. *Port Brisbane* went to Hong Kong breakers in late 1975. *Port Auckland* was converted to a sheep carrier in Singapore in 1976 and ran in the Australia–Arabian Gulf trade as *Mashaallah* for an Iraqi venture, in which Port Line had a share, for three more years until engine trouble forced her demolition in Kaohsiung. *(John G Callis)*

Shown swinging out of the Mediterranean on the last leg of her homeward trip from Australia, Blue Star Line's 11,950gt *Tasmania Star* was delivered by Cammell Laird, Birkenhead, in November 1950, a few weeks ahead of sister *Adelaide Star*, which came from the famous Clydebank yard of John Brown & Company. With overall dimensions of 572 x 73ft and a total cargo capacity of 840,000cu ft, of which 572,000cu ft was insulated, they ranked amongst the largest cargo liners of the day. The superstructure was placed further aft than normal with four holds forward, one more than in the contemporary *English Star* and *Scottish Star*, providing a long foredeck suitable for the carriage of heavy cargoes for which a 60t derrick was provided. Their power plants differed, *Tasmania Star* having three sets of double-reduction steam turbines developing 16,000shp and geared to a single large screw, whilst her twin-screw sister was driven by two six-cylinder Doxford diesels, both outfits providing a comfortable seventeen knots in service and around twenty-one knots on trials. John Brown delivered a second motor vessel, *Wellington Star*, in 1952 and, after a gap of six years, Cammell Laird completed the turbine-driven *Auckland Star* for Blue Star's Bermuda-based subsidiary Salient Shipping, though she reverted to UK registry four years later. The first two ships went to breakers in Kaohsiung and South Korea in 1975. *Wellington Star* was sold a year later to Panamanian owners, renamed *Hawkes Bay* and converted to a livestock carrier in Singapore. She also ended her days in Kaohsiung in 1979, a year after *Auckland Star* had been demolished at Gadani Beach.

Shaw, Savill & Albion's postwar cargo-liner rebuilding programme started with the delivery in 1949 of the single-masted 10,674gt motor ships *Doric* and *Delphic* from Fairfield Shipbuilding & Engineering Company and R & W Hawthorn, Leslie & Company. These vessels both had a forecastle and long bridge deck extended to encompass No 4 hatch. They were closely followed by three 13,594gt steamers of the *Persic* class, which had three-island hulls based on the lines of the preceding cargo/passenger *Corinthic* class. At 14,447dwt and with dimensions of 561 x 72ft, they were amongst the largest reefer ships in the Australasian trade and were driven at seventeen knots by two sets of single-reduction geared turbines. *Persic** came from Cammell Laird in 1949 and sisters *Runic* and *Suevic*, which lacked a mainmast and had kingposts abreast the foremast, were completed by Harland & Wolff, Belfast, in 1950. In February 1961, *Runic* had the misfortune to be wrecked during the tail end of a cyclone on Middleton Reef, 120 miles north of Lord Howe Island, during a trans-Tasman voyage and was declared a constructive total loss. *Persic* passed to Royal Mail Lines as *Derwent* in 1969 and was broken up in Bilbao in 1971–2. *Suevic* outlasted her by three years before machinery problems forced her disposal to Taiwanese breakers in Kaohsiung.

Shaw, Savill & Albion's handsome *Cedric*, seen here at speed off Ushant, and sister *Cymric* could be described as better-balanced developments of the *Doric* design (see page 103). Delivered by Harland & Wolff in November 1952 (*Cedric*) and May 1953 (*Cymric*), they measured 512ft oa on a beam of 69ft and tonnages were 11,232gt and 11,771dwt and insulated capacity amounted to 314,450cu ft. Twin six-cylinder Burmeister & Wain opposed-piston diesels totalling 14,300bhp provided a service speed of around seventeen knots with a knot in reserve. Three more 'C'-class ships followed: *Canopic* from Vickers-Armstrongs in 1954, the Doxford-engined *Cretic* (originally ordered by Rio Cape Line) from Swan, Hunter & Wigham Richardson in 1955 and finally *Carnatic* from Cammell Laird in 1957. They had three full decks with a fourth deck in Nos 2 and 3 holds. *Canopic* and *Carnatic* were given greater insulated capacity for transporting chilled beef. After 1962, they were gradually repainted with light grey hulls to echo the livery being applied to new ships. As a result of the containerisation of the Australia/New Zealand trade, *Cymric*, *Cretic* and *Carnatic* were transferred to Royal Mail Lines management in 1973, becoming *Durango*, *Drina* and *Darro* respectively, whilst *Canopic* and *Cedric* passed into Cairn Line management. *Durango* was scrapped in Kaohsiung in 1975, followed a year later by *Cedric*, which sailed out as *Sea Condor*. *Drina* and *Darro*, which had been sold in 1976–7 and renamed *United Vigour* and *Litska K*, followed their sisters to Kaohsiung breakers in 1979, the latter being renamed *Dimitra* for the delivery voyage. The last to go was *Canopic*, which had become *Capetan Nicolas* in 1975 and as such was finally demolished at Aliaga, Turkey, in 1986.

New ships for South American trades

St Essylt and *St Thomas**, built by J L Thompson & Sons, Sunderland in 1949 for South American Saint Line, caused a stir with their advanced looks, which were largely due to the low streamlined funnel. A third sister, *St John*, was completed in 1954, enabling a monthly direct service to be run from Cardiff to Brazil, Argentina and Uruguay. The design incorporated a long forecastle and the deckhouse was extended around No 4 hatch to the mainmast. They measured 6,889gt and 9,850dwt on dimensions of 472 x 59ft and their cargo capacity amounted to some 632,000cu ft (grain). A single five-cylinder Doxford engine developing 5,300bhp gave a sea speed of fourteen and a half knots. The South American service was acquired by Houlder Brothers in 1961 and the ships were sold off in 1964–5, the first pair going to China Navigation and renamed *Yunnan* and *Yochow* respectively. *St John* became the London-registered *St Marie* and then the Greek *Despina R* in 1967. The China Navigation ships were sold locally to the Prosperity Steamship Company's Panama-registered New Asia Steamship Company in 1971 and, as *Lucky Two* and *Lucky Four*, they were demolished in Kaohsiung and Shanghai in 1979 and 1978 respectively. The former *St John*, which had changed hands a third time in 1974, was broken up as *Valmas* at Visagapatnam in 1979.

Competition on the River Plate run had traditionally been between British and European liner companies, but Argentina's Dodero Line ordered three new motor shelter-deckers from British yards in the late 1940s. *Rio Belen* and *Rio Belgrano* were completed by Cammell Laird & Company, Birkenhead, in 1949 with *Rio Bermejo** following a year later from A Stephen & Sons, Linthouse. They were fine-looking ships and their design incorporated a forecastle and long bridge deck. They had a gross tonnage of 7,143 in the open condition on a deadweight of just over 9,000t and their dimensions were 492ft oa x 62ft feet. Bale capacity was 433,100cu ft and a further 69,284cu ft was set aside for refrigerated cargoes. Propulsion was by means of a ten-cylinder Sulzer, which gave a service speed of fifteen to sixteen knots. They operated mainly from the River Plate to Mediterranean ports and later to the US east coast and were eventually broken up at La Plata in 1982–3.

Compañia Sud Americana de Vapores (CSAV) updated its fleet in 1955 with the handsome 8,300gt steamships *Lebu* and *Andalien**, completed in France by Chantiers de l'Atlantique (Penhoët-Loire), St Nazaire. Their design featured a short forecastle and stump foremast, together with three pairs of kingposts, the forward and aft pairs having cross struts. The tall radar mast was collapsible to permit transit of the Manchester Ship Canal. Main dimensions were 488 x 61ft and they had a deadweight of 10,600t. The five holds had a bale capacity of 459,000cu ft, including refrigerated compartments for the carriage of either meat or fresh fruit. Seventeen derricks, including a single 30t lift, were controlled by sixteen winches. Propulsion was provided by two Parsons geared steam turbines developing 7,500shp and driving a single screw for a speed of just over sixteen knots. *Lebu* caught fire in Quintero Bay on 1 September 1973 and was demolished at Split the following year, just a month or two after her sister had gone to Spanish breakers in Castellon. *(John G Callis)*

Scandinavian tonnage for North Pacific and Asian trades

Bergen shipowner Westfal-Larsen took delivery of three fine-lined, closed shelter-deckers from Kockums, Malmö, in 1950–1 for its Pacific coast of North America service. *Berganger*, *Moldanger* and *Risanger* were 8,050gt and 9,800dwt on overall dimensions of 485 x 61ft and an eight-cylinder Kockums-MAN diesel developing 8,000bhp ensured a comfortable service speed of seventeen knots. They had two full decks and a third deck in Nos 2, 3 and 5 holds, bale capacity amounting to 386,035cu ft with an additional 99,265cu ft for refrigerated cargoes. *Berganger* and *Moldanger* were sold in 1969–70 to China Navigation Company, which gave them the traditional Chinese names of *Shansi* and *Soochow* respectively, the former being converted to side loading by Taikoo Dockyard for Far East–Australia service. In 1977, both passed to Yatco Enterprises, which registered them under its Panamanian subsidiary Compañia de Navegacion Full Moon as *Yat Lee* and *Yat Shing* and they ended their days at the hands of Chinese breakers in 1978–9. Meanwhile, *Risanger* had become Arne Teigens Rederi's *Rytterfjell* in August 1971 and was sold to Greek owners five years later. As *Tofalos G*, she was eventually scrapped in Kaohsiung in 1980. *(John G Callis)*

The Broström group's Svenska Ostasiatiske Kompaniet (Swedish East Asia Company) received the twin-screw eighteen-knot cargo liners *Ceylon**, *Japan*, *Burma* and *Sudan* from Eriksbergs Mekaniska Verkstads, Gothenburg, between 1950 and 1953. Similar in design to *Sumatra*, which had been delivered as a war reparation by Cantieri Riuniti dell'Adriatico, Monfalcone in January 1949, they were completed as open shelter-deckers of 7,693gt and around 9,800dwt on dimensions of 508ft oa x 65ft. Main machinery comprised twin six-cylinder Eriksbergs-Burmeister & Wain diesels rated at 9,700bhp. Their white livery with pale yellow funnel gave them a yacht-like appearance. In 1955, they were followed by the broadly similar *Kyoto, Minikoi* and *Sabang*, which differed principally in having a single kingpost between hatch Nos 2 and 3, as did the smaller *Maltesholm* class built for sister company Svenska Amerika Linjen (Swedish America Line). All of the first four ships were engaged in the Far East trade until the mid-1970s, when all but *Burma* were sold to Singapore's Pacific International Lines and renamed *Kota Pusaka*, *Kota Petani* and *Kota Puri* respectively. They were scrapped in 1979–80 in Kaohsiung, where *Sumatra* had already been demolished as *Mondia II* in 1972. *Burma* became first *Andromachi* in 1976 and then *Eddy* a year later, finally being demolished at Gadani Beach in 1982.

A P Møller was the last company to employ a three-masted, split-superstructure layout, in a series of five similar postwar cargo liners. Three were completed in 1949, *Peter Mærsk* and *Anna Mærsk* by Eriksbergs Mekaniska Verkstads and *Olga Mærsk*, which had a wood-sheathed bridge, from Møller's own Odense shipyard. They measured around 479ft oa on a beam of 61ft. They were followed by *Nicoline Mærsk** and *Jeppesen Mærsk* from Burmeister & Wain in 1951, which were 3ft broader and had an extended poop. In addition, their Burmeister & Wain engines had an additional tenth cylinder, allowing them to develop 11,500bhp for a service speed of seventeen and a quarter knots, compared with the earlier trio's sixteen and a half knots from a 9,000bhp unit (*Olga Maersk* 9,800bhp). *Peter Mærsk* was the first to be sold, becoming Giacomo Costa fu Andrea's *Paola Costa* in 1963. Five years later her two sisters, *Anna* and *Olga*, were sold to a Møller subsidiary and renamed *Clementine* and *Valentine*, being joined by the larger pair as *Nicoline* and *Claudine* in 1971 and 1970 respectively. Between 1974 and 1976, all five went to Eastern buyers, but *Claudine* was wrecked off Manila Bay on 17 August 1974, shortly after being renamed *South Sea*. The others sailed on under various names, *Nicoline* as *Golden Jade*, and were eventually broken up in 1978–9.

A distinctive Clan/PSNC series

Delivered in January 1950, *Clan Shaw* was the first of a series of five 11,000dwt open shelter-deckers ordered by Clan Line Steamers Ltd from Greenock Dockyard Company. *Clan Sinclair* followed three months later but the third and fourth ships were sold to Pacific Steam Navigation Company (PSNC) and completed as *Kenuta* and *Flamenco*. *Clan Sutherland*, completed early in 1951, differed in carrying her boats in gravity davits and in 1960 her 65t heavy derrick was replaced with a 180t derrick on the forward stump mast, as shown in this Fremantle view. Gross measurement was around 8,400t on dimensions of 513ft oa x 66ft and they were readily distinguished by the 'fireman's helmet'-type smoke deflector on the funnel. Service speed was sixteen to seventeen knots provided by three sets of Parsons steam turbines developing 10,340shp and geared to a single screw. A further four ships were delivered in 1954–5: the Clan Line cadet ship *Clan Stewart* (planned as *Clan Skene*), PSNC's *Cotopaxi* (built by W Denny & Bros), *Potosi* and *Pizarro*. In December 1959, *Clan Shaw* and *Clan Sinclair* were transferred to the newly formed Springbok Line subsidiary, becoming *Steenbok* and *Bosbok* in the New Year, but in 1961 they changed their names yet again to *South African Seafarer* and *South African Statesman* after Springbok Line was acquired by the South African Marine Corporation. They were briefly joined by *Clan Stewart* as *South African Sculptor* but in 1962 she reverted to Clan Line and ran for the next five years as Union-Castle Line's *Kinpurnie Castle*. On 1 July 1966, shortly after the *South African* prefix had been shortened, *S A Seafarer* was wrecked near Green Point, Table Bay, and the following year *Kinpurnie Castle* became the Panamanian *Hellenic Med*. *Clan Sutherland* was broken up in Hsinkiang in 1971, *S A Statesman* in Kaohsiung in 1972 and *Hellenic Med* at Gadani Beach in 1978. Of the PSNC ships, *Flamenco* became the pilgrim ship *Pacific Abeto* in 1966 and *Kenuta* was broken up at Tamise in 1971. *Cotopaxi*, *Potosi* and *Pizarro* went to Greece's Gourdomichalis Maritime in 1972 as *Kavo Longos*, *Kavo Peiratis* and *Kavo Maleas*, the latter being scrapped in Kaohsiung in 1974 and the others in Shanghai and Dalmuir in 1976. The former *Flamenco* had the longest career of all, being demolished in her twenty-seventh year at Chittagong in 1981.

A Harrison Line series

Thos & Jas Harrison switched from its traditional three-island/split-superstructure design to a design with a long forecastle and single accommodation block and moved all crew accommodation into a single superstructure amidships in a series of ten similar ships built in three groups. *Astronomer* was the first to be completed by William Doxford & Sons, Sunderland, in 1951, followed by *Wayfarer, Wanderer* and *Arbitrator.* Tonnage measurements were 8,150gt and 9,940dwt on overall dimensions of 460 x 59ft and a four-cylinder oil engine by the builder provided an economical twelve knots. The next pair, *Crofter*, which attended the Coronation Naval Review at Spithead in June 1953, and *Forester* were built by J Readhead & Sons, South Shields in 1951–2. Their funnels, which were later heightened, were mounted close to the bridge as a result of reverting to reciprocating engines with Bauer-Wach exhaust turbines. The final group, completed by Doxfords in 1952–4, comprised the 464ft-long *Governor* (depicted here at Dover), *Diplomat, Barrister* and *Journalist*. They were driven at thirteen and a half knots by four-cylinder Doxford opposed-piston diesels developing 4,800bhp. The last two had no topmasts and a signal mast above the bridge, a feature continued in the similar-sized *Defender* of 1955, which differed in having a short forecastle and which was the precursor of three larger and faster *Administrator*-class ships. The long forecastle ships were sold between 1970 and 1974, mainly to Greek-Cypriot owners and, apart from *Wayfarer*, which was wrecked as *Mitera Zafira* off Constantza in 1973, were broken up after a few more years trading. *Barrister* was the last to go, scrapped as *Georgy* at Castellon in 1984. (*J Mannering*)

River Plate and Caribbean traders

Delivered by Cammell Laird, Birkenhead, in May 1952, the handsome 8,237gt *Romney** was Lamport & Holt's flagship and its last steamship, being propelled by two sets of steam turbines geared to a single screw for a service speed of fifteen knots. She measured 470 x 63ft and her design incorporated a long raised forecastle with accommodation positioned just aft of amidships. She was followed by two broadly similar motor ships, *Raeburn* from Harland & Wolff, Belfast, in November and *Raphael* from Bartram, Sunderland, in the summer of 1953. These differed slightly in superstructure details and in the positioning of boats (*Raeburn* had gravity davits) and their main engines were a seven-cylinder Burmeister & Wain (*Raeburn*) and a six-cylinder Doxford opposed piston unit in *Raphael*, both producing around 7,500bhp. All three carried around 575,000cu ft of general cargo to and from the east coast of South America and were fitted to handle heavy items by means of 55t and 70t derricks on the foremast, which had a removable top section for transit of the Manchester Ship Canal. *Romney* and *Raeburn* were broken up at Faslane in 1978, but the latter had previously been transferred within the Vestey Brothers group, firstly to Blue Star as *Colorado Star* in 1958 then four years later to Austasia Line as *Mahsuri*, finally returning to Lamport & Holt as *Roland* in 1977. *Raphael* became the Cypriot *Pola Rika* in 1976 and was scrapped at Gijon in 1979.

The closed shelter-deckers *Ebro* and *Essequibo* were built for Royal Mail Lines' West Indies and Latin American service in 1952 by Harland & Wolff's Govan shipyard. Their design featured a short forecastle and long superstructure with accommodation for twelve first-class passengers amidships, marking a great advance on the smaller *Brittany* and *Araby*, which operated alongside them. Main particulars were 7,784gt and 8,759dwt in the closed shelter-deck condition on dimensions of 445ft oa x 57ft and they were driven by a six-cylinder Burmeister & Wain developing 4,500bhp for fourteen knots. Provision was made for the carriage of edible oils in deep tanks in No 3 hold. The larger 7,791gt *Escalante* and *Eden* (460 x 62ft), which had a more enclosed forward part of the superstructure and boats raised in gravity davits, were delivered in 1955–6. *Essequibo* became China Navigation Company's *Ningpo* in 1968 and a year later *Ebro* followed her to Hong Kong as Fortunewind Maritime's *Fortune Victory*. These incarnations were brief, however, and they both passed to Burma Five Star Line in 1970 as *Kalemyo* and *Kalewa* and were scrapped in China in 1978–9. *Escalante* was wrecked on the breakwater at St John, New Brunswick on 3 February 1970 on her first voyage as the Panamanian *Manes P*, but *Eden*, which had become Neptune Orient Lines' *Neptune Garnet* the previous year, lasted until sold to Kaohsiung breakers in 1979. (*A Duncan*)

The US 'Mariner' class

In order to provide work for beleaguered US shipyards, the US Maritime Administration ordered twenty-five very fast cargo liners in August 1951. Designed to act as naval auxiliaries in time of war, they were built in groups of five in seven different East, Gulf and West Coast yards and delivered between 1952 and 1955. Designated the C4-S-1 type but better known as the 'Mariner' class on account of the suffix applied to US state nicknames, they cost between $7 million and $9 million each. The first to be delivered was *Keystone Mariner* by the Sun Shipbuilding & Dry Dock Company, Chester, Pennsylvania, in mid-1952. They were large ships with overall dimensions of 564 x 76ft on a draught of just less than 30ft, giving tonnages of some 9,200gt on a corresponding deadweight of 12,900. Seven cargo holds were fitted with the first US examples of MacGregor folding steel hatch covers on the weather deck and flush covers in the tween-decks to permit the use of forklift trucks. Their machinery outfit was the most powerful yet geared to a single screw, consisting of twin turbines with a maximum continuous rating of 19,500shp and a defence overload rating of 22,000shp, the latter allowing *Keystone Mariner* to reach a maximum of twenty-three and a quarter knots on trials in light condition. Advertised sea speed was twenty knots and they were the first cargo liners to have a bulbous forefoot. Pictured here on loaded trials is *Old Colony Mariner* in United States Lines livery.

Several of the early 'Mariners' were completed in time to take part in the Korean War and *Cornhusker Mariner* was wrecked at Pusan and broke in two on 7 July 1953. Of the final deliveries, five were altered for the US Navy and four were completed for Pacific Far East Line. The remainder were operated on behalf of the US Maritime Commission by most US liner companies, many of which found them too large, so they were gradually sold off cheaply to companies engaged in the long-distance trades with additional subsidies to convert them to owners' requirements. American President Lines took four and modified them at Bethlehem Steel, Sparrows Point for its round-the-world service by fitting larger funnels, a glazed passenger observation lounge above the bridge, insulated space and Ebel-type masts as depicted in this view of *President Jackson*. American President Lines later acquired another four vessels and United States Lines took nine, which were given *Pioneer* names. *Pioneer Muse* was wrecked at Kita Daito Jima in 1961 and the remainder were converted to cellular container ships in 1970–1. Another three 'Mariners' were converted to passenger ships: Matson Line's *Mariposa* and *Monterey* in 1956 and American Banner Line's *Atlantic* a year later. The 'Mariner' hull was used for a number of subsequent US cargo liners built in the early 1960s. In their later years, 'Mariners' were operated by a number of other US lines, Waterman Steamship Corporation at one time having eleven in its fleet, but most were scrapped in the 1980s. A few lasted considerably longer, notably the naval and passenger conversions and *Monterey* was into her fifty-third year when broken up at Alang in 2007. (*Airfoto, Malacca*)

Germany rebuilds – Hansa heavy-lift ships

Having lost its four heavy-lift ships during World War II, Hansa Line started to order replacements as soon as shipbuilding restrictions were lifted. The 10,869dwt *Bärenfels*, *Birkenfels* and *Braunfels** were the first in a long line of distinctive series of engines-aft ships, in their case with the bridge placed well forward as in tanker practice. Completed by A G Weser's Seebeck Yard in Bremerhaven in 1951–2, they were of 6,974gt on overall dimensions of 512 x 61ft. They had two holds forward of the bridge and three aft, No 3 having a particularly large hatch measuring 79 x 21ft, which was served by a 165t derrick mounted on the for'd side of the mainmast, which also carried a 30t lift on its after side. Cargo capacity amounted to just under 600,000cu ft (bale) and propulsion was by means of a MAN diesel with an output of 3,820bhp giving thirteen and a half knots. *Uhenfels* of 1959 followed a similar layout but with a normal-sized No 3 hold and a single 50t derrick; however, she was rebuilt by Blohm & Voss in the winter of 1967–8 with two 275t Stülcken masts capable of a record combined lift of 550t. At the same time No 3 hold was enlarged with a 115 x 21ft hatch and she was also widened by about 6ft on either beam to improve stability when loading. *Birkenfels* was lost in collision in April 1966 and *Braunfels* was scrapped in Alicante during the winter of 1971–2 but *Bärenfels* was sold for further trading in 1972, first as *Silver Sky* and from 1976 as *Silver Beach* until broken up in Kaohsiung in 1979. *Uhenfels* became the Greek *Uhenbels* in 1980 and was demolished at Alang five year later.

A joint series for express Far East service

Following the lifting of building restrictions, Hamburg-Amerika Linie and Norddeutscher Lloyd ordered a series of cargo liners to a common design for a joint weekly express service to the Far East. Construction was shared between Deutsche Werft, Hamburg and Lübecker Flender-Werke. Six were allocated to Hamburg-Amerika Linie, beginning with *Braunschweig* and illustrated here by *Leverkusen,* and five to Norddeutscher Lloyd, starting with *Weserstein*, which opened the new service in July 1953. With a gross tonnage of around 6,750 and overall dimensions of 522 or 525 x 63ft, they were driven at just over seventeen knots by 9,000shp steam turbines geared to a single screw. Concurrently, five slightly larger (530ft) but similarly powered *Düsseldorf*-class ships were completed by Howaldtswerke, Hamburg, three for Hapag and two for Norddeutscher Lloyd. These differed in having an extra hold aft and a stump mast in place of twin posts forward as well as between the mainmast and aftermost pair of posts. To meet competition from new twenty-knot ships in the Far East trade, Norddeutscher Lloyd rebuilt all seven of its ships at Bremer Vulkan in 1962–3. A new bow section with a bulbous forefoot was fitted, increasing overall length to 549ft. To this was added a stern bulge to ease water flow and more powerful 14,400bhp diesels were installed, raising speed to nineteen and a half knots. All sixteen ships were absorbed into the merged Hapag-Lloyd concern in September 1970 and were gradually sold off as containerisation spread, the last going in 1985. Two pairs of slightly longer (531ft and 534ft overall) *Düsseldorf*-type ships were delivered to India Steamship Company by Howaldtswerke as *Indian Reliance*, – *Renown* in 1955 and *Indian Resolve*, – *Resource* in 1956.

New Stülcken heavy-lift masts

Germany's Hansa Line caused a sensation in 1954 with the delivery of the heavy-lift cargo liner *Lichtenfels*. Her bridge was placed well forward on a short forecastle, similar to Great Lakes practice, allowing a clear 254ft of deck space for heavy cargoes. She also pioneered the use of an entirely new type of heavy-lift mast jointly developed by her owner and the Stülcken shipyard. Its ease of operation, requiring only three men, was a great improvement on the traditional heavy derrick; *Lichtenfels* was equipped with two such masts, capable of lifting 120t (later raised to 140t) and 30t. Extra large hatches and pillar-less holds permitted heavy loads to be stowed below deck. Tonnage figures were 6,800gt and 8,700dwt on dimensions of 461ft oa x 69ft and she was propelled at just under sixteen knots by two MAN diesels developing 5,600bhp and geared to a single screw. Seven sister ships were completed between 1955 and 1956, *Lindenfels*, *Neuenfels* and *Rabenfels* by Stülcken, *Marienfels*, *Neidenfels* and *Ockenfels* by A G Weser, Bremen, and *Liebenfels* by Weser's Seebeck yard at Bremerhaven. In 1972, *Lichtenfels* was renamed *Silver Dawn* by Stavros Daifas, who over the next six years purchased the rest of the class except *Neidenfels*, which became the Greek *Joanna* in 1972 and was scrapped at Gadani Beach in 1978. Three of the Daifas ships, including *Silver Dawn*, were broken up in Kaohsiung in 1979–80 and one in Chittagong in 1982. Those sold on for further trading lasted longest: *Silver Light* (ex-*Rabenfels*) was demolished at San Esteban as *Penelope V* in 1984, *Silver Glory* (ex-*Ockenfels*) was scrapped as *Ionian Sailor* at Gadani in 1985 and *Silver Bird* (ex-*Liebenfels*) gave thirty-two years of service after changing names three more times, before being broken up as *Gritin II* at Kaohsiung in 1987.

Designed for extra large items of cargo, the Stülckenwerft-built *Treuenfels* of 1960 was a development of the *Lichtenfels* design but had only three cargo holds. The extremely long No 2 hold was served by two 130t Stülcken derricks, which, if required, could be combined to lift 260t. For additional cargo handling, two 5t cranes were mounted on rails alongside the hatches. Her tonnage figures were 9,381gt and 12,700dwt on dimensions of 476 x 63ft and a seven-cylinder MAN diesel developing 5,850bhp drove her at fourteen and a half knots. She was sold to Sea Agent Shipping, Piræus, in 1978 and initially chartered back but was renamed *Treuenbels* in 1980 and broken up at Alang five years later.

An elegant series for Brazil/River Plate trade

Hamburg Südamerikanische DG upgraded its east coast of South America services in 1955–6 with eight new seventeen-knot *Cap* ships, built in four pairs, two each by Lübecker Flender-Werke and Howaldtswerke, Hamburg. Dimensions varied slightly, the Lübeck ships measuring 498 x 62ft or 63ft with the others being some 6ft longer, but each pair had its own individual characteristics. All had short forecastles but *Cap Norte* and *Cap Vilano*, which were developments of *Santa Rita* and *Santa Rosa* completed by Howaldtswerke in 1954, were the only ones to have a poop. The first Lübeck pair, *Cap Blanco* and *Cap Frio**, lacked the post on the forecastle common to the others but had a more extensive superstructure similar to *Cap Norte*. The 1956 deliveries, *Cap Roca* and *Cap Verde* in Lübeck and *Cap Ortegal* and *Cap Finisterre* in Hamburg, looked more alike with larger, more angular funnels and smaller superstructures, which differed as to the number of windows. All eight ships had their reefer capacity enlarged by Howaldtswerke in 1959–60. In 1962–3, they were all switched to Columbus Line linking Australia and New Zealand with the US east coast. *Cap Frio* and *Cap Ortegal* were sold to Afromar Inc. in 1969 and chartered back for two years, after which they were renamed *Karpathos* and *Korinthos* and in 1972 were joined by *Cap Finisterre* as *Penelope II*. Three others were sold between 1969 and 1972 and finally *Cap Norte* and *Cap Vilano* went to the Chinese-controlled Ocean Tramping Company, Hong Kong, and Nan Yang Shipping Company, Macao, in 1973–4 as *Aihua* and *Aimin*. The majority were scrapped between 1979 and 1985. The last to go was the former *Cap Ortegal*, which had become the Saudi *Taibah III* in 1982 and which was demolished at Gadani Beach in 1987 following a three-year lay-up.

The final evolution of traditional Wilhelmsen design

The eighteen-knot trio *Themis*, *Theben* and *Tugela**, completed by Eriksbergs, Gothenburg, in 1953–4 marked the final development of Wilh. Wilhelmsen's instantly recognisable split-superstructure design that could be traced back to *Tourcoing* of 1924 and through more than sixty other ships, twenty-six of them delivered after World War II. The only other company that could be said to come near to Wilhelmsen in terms of lengthy adherence to a similar design was Andrew Weir & Company. Tonnage figures were 7,000gt (10,500dwt) in the open condition or 9,947gt (12,845dwt) with a closed shelter-deck and they measured 510ft oa x 65ft. Main engines were ten-cylinder Burmeister & Wain units developing 9,300bhp in *Themis* and *Theben* and an eight-cylinder 10,000bhp unit in *Tugela*. They ran on Wilhelmsen's Far Eastern or Australian services and were later transferred to transpacific service under Barber Lines management. *Themis* was sold in 1975 and renamed *Toyo* but this was changed to *New Hope* two years later and she was scrapped at Tientsin in 1979. *Tugela* and *Theben* both went to Pacific International Lines of Singapore in 1976–7, becoming *Kota Alam* and *Kota Mas* respectively, and the former was demolished at Kaohsiung in 1982. Her sister, however, had been detained in Basrah since August 1980 just before the Iran–Iraq war. In 2003, she was renamed *Koralmaster* but this was shortened to *Mast* for the tow to Alang where she was demolished the following year.

Further UK deliveries – the Australian wool trade

Designed for the Australian wool trade, the 12,900dwt P&O cargo liners *Ballarat* and *Bendigo* were completed by Alexander Stephen, Linthouse, in 1954. Their waterline dimensions were similar to *Singapore* and *Sunda* (see page 100) but a slightly protruding cruiser stern, as opposed to spoon versions, increased overall length to 527ft. The main external difference lay in the provision of an extra hold forward, which was compensated for by a shorter superstructure, whilst their funnels were fitted with Thornycroft cowl tops. Gross tonnage was a shade under 8,800 and bale capacity around 683,500cu ft. For heavy items of cargo, they were fitted with one 80t and two 15t booms. Main propulsion was again similar to the earlier ships, consisting of three sets of Parsons steam turbines developing 13,000shp and geared to a single screw for a service speed of eighteen knots. They were renamed *Pando Cape* and *Pando Sound** in 1968 following changes to P&O's corporate image and were disposed of four years later, the latter for demolition at Briton Ferry and the former to Ben Line, for which she sailed as *Benledi* until broken up at Inchon in 1978.

Pacific west coast trade

The sixteen-knot sisters *Loch Gowan** and *Loch Loyal* were built by Harland & Wolff, Belfast, in 1954 and 1957 respectively for Royal Mail Lines' west coast of North America service run jointly with Holland-America Line, the latter being Royal Mail's last major cargo ship. Handsome in appearance with a short forecastle and a long bridge deck encompassing No 3 hatch, they shared the same hull dimensions of 503ft oa x 68ft, but their differing gross tonnages of 9,718gt and 11,035gt were due to *Loch Gowan* operating as an open shelter-decker and her sister in the closed condition. Total bale capacity amounted to around 425,000cu ft but *Loch Loyal*'s 257,300cu ft of insulated space was some 116,000cu ft more than that of her sister. Cargo gear included a 30t derrick on the forward side of the mainmast. As to propulsion, *Loch Gowan* had three steam turbines geared to a single screw but *Loch Loyal* was a motorship with a seven-cylinder Burmeister & Wain developing 10,300bhp. Neither was destined for lengthy service and *Loch Loyal* was crippled by an engine-room fire in 1969, the same year that Johnson Line's first cellular container ships entered the North Pacific trade. *Loch Gowan* went to Kaohsiung breakers in 1970 and the following year her sister was taken by Greece's Aegis Group and renamed *Aegis Loyal*, finally being scrapped in Shanghai in 1974.

India trade

Thos & Jno Brocklebank's 9,748gt *Maipura*, delivered by William Hamilton & Company in 1952, was the first since its *Mahronda* quartet of 1905–6 to have a composite superstructure in place of the traditional trunked No 3 hatch between bridge and funnel. This trend was continued in the smaller *Maskeliya* and *Maturata* (7,350gt, 472 x 59ft), products of the same builder in 1954–5, which were rendered more distinctive by their three bipod masts and a shorter, dome-topped funnel. They also had a smaller, two-step superstructure with boats on different decks and the bridge deck was extended aft to include the short No 4 hatch. This design was further modified for the subsequent five-ship *Masirah* class completed by William Hamilton & Company between 1957 and 1960 and illustrated here by *Mangla* at Aden. These had an enlarged funnel and superstructure with boats carried at the same level and measured around 8,700gt on a deadweight of 10,530dwt. Their dimensions of 497ft oa x 63ft placed them between *Maipura* and *Maskeliya* but they had the same main machinery: three sets of Rowan steam turbines driving a single screw through single-reduction gearing for fifteen knots. In 1968, they passed to Cunard-Brocklebank management and in 1971, *Makrana* and *Mawana* were sold to the Papalios Group and renamed *Aegis Glory* and *Aegis Legend*, being scrapped in Shanghai in 1974, *Aegis Glory* having become *Aegis Eternity* in 1972. In the same year, *Masirah*, *Mangla* and *Mathura* had passed to New York-Greek-run Marchessini Lines as *Eurysthenes*, *Eurypylus* and *Eurytion* but were subsequently dogged by misfortune. *Eurysthenes* had to be broken up in Kaohsiung in 1974 after grounding in the San Bernardino Strait and *Eurypylus* followed her to Taiwan two years later after suffering an engine-room explosion off the Californian coast in 1975. *Eurytion* passed to Kuwaiti ownership as *Alwaha* in 1977 but was almost immediately gutted by an engine-room fire and demolished at Gadani Beach in 1978.

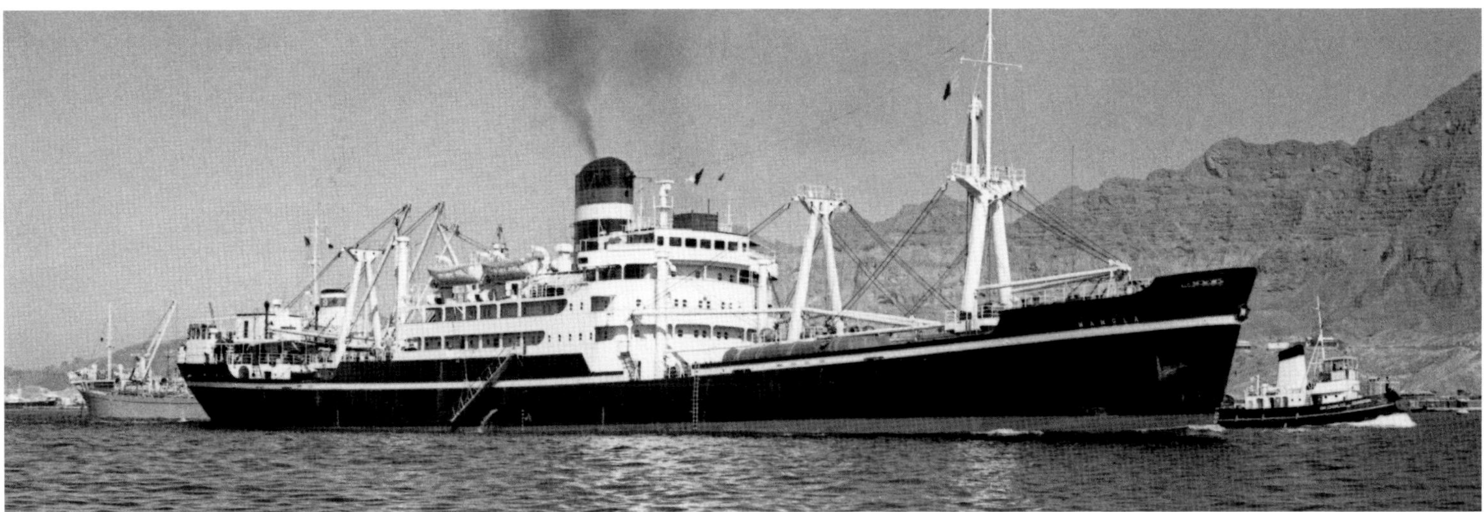

Eastern traders

China Navigation Company's 5,832gt *Chungking* was the first in a series of eight ships built by Taikoo Dockyard, Hong Kong, between 1955 and 1961, and which could be divided into two groups of four, the 'C'-class (illustrated here by *Chekiang*) and the 5,957gt 'K'-class. Although sharing the same dimensions (422 x 56ft) and main machinery (four-cylinder Doxford engines developing 4,450bhp for fourteen and a half knots), the 'K's had an enclosed promenade deck and *Kweilin*, the final delivery in 1962, was further distinguished by having three bipod masts in place of goalposts. *Kwangtung* was chartered to Crusader Shipping for the New Zealand–Japan trade in March 1965 and renamed *Norman*, the same name being continued by *Kweichow*, which replaced her a year later until 1968. *Chekiang* and *Chefoo* were converted to side loaders in 1969 and renamed *Coral Chief* and *Island Chief* for Australian service. *Kwangsi* was similarly converted in 1971, becoming *New Guinea Chief* for the Australia–New Guinea run. All eight ships later served a variety owners, *Chefoo* and *Kwangsi* going to Straits Steamship Company in 1978 and ending their days as *Straits Hope* and *Straits Star*, the former after a thirty-four-year career. *Chekiang* and *Kweilin* became Pacific International Lines' *Kota Buana* and *Kota Berjaya*. Lead ship *Chungking* passed though two Hong Kong owners and survived being blown ashore in Typhoon Rose in August 1971, before being sold to Vietnam in 1977 and renamed *Song Gianh*. She was deleted from the register in 1992 and it can be assumed that she outlived *Chefoo* by a year or two.

New French tonnage

The ailing French liner company Cyprien Fabre & Company placed orders in the early 1950s for two new cargo ships to boost its Canada and Great Lakes service. *Duquesne* was completed by Forges et Chantiers de la Mediterranée, La Seyne, in 1954 and *Frontenac* by Chantier et Ateliers de Provence, Port de Bouc, in the following year, which also saw Cyprien Fabre & Company merging with another Marseilles company, Compagnie Fraissinet. They measured 5,788gt and 7,487dwt on dimensions of 449 x 60ft and were fitted with bipod masts whilst the lower deck of their accommodation block was extended aft around No 4 hatch. The company's problems continued, so the two ships were sold to Chargeurs Réunis in 1956 and renamed *Manga* and *Maroua*. This period lasted only five years before they were resold to China Navigation Company and renamed *Tsingtao* and *Tientsin* for operation between Hong Kong and Australia, *Tientsin* being depicted in Sydney Harbour. *Tsingtao* bore several subsequent names whilst under Swire Group ownership; *Island Chief* between 1968 and 1970, *Tauloto* in 1972, *Soochow* in 1973 and finally *Wenchow* in 1977 before being scrapped in Kaohsiung in 1980. *Tientsin* was renamed *Six Stars* between 1969 and 1971 and was sold to Somalia in 1973, retaining her name until broken up in Shanghai in 1975.

Well-known French liner company Messageries Maritimes was not noted for operating cargo ships before World War II, having relied mainly on a handful of former German ships after World War I and a number of Liberty ships after World War II. Replacement of these Liberty ships began with the ten-ship *Godavery* class, which had the distinctive rounded top funnel adopted for all the company's new ships after 1952 and illustrated here by the second ship of the class, *Moonie*, in the North Sea. Designed for a variety of services including Africa, Asia and Australia, they were completed between 1955 and 1958, the first two by Chantier et Ateliers de Provence, Port de Bouc, and the remainder by Chantiers Navale de La Ciotat. Tonnages averaged 7,000gt and 8,900dwt on dimensions of 489 x 62ft and they were driven at sixteen knots by nine-cylinder Burmeister & Wain engines rated at 8,300bhp. *Sindh* was trapped in the Suez Canal for eight years following the Six Day War and all were sold between 1975 and 1978, *Kouang Si* and *Yang-Tse* going directly to breakers in Kaohsiung and Whampoa and the others for further trading. The last to be scrapped was *Si Kiang* as the Greek *Takis* at Aliaga in 1985. The design was enlarged upon for five 7,474gt *Maori*-class ships (514 x 65ft) completed at Chantiers Navale de La Ciotat for Far East service between 1958 and 1960, and which had long, very flaired forecastles and 13,450bhp diesels for eighteen knots. Five identical 'V'-class ships led by *Vivarais* followed for Australian and Pacific routes; three more 'V's led by *Var* in 1964 had raised poops. In 1972–3, Portugal's Lisnave shipyard lengthened six of the 'V's by the insertion of a new 60ft-long cellular hold with a capacity of forty-four 20ft containers served by a 5t crane.

British-built ships for African and Asian trades

In the mid-1950s, British India Steam Navigation Company built four 8,500gt 'N'-class ships to a new design for its Australian and East African services. *Nuddea* and *Nardana* came from Barclay, Curle & Company in 1954 and 1956 whilst *Nowshera* and *Nyanza* were products of Scotts' Shipbuilding & Engineering Company in 1955 and 1956. *Nyanza*'s finely balanced profile is shown to advantage in this October 1958 view taken from the Mid Barrow light vessel. The lead ship, *Nuddea*, differed in having her masts mounted on the forward- and aftermost masthouses. Overall length was 514ft on a beam of 68ft and they were propelled by three-stage steam turbines geared to a single screw for a normal sea speed of sixteen to seventeen knots. *Nardana* and *Nyanza*, however, which lacked the 50t and 25t jumbo derricks of the earlier ships, were fitted with extra nozzles for defence purposes, allowing them to steam at twenty knots if required. In 1963–4 they were sold to P&O and, as *Baradine* and *Balranald*, traded first to Australia and later to the Far East and the Arabian Gulf. Returned to British India Steam Navigation Company in 1968, they briefly passed into P&O's General Cargo Division in the early 1970s but were sold in 1973–4 along with *Nowshera* to Arya National Shipping Line of Iran, becoming *Arya Pand*, *Arya Gol* and *Arya Chehr* respectively. The latter was broken up in Tsingtao in 1976 and the others at Gadani Beach in 1976–7. Lead ship *Nuddea* had preceded them to the scrapyard, going direct to Kaohsiung without change of name in 1976. (*John G Callis*)

Union-Castle Line's 10,800dwt sisters *Tantallon Castle* and *Tintagel Castle** were single-screw motor vessels built by Harland & Wolff, Belfast in 1954–5. Designed for service from South Africa to Britain as well as to the United States, they were neat-looking ships and were 7,448gt on dimensions of 495ft oa x 66ft. An eight-cylinder Burmeister & Wain diesel of 10,600bhp burning heavy fuel oil provided a service speed of sixteen and a half knots. They were the last Union-Castle cargo ships to have a black-painted hull, future deliveries adopting the well-known lavender shade of the passenger liners. After relatively short careers, they were sold to Cypriot owners in 1971, *Tantallon Castle* as *Aris II* (becoming *Aris* in 1972) and *Tintagel Castle* as *Armar* and were demolished seven years later at Aioi and Kaohsiung respectively.

Ben Line Steamers broke away from its wartime-influenced designs with the seventeen-knot *Benreoch* in 1951. She was followed by three modified 12,000dwt sisters completed in successive years from 1955 by Charles Connell & Company's Scotstoun yard. *Benvrackie*, seen here leaving Singapore, *Bendoran* and *Benlomond*. were arguably better looking than *Benreoch*. *Benreoch* had two sets of posts on a long forecastle, whereas the design of the other three incorporated an extra sixth hatch, but all four shared the same overall hull dimensions of 504 x 64ft. *Bendoran* and *Benlomond* differed from the other two in carrying their boats in gravity davits. Two sets of double-reduction geared turbines with a maximum output of 9,350shp drove a single screw for a service speed of seventeen and a half knots. *Benvrackie* was the first Ben Line ship to supplement its cargo-handling gear with two deck cranes mounted forward of the funnel to serve the trunked No 4 hatch. *Bendoran* was the first company ship to cost more than £1 million. All four ended their days at the hands of Kaohsiung breakers, *Benvrackie* arriving in November 1975, *Bendoran* and *Benlomond* in 1977 and *Benreoch* in 1979, after sailing as the Greek *Tudis* since 1976.

Japanese fleet reconstruction – early turbine ships

Some of Japan's new cargo liners were turbine driven due to lack of available materials for building diesel engines. An example was Iino Lines' *Yasushima Maru**, completed by Hitachi Zosen, Innoshima, in 1954 and shown here on trials, during which she recorded a speed of more than twenty knots. Together with near sister *Tsuneshima Maru*, completed a year earlier by Harima Shipbuilding & Engineering Company, Aioi, she measured 9,440gt and 12,227dwt on overall dimensions of 508 x 64ft and was unusual in having a three-deck superstructure. In 1956, Iino Lines acquired the similar but slightly smaller *Nikko Maru*, built by Hitachi for Nissan in 1952, and renamed her *Takeshima Maru*. All three adopted the livery of Kawasaki Line following the merger with Iino in 1964. They were sold in 1970, *Takeshima Maru* and *Tsuneshima Maru* becoming *May* and *June* and the latter briefly *Galion* before both were scrapped at Kaohsiung in 1973. *Yasushima Maru* was renamed *Venus Argosy* and broken up at Split in 1978.

Mitsui Line's 'H' and 'M' classes

Mitsui Steamship Company began an eighteen-ship postwar reconstruction programme at Mitsui's Tamano yard with five 'A'-class vessels (499ft oa x 64ft) in 1951–2 and these were followed by five more powerful 'H'-class vessels delivered in 1954–5. The 'H'-class vessels had outward sloping cruiser rather than cruiser spoon stems. The first three *Harunasan Maru*, *Hakonesan Maru* and *Hoeisan Maru* measured 505ft on the same beam. Enlarged dimensions of 514 x 65ft were adopted for *Hagurosan Maru** and *Hodakasan Maru*, which were built for round-the-world service in 1955, and eight 'M'-class ships which followed between 1956 and 1959. The 'M'-class ships had four goalpost masts and a more substantial radar mast mounted above the bridge. Tonnages averaged 9,500gt and 11,400dwt and all had turbo-charged nine-cylinder Burmeister & Wain engines developing 11,250bhp for seventeen and a half knots. The subsequent *Kinkasan Maru* and *Kasugasan Maru* completed for the Great Lakes trade in 1961–2, were notable as the first automated ships with bridge control of their engines in a move to reduce crew numbers. Mitsui Steamship Company merged with Osaka Shosen Kaisha in 1964 and its smart livery of green hull, buff upperworks and grey funnel with three white rings was replaced by the uniform blue hull and red funnel adopted by Mitsui-OSK Lines. All the 'H'- and 'M'-class ships were disposed of between 1973 and 1980, only *Mogamisan* –, *Manjusan* –, *Mayasan* – and *Kinkasan Maru* going direct to breakers in 1979–80 and the others traded on for a variety of eastern owners. The final deliveries in the 'M' series, *Momijisan Maru* and *Matsudosan Maru*, were the last to be scrapped as *Han Garan* and *Han Nuri* in Pusan in 1984.

Variations on an OSK theme

Osaka Shosen Kaisha's rebuilding programme undertaken by Mitsubishi's Kobe yard was based on three different hull sizes and the ships were built in groups of two or three, which varied slightly from each other in layout and engine power. The larger ships had an overall length of 512ft on a beam of 64ft and began with the *Panama Maru* trio in 1952, followed by *Philippine Maru** and *Arizona Maru* in 1955–6, all of which had four goalpost masts. The fore and aft goalposts were replaced by single masts from *Havana Maru* and *Honolulu Maru* of 1957–8 onwards, whilst the remaining ships were distinguished by lower superstructures, some of which were partially enclosed. All were driven by Sulzer diesels and output was gradually increased from 10,000bhp for sixteen and a half knots in the initial trio to 12,000bhp for seventeen and a half knots and finally 13,000bhp for more than eighteen knots in the final trio *Hague* –, *Norfolk* – and *Tacoma Maru* of 1961–2. All changed livery after becoming part of the merged Mitsui-OSK fleet in 1964 and they were disposed of between 1973 and 1980. The last to be broken up was the former *Seattle Maru* as the Saudi *Loutfallah* in Karachi in 1985.

NYK's fast 'S' class

Nippon Yusen Kaisha's postwar 'A'-class ships retained the long bridge deck of the prewar 'N' and 'A' classes (see page 74) but this was dropped in the subsequent fifteen-ship 'S' series from Mitsubishi, which began with *Sagami Maru* in 1955 and ended with *Sapporo Maru* in 1961. Seven were built in Yokohama and the remainder in Nagasaki, ships from the latter yard being distinguished by fewer and thicker vertical stanchions in their superstructure, as depicted in this view of *Suruga Maru* in Sydney. Main machinery also differed between the ships, the seven from the Yokohama yard having eight-cylinder MAN diesels whilst the Nagasaki ships had nine-cylinder UEC units. All the ships were turbo-charged, however, and produced 12,000bhp (up-rated to 13,000bhp in the final two ships) for around eighteen knots in service and more than twenty knots on trials. Their design owed much to the prewar twin-screw *Saiko Maru* class but in contrast all four masts were goalposts and topmasts were repositioned on those nearest to the superstructure. They measured 9,300gt and 11,800dwt on overall dimensions of 514ft (Yokohama deliveries 509ft) x 64ft and operated on their owner's Europe, US and westbound round-the-world services, moving to others routes as containerisation was introduced. *Sumida Maru* and *Sapporo Maru* had their refrigerated capacity increased in the summer of 1970 for serving the east coast of South America. Most were disposed after about twenty years' trading, mainly to Far Eastern buyers.

New UK designs for Australia/New Zealand trade

Port Line's 11,000dwt *Port Sydney** and *Port Melbourne* continued the streamlined look introduced by *Port Brisbane* (see page 103) but had a much lower superstructure with their bridge positioned abaft No 3 hatch on a long bridge deck. Built by Swan, Hunter & Wigham Richardson, Wallsend, and Harland & Wolff, Belfast, in 1955, they measured 533ft oa x 70ft and were propelled at seventeen and a half knots by twin six-cylinder diesels developing 13,200bhp, by Burmeister & Wain and Doxford respectively. Three of the six holds were insulated for the carriage of meat, dairy produce and fruit and cargo gear included a 70t derrick at No 2 hatch and a single crane serving Nos 4 and 5. In 1972, they were sold to the Carras Group and renamed *Therisos Express* and *Akrotiri Express* with the intention of converting them to car ferries. Instead, they were renamed *Daphne* and *Danae* in 1974 and converted at Chalkis Shipyard over the next two years into up-market, 450-passenger cruise ships of 15,833gt. The venture was not a success and they were offered for charter, *Daphne* being taken by Lauro in 1978–9; Costa Cruises subsequently bought them both in 1984. *Danae* briefly bore the name *Anar* in 1992 before becoming *Starlight Princess* then *Baltica* in 1994 and finally *Princess Danae* in 1996. Her sister was renamed *Switzerland* in 1996, *Ocean Odyssey* and then *Ocean Monarch* in 2002. Both were still in service in 2008 after more than fifty years, a tribute to their original builders.

With UK yards fully committed, Vestey Brothers turned to Germany's Bremer Vulkan for a series of medium-sized ships for Blue Star Line, built under fixed-price contract with penalties for late delivery. *Canberra Star, Hobart Star* and *Newcastle Star* were completed in 1956 and *Gladstone Star** and *Townsville Star* a year later. Only *Newcastle Star* ended up being for Blue Star account, the rest being registered to Bermuda subsidiary Salient Shipping. Their design featured a curved stem and cruiser spoon stern but otherwise followed traditional Blue Star practice with just a single mast; the first three later had a single crane installed aft. Tonnages were 8,257gt and 12,200dwt on dimensions of 519ft oa x 70ft but the 1957 pair were 20ft longer with the forecastle extended to the foremast and an extra post forward, equivalent tonnage figures being 10,635gt and 12,300dwt. All five shared the same ten-cylinder MAN machinery rated at 11,250bhp for a speed of around seventeen and a half knots. They traded on Australasian routes until 1972, when *Hobart Star* was transferred to the South American run and renamed *Buenos Aires Star*, however, collision damage after only one voyage resulted in *Canberra Star* replacing her as *Buenos Aires Star*. *Newcastle Star* then joined the latter as *Montevideo Star* but was laid up in 1975 and sold the following year to Cyprus' Conquest Shipping as *Golden Madonna*. *Hobart Star* went to Greek owners in 1978 becoming *Aegean Prosperity* and both *Aegean Prosperity* and *Golden Madonna* were scrapped in Kaohsiung in 1980, one year after *Canberra Star* had met a similar fate. Of the 1957 pair, *Townsville Star* went to Kaohsiung breakers in 1980 after being trapped at Khorramshahr for two months by the Iran–Iraq war and *Gladstone Star* was demolished at Gadani Beach in 1982 after sailing out as *Maltese Gladys*. The 10,619gt *Queensland Star* and *Rockhampton Star* (507 x 68ft) completed by Fairfield and Cammell Laird in 1957 and 1958 to serve northern Queensland ports, were broadly similar but with forecastles extended to incorporate No 2 hatch.

Concurrent with the Blue Star order described above, Bremer Vulkan also completed three interesting ships for Shaw, Savill & Albion Company in 1956–7. The 6,497gt *Arabic, Afric** and *Aramaic* were unusual in having no refrigerated capacity, being designed for increasing amounts of general cargo being exported from Australia and New Zealand, in particular wool, tallow and hides. Their curved bow and exaggerated sheer line, coupled with a streamlined superstructure, gave them a pleasantly racy appearance and they were of similar engine power and speed to the Blue Star ships. Dimensions were 475ft oa x 64ft on a deadweight of 9,240dwt and the bale capacity of the five holds amounted to 533,650cu ft. Cargo gear included 50t and 25t jumbo derricks mounted on the forward side of the two masts. A fourth ship, *Alaric*, which came from Harland & Wolff's Govan yard in 1958, differed both in appearance and in being fitted with insulated space. In 1968, the German-built trio were transferred within the owning Furness Withy Group to Pacific Steam Navigation Company and renamed *Oroya, Orita* and *Oropesa* respectively; in 1970, the first and last briefly held the names *Pacific Ranger* and *Pacific Exporter*. In 1972, all three were sold to Hong Kong Islands Shipping, becoming *Lamma Island, Hongkong Island* and *Lantao Island* respectively. The latter was scrapped in Kaohsiung in 1982 and her sisters at Inchon a year later. Meanwhile, the former *Alaric* had been demolished in Bombay in 1979, having sailed for Iranian owners as *Iran Niru* from 1972 and as *Rumi* from 1976.

Clan Line received the handsome 9,300gt steamers *Argyllshire* and *Ayrshire* (seen leaving Aden) from Greenock Dockyard in 1956–7. Designed for Australian service, they continued the 'fireman's helmet' funnel top introduced with *Clan Shaw* (see page 106) but had a long forecastle in addition to a poop. Deadweight tonnage was 11,240 and they measured 535ft oa x 69ft, allowing a sixth hold that differentiated them from the immediately preceding *Clan Robertson* and *Clan Ross*. Bale capacity amounted to some 600,000cu ft, of which more than half was insulated in hold, Nos 2, 3, 4 and upper 5. Cargo-handling gear included a 105t heavy derrick serving No 2 hatch and 40t lifts for Nos 3 and 5. Three steam turbines geared to a single screw developed a maximum of 11,500shp but a service rating of 10,500shp guaranteed a speed of seventeen knots. It was traditional for Clan Line to employ Lascar ratings and this generally resulted in large crews, that of these particular ships amounting to twenty-eight officers and seventy crew, with capacity for up to 12 passengers. *Ayrshire* had the misfortune to ground on Abd al Kuri Island at the southern end of the Red Sea on 23 March 1965 and was abandoned after attempts to refloat her failed. *Argyllshire* was sold to Liberia's Gulf East Marine in 1975 and renamed *Schivago* but went to Kaohsiung breakers two years later.

New Zealand Shipping Company's 13,314gt *Otaio*, seen passing under the Sydney Harbour Bridge, was the last major UK cadet training ship. Built by John Brown & Company at Clydebank in 1958, she could accommodate forty deck and thirty engineering cadets together with their instructors. She was essentially a development of the company's *Otaki* and Federal Steam Navigation Company's *Essex*, sharing the same dimensions of 526ft oa x 73ft. Externally, *Otaio* differed from *Otaki* and *Essex* in a number of ways, having a curved stem, the foremast placed one hold further forward and a long bridge deck containing three-berth cabins, classrooms, a recreation room and an engineering workshop. Her machinery also differed, comprising twin six-cylinder 6,200bhp Doxford diesels, each driving a screw and giving a speed of seventeen knots, whereas the earlier ships had twin twelve-cylinder Sulzers developing a combined 11,400bhp and geared to a single screw. Because of her other duties, *Otaio*'s 429,300cu ft of insulated space was around 40,000cu ft less than in the earlier pair. She adopted the Federal funnel markings in 1966 and then the blue of the P&O General Cargo Division in 1971. Sold in 1976, she continued her training activities as the grey-hulled *Eastern Academy* for Gulf Shipping Lines and was finally broken up at Gadani Beach in 1982.

Scandinavian owners adopt composite superstructures

A P Møller had introduced a new layout with the 6,462gt *Chastine Mærsk*, completed at its own Odense shipyard in 1953, and her sisters *Maren Maersk* and *Johannes Mærsk*, which were delivered by Kieler Howaldtswerke. Their hulls measured 489ft oa x 63ft and incorporated a long forecastle and a poop extending forward to the mainmast. The lead ship differed in having two 10t cranes between Nos 2 and 3 hatches, the others having a normal stump mast mounting conventional derricks. Propulsion was by means of a ten-cylinder Burmeister & Wain diesel developing 11,400bhp for seventeen and a half knots. Five similar but larger versions (498ft oa x 64ft) followed between 1954 and 1956: *Susan Mærsk* and *Rita Mærsk* from Nakskov and *Sally Mærsk*, *Effie Mærsk* and *Marit Mærsk* from Odense. These had more powerful nine-cylinder Burmeister & Wain engines developing 12,500bhp and giving more than eighteen knots in service. *Sally* –, *Effie* – and *Marit Mærsk* were lengthened to 539ft oa in 1965–6 by the insertion of an extra hold, increasing gross displacement to just over 7,000gt. Finally, five 'L'-class ships with similar dimensions were delivered between 1956 and 1958, *Lica* –, *Luna* –* and *Lexa Mærsk* by A G Weser and *Leda* – and *Laust Mærsk* by the Odense shipyard. They were broadly similar to the earlier ships but had a shorter poop and an eight-cylinder 10,000bhp Burmeister & Wain diesel for seventeen and a half knots. *Laust Mærsk* was wrecked in Tokyo Bay following collision with *Alcoa Pioneer* on 5 February 1961. Three were broken up in 1980, *Lica* – and *Lexa Mærsk* in Kaohsiung and *Luna Mærsk* at Gadani Beach. *Leda Mærsk* was sold to Saudi Arabia in 1981, becoming *Saudi Cloud* and was demolished at Alang in 1984.

Norway's Høegh Line had also favoured split superstructures but in 1956 it took delivery of the 9,191gt sisters *Høegh Cape** and *Høegh Cliff* from Deutsche Werft, Hamburg, for its Straits/India–US trade. Their typical German design owed much to *Høegh Clipper*, which had been completed two years earlier by Kieler Howaldtswerke but which was sold almost immediately to Messageries Maritimes and renamed *Donai*. They measured 496ft oa x 64ft on a deadweight of 10,400 and were driven at sixteen knots by a seven-cylinder Burmeister & Wain diesel developing 8,750bhp. In the summer of 1967, they were sold to Indo-China Steam Navigation Company and renamed *Eastern Cape* and *Eastern Cliff*. Disposed of again five years later, the former became Pacific International Lines' *Kota Tanjong* and was scrapped in Bombay in 1983, whilst her sister went to the People's Republic of China as *Bi Hua*. She was renamed *Hong Qi 134* in 1979 and was reported to be still in existence as late as 2003.

A Belgian series for African trades

Compagnie Maritime Belge followed up its seven *Lubumbashi*-class 8,700gt cargo liners with a series of thirteen *Moanda*-class ships for its African services. All but two were given Congolese place names, the exceptions being *Monthouet* and *Montalto*, which were completed as training ships with an extra accommodation deck. Ten were built by Cockerill Ougrée, Hoboken, between 1957 and 1962 and *Mol** and *Congo Zole*, which had a stump mast in place of the second bipod, by De Schelde, Flushing, in 1962. Tonnage measurements were 8,770gt and around 12,800dwt on dimensions of 482ft oa x 62ft and the first five deliveries had a thirteen-knot service speed for West African service, whilst the remainder were given an extra knot for the longer East African route. Finally, the larger and more automated 15,300dwt *Mokaria* was completed by Boel & Sons in 1964. *Congo Moko* and *Congo Zole* were transferred to Compagnie Maritime Congolese in 1967 and renamed *Joseph Okito* and *Maurice Mpolo*. The remainder were disposed of in the 1970s, only *Mokaria* lasting until 1983.

CHAPTER

9

New Designs and Innovation

By the mid-1950s, most companies had completed their postwar fleet reconstruction programmes and attention was turned to new and more efficient designs. Engines began to be positioned further aft or in some cases right aft whilst retaining a navigating bridge amidships. Both measures had the effect of shortening the shaft tunnel and providing additional space for cargo. Attention began to be focused on ways to speed up cargo handling and Scandinavian shipowners led the way in the development of multiple hatches, a concept which was later refined into the 'open ship' type in which the hatches covered most of the upper deck and were generally served by electric cranes rather than derricks. In terms of propulsion, lightweight, medium-speed diesels also began to make an appearance.

The period was also marked by the beginnings of a remarkable expansion in the merchant fleets of the Communist Bloc, ships for the Soviet Union being built in long series in domestic shipyards as well as in those of Finland, Poland, East Germany and Yugoslavia. Meanwhile, steamship lines in the United States, most of which were still operating World War II-built tonnage, embarked on a major reconstruction programme, whilst at the same time a number of third-world countries began to invest in their own merchant fleets, encouraged by the UNCTAD (United Nations Conference on Trade and Development) agreement of 1955, which allowed them to carry 40 per cent of their trade in their own ships, a further 40 per cent being allotted to the established liner companies and the remaining 20 per cent to outsiders. All of this resulted in greater competition for the previously dominant British liner companies.

Note: An asterisk in a caption indicates the vessel shown in the photograph.

Engines moved further aft

Fred Olsen & Co was one of the first companies to look at ways of speeding up cargo handling and experimented with fork-lift trucks and pallets in a series of medium-sized Canaries traders. The larger *Burrard* and *Bolinas**, built to join the earlier *Buffalo* on its North Europe–Pacific coast of North America service, were delivered by Akers MV, Oslo and Bergens MV in 1956. They measured 9,300gt and 11,300dwt in the closed condition on overall dimensions of 508 x 65ft and were propelled at seventeen knots by a six-cylinder Burmeister & Wain diesel rated at 8,600bhp. They had two continuous decks, a third deck in all but No 6 hold and a fourth in No 4 hold, whilst bale capacity amounted to 431,590cu ft with a further 157,300cu ft set aside for refrigerated cargo. The fore and aft sets of hatches were joined by a continuous coaming inside of which was a set of rails, allowing the three 5t electric cranes, which were mounted on travelling platforms to serve any hold either singly or (forward only) in pairs. Each hatch was also served by two derricks and the posts supporting those between Nos 2 and 3 hatches were set wide enough apart to allow the cranes to pass between them. The crane platforms were also used to open and close the MacGregor-Comarain single-pull hatch covers. *Burrard* was briefly Olsen & Ugelstad's *Ternefjell* in 1970 but the following year was sold with her sister to Everett-Orient Line for which both ships traded in Eastern waters as *Rutheverett* and *Vinceeverett*, until the former was wrecked on 30 June 1976 and subsequently broke her back. *Vinceeverett* was broken up in Kaohsiung in 1979. (*John G Callis*)

A growing tendency to position machinery further aft could be discerned in 1956, spearheaded by Scandinavian owners such as Sweden's Broström Group with the Levant trader *Tavastland* and Norwegian shipowner Peter Meyer. The latter's 6,116gt *Havjo*, completed by Öresundsvarvet, Landskrona, and pictured passing Doel inbound for Antwerp, was designed for transatlantic service with a long forecastle and was unusual in having four bipod masts forward of the accommodation block, which extended into the poop. Overall measurement was 469ft on a beam of 64ft and her 9,200dwt capacity included twenty-one separate cargo compartments, some refrigerated, which were served by an array of twenty-two derricks. Main propulsion was provided by an eight-cylinder Götaverken diesel developing 7,500bhp for a speed of seventeen knots. Subsequent Meyer tonnage followed the same basic design with different masting arrangements but the company's final cargo liners, the Lübeck-built *Havsul* and *Havlom*, had conventionally placed machinery and were fitted with heavy-lift masts, in *Havlom*'s case a Stülcken. Increasing competition from container and ro-ro ships forced Meyer to close its liner service in 1972 and the remaining ships were sold to the People's Republic of China, *Havjo* being renamed *Gaopeng*. She was broken up at Qinghuangdao in 1985 but three of her former running mates lasted until the early 1990s, two being demolished in China and the former *Havtjeld* as *De Du* (briefly *Gaoyu* 1972–3) at Alang in 1992.

The Danish East Asiatic Company's 8,797gt *Bogota**, completed in 1956, had machinery placed right aft but, as in tanker practice, she retained a separate bridge structure forward of amidships, which housed senior officers and a few passengers. This layout had previously been confined to smaller vessels, such as Lloyd Triestino's four 5,449gt *Adige*-class ships of 1950–1 and Hansa Line's heavy-lift tonnage, but *Bogota* and her five sisters could claim to be both the largest and fastest, with a service speed of seventeen and a half knots provided by an eight-cylinder Burmeister & Wain diesel rated at 10,000bhp. *Bogota, Beira, Basra* and *Boribana* were products of Burmeister & Wain, whilst *Boma* and *Busuanga* came from the East Asiatic's own Nakskov yard. The 498 x 64ft hulls featured a long forecastle and a very short poop joined to the after accommodation block, whilst the five cargo holds had a bale capacity of 570,450cu ft and were served by twenty-two derricks ranging from 5t to 10t and including 20t and 60t lifts mounted on the two bipod masts. The 10,090gt *Ayuthia* and *Asmara*, delivered in 1960–1, were similar in layout but dimensionally larger at 524 x 68ft. As to their fates, *Beira* and *Bogota* were sold to Nigeria in 1975 and 1977, the former being scrapped as *Ifewara* at Gadani Beach in 1982 whilst the latter caught fire as *Falcon Glory* and grounded at Port Harcourt on 9 March 1979. Refloated in 1980, she was beached and became a total loss. *Busuanga, Basra* and *Boribana* went to Indonesia, *Busuanga* in 1976 as *Lumoso*, being demolished in Kaohsiung in 1979, and the latter two to Trikora Lloyd in 1977 as *Asahan* and *Pomalaa*, which were broken up respectively in Taiwan in 1985 and China in 1984. *Boma* was renamed *Sibonga* in 1978 but quickly sold to Hong Kong Islands Shipping Company as *Ngan Chau* and was cut up at Kaohsiung in 1980. Of the larger 'A'-ships, *Asmara* became the Panamanian flag *Man Fung* in 1978 and two years later the Greek *Aspassia M*, being scrapped in 1985, two years after sister *Ayuthia*, which had traded as *Torm Jessie* since 1980, had been demolished in Bombay.

Medium-speed diesels and multiple hatches

In the mid-1950s, the ever-innovative Johnson Line obtained a license from Gustav Pielstick to manufacture his medium-speed diesel engines that were formerly used in U-boats. Trial six-cylinder units were fitted to the 1925-built sisters *Axel Johnson* and *Annie Johnson* in 1957. Later the same year, four twelve-cylinder units developing 12,000bhp and geared to two screws were installed in the clean-lined *Rio de Janeiro*, depicted here at speed in the English Channel. These were much smaller than the traditional slow-speed engines and saved weight and space. Designed for the company's east coast of South America service, she was the first of six 9,000dwt closed shelter-deckers, the others being *Buenos Aires, Montevideo, Santos, Brasilia* and *Rosario*, completed by Johnson's own Lindholmens yard in Gothenburg by 1960, and they represented a development of the *Seattle* class (see page 98), with light streamlined masts mounted at the break of the long forecastle and above the bridge. Another innovation was multiple hatches, Nos 3 and 4 holds being divided longitudinally into three sections, the outer holds for refrigerated cargoes, and each being accessed through its own hatch with those on the wings being smaller than the centre hatch. Gross measurement was 8,495t on overall dimensions of 490 x 63ft and cargo handling was by means of ten 5t and two 7.5t electro-hydraulic cranes. *Bahia Blanca*, a late delivery in 1964, was fitted with a bipod mast carrying a 70t heavy-lift derrick. Between 1968 and 1969, all seven were converted to part container ships by the insertion of a 60 TEU cellular hold forward of the bridge with provision for a similar number of boxes to be stowed on deck, handling being undertaken by a new 25t crane. This action prolonged the ships' lives for another decade or so and *Rio de Janeiro* was disposed of in 1980, making her way to Barcelona for demolition as *Ris 8*. *Bahia Blanca* was the last survivor of the class, being broken up in Chittagong in 1985–6 as *Chimera* after briefly holding the name *Bahia*. (*John G Callis*)

New Indian tonnage

Scindia Steam Navigation Company, established in Bombay in 1919, began to replace its fleet of second-hand ships with new buildings in the mid-1950s. These comprised three basic types: two fourteen-and-three-quarter-knot *Jalazad*-types of 499 x 61ft in 1955–6, four twelve-knot *Jalavihar*-types of 476 x 58ft from Indian shipyards between 1955 and 1958 and six 17.2-knot *Jaladhan*-class ships from Lübecker Flender-Werke in 1956–7. The latter class, illustrated here by *Jaladhir*, had a long forecastle and short poop and measured 6,527gt on dimensions of 509ft oa x 64ft. They operated on services to Europe and the United States and had a bale capacity of 598,104cu ft and a small amount of insulated space. A sea speed of seventeen knots was maintained by a nine-cylinder MAN diesel developing 8,100bhp. The lead ship was sold to Liberian registered owners in 1971 and renamed *Uniworld*, her sisters all going for scrap between 1980 and 1983. The modified *Jaladuta* and *Jaladurga*, completed by Lübecker Flender-Werke in 1959 and 1960, were 4ft shorter and had seven-cylinder turbo-charged MAN engines of 7,860bhp. They were broken up in Calcutta in 1983 and 1985 respectively.

India Steamship followed up its four 'R'-class ships (see page 109) with six smaller sisters from Howaldtswerke, Hamburg beginning with the 7,275gt *Indian Splendour* in 1957 and ending with *Indian Triumph* in July 1960. Their hulls measured 508 x 66ft and incorporated a short forecastle and poop. Bale cargo space amounted to 553,954cu ft with an additional 8,990cu ft of insulated space. Cargo-handling gear comprised single 40t and 30t jumbos, together with six 10t and twelve 5t lifts. The series differed in way of main machinery; *Indian Splendour*, -*Success** and – *Tradition* had 9,900shp steam turbines geared to a single screw and the other four had eight-cylinder MAN diesels of similar power, all being capable of maintaining seventeen and a half knots in service. The turbine ships were hard hit by the escalation in oil prices in the 1970s and *Indian Tradition* was scrapped at Mormugao in 1978, followed a year later by her two sisters in Bombay. *Indian Strength* was sold to Iranian owners as *Faulad Sardar* in 1979 and became *Success* two years later, but was sunk in the Arabian Gulf on 11 January 1982 by aircraft missile attack. *Indian Triumph* was demolished at Calcutta in 1985, *Indian Trust* soon afterwards and *Indian Security* was the last to go, being broken up in Bombay in the winter of 1987–8. (*A Duncan*)

New series for the Eastern Bloc

The year 1955 marked the beginnings of what was to become an unprecedented expansion in the size of the Communist Bloc merchant fleet. Ships were built in series to standard designs and smart new liner tonnage was epitomised by Poland's B-54 type, led by *Marceli Nowotko* in 1956. A further forty ships had been completed to the same hull design by 1964, twenty-nine at Gdansk and twelve at Szczecin and, of these, Polish Ocean Lines received twenty, the USSR nine and Cuba three, with the remainder split between owners in China, France, Indonesia and Switzerland. They were good-looking vessels with a long forecastle and the lower deck of the accommodation block, which varied slightly in design as the series progressed, extended around No 4 hold, though the latter feature was dropped in the Szczecin deliveries *Divnogorsk* and *Mednogorsk* for the USSR and the final six B454 variations. The first five Gdansk deliveries had single masts and a single post aft, but the post was dropped from hull No 8, *Reymont*, and all subsequent ships had three bipod masts. Tonnage figures were 6,660gt and 10,460dwt and they measured 505ft oa x 64ft. Main propulsion was either by an eight-cylinder Fiat or a six-cylinder Sulzer, each producing around 8,000bhp for a service speed of sixteen and a half knots. *Boleslaw Beirut* and *Djakarta* were trapped in the Suez Canal by the Six Day War in 1967 and the Cuban *Aracelio Iglesias* was wrecked off Hainan Island in 1970. The trapped ships were sold to Greece on release in 1975, becoming *Fay III* and *Manina III*, the latter being wrecked on 30 March 1981. By this time, some had already been broken up, *Reymont* after catching fire off Bornholm on 16 April 1979, and the process continued throughout the 1980s. The Russian *Solnechnogorsk* (1958) was scrapped in 1995 and, although details are hard to come by, it would appear that the Chinese *Chi Cheng* (built as *Guo Ji* in 1962 and serving as Albania's *Internacional* from 1963 to 1978) and *Zhen Xing* (built as Polish *Konopnicka* and serving as *Yi Xing* from 1979 to 1983) might just have made it into the twenty-first century.

East Germany's 9,247gt *Frieden** completed by Warnowwerft VEB, Warnemünde, in 1957 was the forerunner of a series of standard cargo liners that had a tanker-like profile with separate bridge and engines aft. They bore little resemblance to East Asiatic Company's *Bogota* class (see page 123) on account of having single cranes fore and aft and an array of tall, closely spaced twin masts and posts topped by conspicuous ventilators. Most of the fourteen sisters delivered by 1961 had taller funnels, and two of which were launched as *Volkerfreundschaft* and *Solidaritat* but completed as the Czech *Dukla* and Polish *Zeromski*, the latter becoming the Czech *Orava* in 1959. The final delivery was the Cuban *Sierra Maestra*. Deadweight tonnage averaged 13,000t on dimensions of 518 x 66ft and four Halberstadt-MAN engines geared to twin screws gave a speed of sixteen knots. *Magdeburg* was beached in the Thames following a collision with Nippon Yusen Kaisha's *Yamashiro Maru* (see page 148) on 27 October 1964 but was later raised, only to sink in tow off Brest on 17 December 1965. The two Czech ships were sold to China in 1965 as *Lanzhou* (later *Sui Jiu Lao 8*) and *Hangzhou*. In 1970, *Dresden* was preserved at Rostock's shipbuilding museum as *Traditionsschiff Frieden*. The majority of the class was sold or scrapped between 1977 and 1980, *Freundschaft* briefly becoming *Eurabia Friendship*, whilst *Leipzig*, *Karl Marx-Stadt* and *Gera* went to Saudi Arabia as *Saudi Independence*, *– Trader* and *– Pride* and were scrapped in India in 1984. The two Chinese ships lasted a few more years and are assumed to have been demolished in the late 1980s.

New UK designs

The 8,539gt *Menelaus** built by Caledon Shipbuilding & Engineering, Dundee, in 1957, was the first in the Blue Funnel fleet to be fitted with MacGregor steel hatch covers. She retained Holt's traditional three-island hull but differed from the preceding *Achilles* class in having her accommodation block positioned at the after end of the long bridge deck. Other differences included unstayed masts and a different hull form, dimensions being 495ft oa x 65ft. Deadweight measurement was around 9,700t and main machinery a six-cylinder Harland-Burmeister & Wain developing 8,500bhp for sixteen and a half knots. Five cargo oil tanks in Nos 3 and 4 holds had a capacity of around 2,000t. *Menestheus*, *Machaon* and *Maron* followed from Caledon in successive years and Vickers-Armstrongs' High Walker yard delivered *Memnon* and *Melampus* in 1959 and 1960. The latter was trapped in the Suez Canal by the Six-Day War in 1967 and in 1975 *Maron* and *Memnon* were renamed *Rhexenor* and *Stentor* for Southeast Asia-Australia service. By 1977 all but *Melampus* had been transferred to Elder Dempster Lines and given yellow funnels and 'O' names. This phase in their careers was brief and they were sold in 1978 to the Thenamaris Group and sold to Far Eastern breakers a year later. Greek owners also bought the abandoned *Melampus*, which had been released from Suez in 1975, and traded her as *Annoula II* following a refit. She was eventually demolished at Gadani Beach in 1982.

In an echo of its order for eighteen identical motor ships in the 1920s (see page 59) Andrew Weir's Bank Line continued its postwar fleet replacement programme in the 1950s with two long series of similar ships for its round-the-world and many other services. The first to be completed was the 6,300gt *Firbank* by Wm Doxford & Sons, Sunderland, in January 1957, followed two months later by the 6,500gt *Cloverbank* from Harland & Wolff, Belfast, and which was an enlarged version of the preceding six-ship *Beaverbank* class. *Firbank* measured 487 x 62ft whilst the Belfast-built ship was 4ft shorter but 1ft greater in beam. Both shared the same basic five-hold layout with short forecastle but the Belfast ships also had a poop with an extra set of posts and a cruiser stern, in contrast to the cruiser spoon version of the Sunderland ships. There were also differences in funnel and superstructure, *Firbank* having a straight rather than the rounded top of the *Cloverbank* series. From the thirteenth Doxford-built ship, *Testbank*, onwards, topmasts were dropped in place of a single mast above the bridge and somewhat surprisingly three of the east coast series, *Northbank** (1957), *Forresbank* and *Trentbank* (both 1962), emulated the Belfast ships in having an extra pair of posts aft mounted on a poop. The Doxford-built series ended with *Sprucebank*, the twenty-first delivery, in 1963. The following year Harland & Wolff, which had amended its funnel design with *Springbank* in 1962, completed its seventeenth and final ship, *Weybank*, which, with the preceding *Roybank*, had a signal mast mounted on the funnel. Two were lost in Bank Line service: *Levernbank* (1961) stranded off Matarani on 9 July 1973 and sank two days later and *Lindenbank* (1961) was wrecked off Fanning Island on 17 August 1975. The remainder were all sold between 1970 and 1979, six becoming casualties under other flags; the former *Laurelbank* and *Hollybank* were the last to be scrapped, in 1990.

German and Dutch developments

Hamburg-America Lines' powerful-looking *Dresden* and *München** were Germany's largest cargo liners when delivered in 1957–8 by A G Weser; *München*, depicted here at anchor off Singapore, was distinguished by a slightly taller funnel. Shelter-deckers, they measured 9,040gt (13,860dwt) in the open condition and 12,490gt (16,960dwt) in the closed condition on overall dimensions of 545 x 73ft. A ten-cylinder two-stroke, single-acting Krupp-Burmeister & Wain engine developed 12,500bhp for a sea speed of eighteen knots. All seven hatches were fitted with MacGregor sliding steel covers and a comprehensive outfit of twenty-eight derricks ranging from 3t to 60t was backed up by twenty-six winches. Designed for the Far East run, they had only limited reefer space but were fitted with deep tanks for latex and teak oil. They were sold to Rickmers Line in 1970, becoming *Sophie Rickmers* and *Etha* (*Etha Rickmers* from 1975) and traded to China until scrapped in Shanghai in 1986.

Nederland Line's largest postwar cargo ships were the 10,783gt *Karimata* and *Karimun*, completed in Rotterdam by P Smit Jr and Rotterdam Drydock Company in 1953. The design was later modified for the four-ship 10,891gt *Karachi* class, which were 5ft longer at 536ft overall on a beam of 67ft. *Karachi* and *Karakorum* were completed at C van der Giessen's Krimpen yard in 1958 with *Neder Waal** and *Neder Weser* following from the same yard and P Smit Jr, Rotterdam, respectively a year later. The latter names were substituted for the more romantic sounding *Karikal* and *Karpatos* before launch. Handsome three-deck ships, they were notable for four very tall masts and a five-deck superstructure positioned two-thirds of the way along the hull. Deadweight amounted to 12,600t and the first three were propelled by a nine-cylinder Stork diesel rated at 10,500bhp, whilst *Neder Weser* had a similar-powered Burmeister & Wain unit, sea speed being seventeen and a half knots. In 1963, Nederland Line and Royal Rotterdam Lloyd formed Nedlloyd Lines, each leasing twenty-five ships to the new concern, which had the white initials NLL in a blue diamond or roundel added to their funnels. In 1970, Nederland Line vessels were transferred to the new Royal Nedlloyd along with vessels of Royal Rotterdam Lloyd and United Netherlands Navigation Company. *Karachi* was renamed *Kapelle* in 1972 and all four adopted the *Nedlloyd* prefix in 1977. The three Giessen-built ships were sold to Pacific International Lines in 1978–9 and renamed *Kota Dewi*, *Kota Dewa* and *Kota Jati*. *Kota Dewi* was lost after collision on 22 November 1978. The others were broken up at Nantong and Shanghai in 1984, the same year that the fourth sister, which had become *Saudi Al-Damman* in 1981, was demolished in Kaohsiung.

Royal Rotterdam Lloyd took delivery of the 8,722gt *Schelde Lloyd* from Howaldtswerke, Hamburg in 1958. She was a development of the company's eight-ship *Maas Lloyd* class begun in 1956 and shared a similar design with long forecastle and half-height poop, the only external differences being a rounded funnel top and taller pairs of white painted posts on the superstructure. Dimensionally, however, she was larger, at 545ft oa x 70ft (*Maas Lloyd* was 529 x 66ft) and was propelled by a ten-cylinder MAN engine rated at 10,500bhp for a sea speed of around eighteen knots. *Schie Lloyd* (depicted here in Singapore) followed in 1959 and after a gap of two years *Seine Lloyd* was completed by Van der Giessen, Krimpen. All three were transferred to the newly formed Koninklijke Nedlloyd in 1970 and were renamed *Nedlloyd Schelde*, *– Schie* and *– Seine* in 1977. Their disposal came in 1982: *Nedlloyd Seine* went to breakers in Ko Sichang, *Nedlloyd Schelde* was sold to Pacific International Lines and renamed *Kota Wangi* and *Nedlloyd Schie* went to Saudi Arabia, first as *Saudi Al Jubail* and then a year later *Saudi Mohamed Reza*. Both were scrapped in Kaohsiung in 1984.

British three-quarters-aft designs

Delivered by Greenock Dockyard in 1958, Clan Line Steamers' 7,413gt *Clan Maciver** was the first British cargo liner to adopt a three-quarters-aft layout but her superstructure closely resembled that of the preceding *Clan Malcolm* class. She had a long forecastle and a short poop merged with the accommodation, her design setting the pattern for eleven subsequent ships built in three groups. With an overall length of 494ft on a beam of 62ft, she was propelled by a five-cylinder Doxford diesel rated at 5,400bhp for fourteen knots. She was followed by two sisters, *Clan Macindoe* from John Brown & Company in 1959 and Clan *Macilwraith* from Greenock Dockyard in 1960, both of which had three bipod masts. All were sold in 1979, becoming the Panamanian-flagged *Trinity Pride*, Gulf Shipping Lines' *Gulf Heron* and Guan Guan Shipping's *Golden City* respectively. *Trinity Pride* and *Gulf Heron* lasted no longer than 1980, the former being scrapped in Shanghai and *Gulf Heron* becoming a total loss after being shelled in the Shatt al Arab in September during the Iran–Iraq war. *Golden City* caught fire in the Malacca Strait on 17 July 1986 and was demolished at Jurong later that year. The five-ship *Clan Fergusson* class completed by Swan, Hunter & Wigham Richardson and the identical *Glan Graham* and *Clan Grant* delivered by Greenock Dockyard in 1962 were around 10ft shorter and had single stump masts and just a single set of posts aft. Greenock also built the 507ft oa *Clan Macnab* in 1961, sister *Clan Macnair* following from John Brown in 1962. Only the latter had a Doxford engine, the rest being fitted with more powerful six-cylinder Sulzer units for more than fifteen knots. In 1962–3, Greenock Dockyard went on to complete the three-ship *Clan Macgillivray* class, which were notable as the first British ships with remote control of the main engine from a separate control room. Measuring 508ft x 63ft, they had a modified superstructure and no poop; the similar Burmeister & Wain-propelled *Clan Alpine*, completed by Scotts' Shipbuilding in 1967, was the last ship built for Clan Line.

British India Steam Navigation Company was another company to follow the trend towards the three-quarters-aft layout with its five-ship *Bulimba* class (6,796gt/7599dwt) built at Harland & Wolff's Govan yard between 1959 and 1961. Designed for service between Australia, Asia and the Arabian Gulf, they had a streamlined appearance with long sweeping hances between a short forecastle and long combined bridge and poop, and a heavily raked foremast and mainmast attached to a tapered sloping funnel. The forward hances gave rise to cargo-handling problems and were less extreme from the third ship onwards, both *Bulimba* and *Bankura* having theirs modified accordingly. Cargo handling was by five 3t centreline cranes and four derricks and they were the first British ships to have hydraulic flush-fitting 'tweendeck hatch covers. Main machinery consisted of a six-cylinder Harland-Burmeister & Wain with a maximum continuous output of 6,700bhp for a service speed of sixteen knots. All were disposed of in 1971, two to Sudan Shipping Line and the others to Indian and Eastern buyers. The former *Bulimba*, which had been the Malaysian *Bunga Kenanga* in the interim, was wrecked as *Seasprite* on 30 June 1979. *Barpeta* was demolished at Gadani Beach as *Spijkenisse* in 1980 and *Bankura* at Bhavnagar as *Cherry Singa* in 1983. *Bamora* and *Bombala** ended up in Chinese hands as *Yang Zi Jiang No 3* and *Zhen Zhu Quan* (later *Su Cheng*), the latter being broken up at Alang in 1996 and the former still existing as late as 1999.

Ellerman Lines' first three-quarters-aft designed ship was the 9,914gt *City of Melbourne* built by A Stephen & Sons in 1957 for Australian service. Notable for her powerful twelve-cylinder Sulzer engine, which developed 18,900bhp on test bed trials, she measured 542ft oa x 71ft. She was followed by five smaller ships of around 510 x 67ft, *City of Sydney** (1961), *City of Canberra* (1962) and *City of Adelaide* (1964) from Barclay, Curle & Company, Glasgow and *City of Eastbourne* and *City of Glasgow* from Vickers-Armstrongs, Newcastle, in 1962–3. These had a more compact superstructure and their mast arrangements varied, *City of Sydney*'s mainmast being replaced by a pair of posts in *City of Canberra* and *City of Adelaide*, whilst the Vickers-built ships had four masts forward, only that nearest to the bridge having a topmast, and a long forecastle. Engines were nine-cylinder Sulzers in the first three ships and eight-cylinder units in the Vickers pair, power varying between 10,300 and 14,200bhp for speeds of around eighteen knots. *City of Sydney*, – *Eastbourne* and – *Glasgow* were renamed *City of Montreal*, – *Toronto* and – *Ottawa* for St Lawrence service in 1971 and *City of Adelaide* was chartered to Hamburg-South America as *Cap Cleveland* in 1972, becoming *City of Canterbury* on her return in 1973. *City of Canterbury* was sold to Compagnie Maritime Belge in 1976 as *Rubens* and scrapped as *A L Pioneer* at Chittagong in 1983, whilst *City of Montreal* became the Panamanian *Yat Fei* in 1977 and was demolished at Kaohsiung in 1979. The other three went to Singapore owners in 1978, *City of Canberra* becoming Gold Shipping Pty's *Tasgold* and sisters *City of Toronto* and *City of Ottawa* becoming Pacific International Lines' *Kota Cantik* and *Kota Cahaya*. *Tasgold* was scrapped in Kaohsiung in 1980 and the other two at Kaohsiung in 1984 and at Nantong in 1985 respectively.

Continental three-quarters-aft designs

A most unusual layout distinguished the 9,186gt sisters *Magellan, Maryland**, *Michigan* and *Mississippi* completed for Compagnie Générale Transatlantique's northwest Pacific service by Ateliers et Chantiers de Provence, Port de Bouc, in 1958–9. They were amongst the last cargo liners to feature a split superstructure incorporating a trunked hatch but in their case it was further aft than usual with just a single hatch positioned abaft the machinery. Closed shelter-deckers with three decks, they had a long forecastle and *Magellan* differed forward in having single posts and a single mast with 30t and 20t heavy-lift derricks as well as fewer windows on either side of the bridge block. Length overall was just over 490ft on a beam of 62ft and they were propelled by the first examples of six-cylinder turbo-charged Doxford diesels with electric blowers in place of scavenge pumps, which produced 9,000bhp for a service speed of sixteen knots. *Maryland* and *Michigan* became Singapore Islands Line's *Senang Island* and *Brani Island* in 1976, the latter being demolished at Gadani Beach in 1980 after grounding north of the Saudi port of Gizan on 19 July, whilst her sister went to the same breakers a year later. *Mississippi*, which had more refrigerated space than her sisters, had gone to Kaohsiung breakers in 1978 and *Magellan* was sold in the same year to the Thenamaris group and was scrapped as *Elbreeze* at Gadani Beach the following winter.

Following on from its engines-aft, fourteen-ship, 3,585gt *Jason* series, Koninklijke Nederlandsche Stoomboot Maats. (KNSM) built fourteen more ships of 5,100gt between 1959 and 1963, beginning with *Achilles* and ending with *Hercules*, both of which came from NV Scheepsbouwwerf Gebroeders Pot, Bolnes, which was responsible for six, a further five coming from C van der Giessen & Zonen, Krimpen, two from Amsterdamsche Droogdok Mij NV and a single unit from A Vuyk & Zonen, Capelle. They measured 401ft oa by 58ft on a deadweight of 7,140 and differed from the *Jason* series in having a fourth hold abaft the main machinery, which consisted of a seven-cylinder Stork developing 6,000bhp for seventeen and a half knots. *Sophocles* sank after fire and explosion on 19 February 1965. The remaining ships were lengthened to 456ft by the insertion of an extra hold between October 1966 and July 1970 by three Dutch shipyards, predominantly Boele's Scheepswerven & Machinefabriek NV, Bolnes. Most were sold to Greece between 1977 and 1979 and broken up in the second half of the 1980s but in 1979 *Ganymedes** went to Honduras as *Cosmos* and *Hercules* became the Peruvian *Yacu Caspi*. As the last to be delivered, it was fitting that *Hercules* was also the last to be scrapped – as *Amazon I* at Alang in 1995.

Far East pacesetters

Secret plans put together by Ben Line Steamers and Charles Connell & Company's naval architect William Paterson for a revolutionary new twenty-knot vessel – the first time such a speed had been attempted on the Europe–Far East run – reached fruition in 1959 with the delivery of the elegant 11,463gt *Benloyal**. Initially advertised as a nineteen-knot ship, her design featured a long raised forecastle and poop on dimensions of 550ft oa x 71ft. Main machinery, which was placed in the two-thirds-aft position, consisted of two Rowan-Pametrada steam turbines with a maximum continuous rating of 15,500shp. Her hull lines were so fine that she required 500t of permanent concrete ballast to maintain stability. In addition to a comprehensive array of derricks, she mounted two cranes abaft her superstructure, which provided well-appointed accommodation for twelve passengers. Three hull sisters were completed as full-scantling ships with shorter forecastles and no forward extension of the superstructure in order to improve stability: *Bengloe* and identical motorships *Benvalla* and *Benarmin*, which had ten-cylinder Sulzer diesels developing 15,000bhp. Following containerisation of the Far East service in 1972, the two motorships were sold to China for further trading as *Yichun* (later *Hua Chun*) and *Yong Chun*. *Benloyal* and *Bengloe* were transferred to secondary services and broken up in 1978 in Busan and Hong Kong respectively. The three diesel ships were broken up in China in 1992.

More communist shipping

The Soviet Union's first home-built liner tonnage comprised the six-ship *Dneproges* series, which came from the Nosenko shipyard at Nikolayev in 1956–7. Four-hold ships with the bridge amidships and engines aft, they had a deadweight measurement of 7,100t and a length of 430ft. They were soon eclipsed by the very much larger and more impressive *Leninskiy Komsomol*, which emerged from the Kherson shipyard in 1959. She could be described as the Soviet Union's answer to the American 'Mariner' class (see page 108), with broadly similar overall dimensions of 558 x 72ft, and was the prototype of a series that would eventually number twenty-five ships, five of which were built at Nikolayev by the Nosenko shipyard. Tonnage figures averaged 11,300gt and 16,000dwt and they were driven at nineteen knots by two Kirov steam turbines developing 13,000shp and geared to a single screw. All shared similar hulls incorporating a long forecastle and short poop but only the first two deliveries from each yard were equipped with four bipod masts and conventional derricks, the remainder having two pole masts and twelve 5t electric deck cranes as illustrated here by *Akademik Shimanskiy*. Heavy-lift capacity common to all comprised two 60t jumbo derricks. *Parizhskaya Kommuna*, the final ship, delivered in late 1968, was the only conventional cargo liner to be powered by gas turbines, her two units developing 11,800shp. *Khimik Zhelinsky* was trapped in the Shatt al Arab waterway in February 1981 and later sunk but the majority were broken up between 1984 and 1989, just three lasting into the early 1990s.

Yugoslavia built a number of cargo liners for domestic account interspersed with series for the Soviet Union and exports to other countries. Yugoslav Line (Jugolinija) took delivery of three fast cargo liners, *Trebinje*, *Jesenice* and *Primorje**, for its Far East service in 1960–1 and these were joined by a fourth sister, *Kostrena*, in 1963. Measuring around 7,400gt and 10,350dwt on dimensions of 509ft oa x 68ft, they were driven by single eight-cylinder CRDA-Sulzer diesels with an output of 10,400bhp providing a service speed of more than eighteen knots. Their pale yellow hulls sat well with the company's funnel colours of blue with a red star on a broad white band. *Trebinje* was sold to Greece in 1968 and renamed *Kapastamati*, becoming *Champex* three years later and being scrapped at Alang in 1983. *Primorje* was demolished at Split in 1985 and *Jesenice* at Alang in 1987, the same year that the youngest sister, *Kostrena*, was renamed *Rena* for a single voyage to Kaohsiung where she was cut up in 1988.

The final conventional designs for Scandinavia

Wilh. Wilhelmsen had switched from its traditional split-superstructure design to a composite accommodation block with the Dutch-built *Troubadour* in 1954 but retained a raised forecastle and poop. Just ten of the company's cargo liners followed this layout, culminating in the powerful 9,450gt *Tagaytay** quartet completed by Deutsche Werft, Hamburg, between 1958 and 1960. Overall dimensions were 524 x 66ft. They differed in engine power, however, *Tagaytay* and *Tai Ping* being fitted with nine-cylinder Burmeister & Wain diesels developing 11,200bhp, whilst *Tarantel* and *Traviata* had an extra cylinder for 12,500bhp, speeds being in the eighteen to nineteen knot range. In 1970, all four had two cellular container holds served by a 25t crane inserted in Japan, increasing overall length to 617ft and tonnage to 11,754gt. Seven years later they were transferred to the Singapore flag under Barber Line management, just *Traviata* being renamed *Tema*. *Tarantel* and *Tai Ping* were sold to Mediterranean Shipping Company in 1978–9, becoming *Regina S* and *Gina* respectively, and both were scrapped in Chittagong in 1984. *Tagaytay* and *Tema* went to Hong Kong Islands Shipping Company in 1979, becoming *Apli Chau* and *Sunshine Islands* respectively. *Sunshine Islands* was renamed *Lamtong Chau* in 1982, after colliding with the Panamanian car carrier *Vantage* in the East China Sea. Both *Apli Chau* and *Lamtong Chau* were demolished in Kaohsiung in 1984.

The handsome sisters *Fernlake* and *Fernview*, delivered by Götaverken, Gothenburg in 1961, were Fearnley & Eger's final and fastest conventional cargo liners. With tonnages of 9,699gt and 10,000dwt, they had a long forecastle and poop in a hull measuring 510ft oa x 68ft. The main engine was a nine-cylinder Götaverken diesel developing 11,300bhp, which provided a service speed of around nineteen knots in the open shelter-deck condition. They were employed in Barber Line's US east coast–Far East Straits service in conjunction with A F Klaveness & Company and Wilh. Wilhelmsen and later adopted the new Barber colours of orange hull and pale green upperworks, as seen in this view of *Fernlake* off Singapore. The insertion of a container hold in 1970 increased overall length to 573ft and tonnage to 11,500gt and 12,600dwt. *Fernlake* and *Fernview* were sold to Wilh. Wilhelmsen in 1976–7 and renamed *Tampa* and *Texas* respectively, but were sold again in 1982, the former briefly holding the names *Blue Advance* and *Sea Adventure* before being scrapped at Chittagong later that year. *Texas* traded as *Khaled* until demolished at Alang in 1986.

The Oslo shipowner Sigurd Herlofson's *Black Osprey* and *Black Swan** were operated by Black Diamond Steamship Corporation of New York on a long-established service linking the US east coast with ports in northern Europe. Completed by Kockums MV, Malmö, in 1960–1, they were open shelter-deckers with a long forecastle and three of the five holds positioned forward of a short bridge deck. Bale capacity amounted to some 570,000cu ft while thirty cars could be carried in a space immediately below the superstructure accessed through the 'tween deck. They measured 484ft oa x 61ft and had a service speed of seventeen and a half knots provided by an eight-cylinder MAN diesel developing 7,200bhp. Despite the general switch-over to container and ro-ro modes in the North Atlantic trade, these ships soldiered on until 1976, when the service closed and they were disposed of. *Black Osprey* went to Panamanian owners as *Jody* and arrived at Alang for breaking in December 1983, whilst her sister became the Greek *Nissos Myconos* and briefly held the name *Valiant No 1* before being demolished at Huangpu in 1985.

The North Atlantic trade

Andania and *Alaunia**, completed by William Hamilton & Company, Port Glasgow, in 1960, began a major renewal of Cunard Line's North Atlantic cargo services. Measuring just over 7,000gt and 9,150dwt, they had three-island hulls with an overall length of 490ft on a moulded beam of 63ft. Their appearance was fairly conventional apart from the smoke-deflecting funnel top, which was added after delivery. They were driven by double-reduction Rowan-built turbines developing 10,000shp and driving a single screw for a speed of seventeen and a half knots. They normally ran from UK northwest ports to Canada in summer and the Mexican Gulf in winter. In 1969, they were transferred to sister company Cunard-Brocklebank and renamed *Macharda* and *Malancha*, only to be sold two years later to Liberian-registered owners, becoming *Humi Mahis* and *Humi Nasita*. In 1973, they were sold to the China-owned Ocean Tramping Company and were renamed *Yung Jian* and *Yungming* but these names were changed yet again to *Hong Qi 107* and *Hong Qi 108* on transfer to China Ocean Shipping Company in 1975. The former was scrapped in China in 1986 and the latter is presumed to have been broken up by 1990.

New York-based P D Marchessini operated a liner service to northern Europe under the title Marchessini Lines. Its impressive *Eurymachus* was the first of four shelter-deckers completed by A G Weser's Seebeck yard in Bremerhaven in 1960–1 for its Compania Maritima San Basilio subsidiary. The design incorporated a long forecastle with a well-raked bow and a substantial superstructure, topped by a large red funnel rendered more prominent by a blue five-pointed star in a white circle. Tonnages in the closed shelter-deck condition were 9,655gt and 13,315dwt and a Weser/Bremer-Werft geared steam turbine with a maximum continuous rating of 7,700shp gave a speed of around seventeen knots. All six hatches were fitted with MacGregor covers and cargo gear consisted of one 50t and one 25t boom for heavy cargo, together with two 5–10t and sixteen 5t derricks. *Eurygenes* was abandoned after catching fire some 600 miles east of New York on 21 October 1973 and was declared a constructive total loss after being towed to New York. She went to Hamburg breakers in 1974. The same year also saw the sale of *Eurymachus* and *Eurybates** without change of name to Ta Chi Navigation, Panama, *Eurylochus* following a year later in 1975. *Eurymachus* was scrapped in Taiwan in 1977 but the other two became the Kuwaiti *Al Wasseem* and *Al Mahrouza* in 1980 and 1977 respectively, being demolished in Pakistan in 1980 and 1981.

Anchor Line's first modern-looking ship was the 5,704gt *Sidonia** completed by van der Giessen, Krimpen, in 1961. Designed to operate on the London–New York run in conjunction with Cunard's *Andania* and *Alaunia*, she featured a short forecastle and four bipod masts with engines positioned well aft. Hull measurements were 472ft oa x 61ft and a six-cylinder Stork diesel developing 8,500bhp provided a sea speed of sixteen knots. In 1965, she was joined by two near sisters, the similar sized *Sicilia* from Bartram & Sons, Sunderland, and the slightly larger *Elysia* (485 x 63ft) from R & W Hawthorn, Leslie & Company, Newcastle, both of which had more open superstructures. *Sidonia*, which had proved too small for the North Atlantic trade, went to China Navigation Company in 1967 as *Hupeh*, *Elysia* became Strick's *Armanistan* in 1968, whilst *Sicilia* became Zim Line's *Anat*. The latter passed to Greece as *Golemi* in 1981 and was scrapped at Gadani Beach in 1986. *Armanistan* became P&O's *Strathavoch* in 1975 and Hong Kong Island Shipping's *Sharp Island* in 1978, before going to Taiwan breakers in 1983. The former *Sidonia* passed through two different Panamanian hands as *Sun Opal* and then *New United* in 1982 and was finally broken up in Kaoshiung in the winter of 1985–6.

New Germans for Australian trade

Norddeutscher Lloyd's first ships with engines placed three-quarters aft were the three-ship, 8,500dwt *Burgenstein* class built by Bremer Vulkan between 1958 and 1960 for the west coast of South America trade. The larger *Regenstein* and *Riederstein* were also delivered in 1960 by Howaldtswerke, Hamburg, for the company's Australian service, the former seen here moored in Athol Bay, whilst awaiting a berth in Sydney. Measuring 7,375gt and 10,090dwt on an overall length of 527 x 65ft beam, they differed from the *Burgenstein* class in having a long forecastle, two hatches aft of the superstructure and no poop. Their main engine was a nine-cylinder MAN diesel rated at 9,000bhp for a speed of seventeen and a half knots. In 1968, their decks were altered to be more container friendly and they passed into the combined Hapag-Lloyd fleet in September 1970. Sold six years later without change of name, they were eventually broken up in China in 1984.

Hamburg-America Line built five new ships for its Australian service between 1960 and 1962. The 9,365gt (11,100dwt) *Munsterland* and *Kulmerland* came from Deutsche Werft and the similar *Blumenthal*, *Nürnberg* and *Wolfsburg** from Howaldtswerke, Hamburg. The latter three were 4ft longer at 520ft but all had a beam of 63ft. Engines were common to all in the shape of an eight-cylinder MAN diesel developing 10,000bhp for a service speed of seventeen to eighteen knots. *Munsterland* gained notoriety when trapped on 5 June 1967 along with thirteen other ships in the Suez Canal during the Six Day War. She and another German ship, *Nordwind*, were regularly steamed during their lengthy sojourn and steamed back to a triumphant welcome in Hamburg when finally released in May 1975. *Kulmerland*, *Nürnberg* and *Wolfsburg* were sold to Portugal in 1971 and became Companhia Nacional de Navegacao's *Manica* and Insulana de Navegacao's *Congo* and *Muxima* respectively, and the latter two were absorbed into the fleet of Companhia Portuguesa de Transportes Maritimos in 1974. *Blumenthal* went to Angola in 1971 and was renamed *N'gola*. *Munsterland* became *Munsterlandes* in 1980 and was scrapped at Fujian four years later. *Manica* and *Congo* were demolished at Lisbon and Kaohsiung respectively in 1986, and *Muxima*, which had been renamed *Vasco Fernandez* in 1985, at Ningbo in 1987. *N'gola* was the last to go, being hulked at Luanda in July 1992 and stripped over the next few years.

A handsome Dutch series

United Netherlands Navigation Company's nine 'S'-class vessels were developments of the 1957-built *Zaankerk* trio. They were completed between 1960 and 1962, *Serooskerk*, *Simonskerk**, *Sloterkerk* (chartered from Nederland Tank & Paketvaart), *Schiekerk* and *Spaarnekerk* by P Smit Jr, Rotterdam, *Streefkerk* by Nederlandsche Dok Maats., Amsterdam and *Steenkerk*, *Servaaskerk* and *Sinoutskerk* by C van der Giessen, Krimpen. They were fine-looking ships with a nice sheer line and short forecastle and were distinguished by a tall superstructure amidships and very tall masts and posts. Note also the exaggerated cruiser spoon stern common to many Dutch-built ships. Tonnages were 9,820gt and approximately 12,000dwt on overall dimensions of 528 x 69ft and main propulsion was by either a nine-cylinder Smit-Burmeister & Wain or a ten-cylinder Stork, both developing around 10,600bhp for eighteen knots. The series passed to the newly formed Royal Nedlloyd on 1 July 1970, the same year seeing all but the first two deliveries – *Serooskerk* and *Simonskerk* – having a cellular container hold with two cranes inserted forward of the bridge by Wilton-Fijenoord NV. In 1973, *Sloterkerk*, *Schiekerk* and *Servaaskerk* were transferred to Royal Interocean Lines service and renamed *Straat Fukuoka*, – *Fresco* and – *Forcados*. The *Straat* prefix was replaced in 1977 by *Nedlloyd* which was applied to all group ships. The unaltered pair were disposed of in 1981, going to Saudi National Lines as *Saudi Eagle* and *Saudi Falcon* and were broken up in China three years later. *Steenkerk* was demolished at Inchon in 1983 and the three remaining *–kerks*, together with *Nedlloyd Fukuoka* at Kaohsiung in 1983–4. *Nedlloyd Forcados* and *Nedlloyd Fresco* changed hands in 1983, the former becoming the Panamanian *New Horse* and being broken up at Zhongshan in 1984, whilst the latter sailed as Pacific Asia's *Kota Wisata* until demolished at Xingjang in 1986.

A Blue Star quintet

Blue Star Line took delivery of five smaller ships from Bartram & Sons, Sunderland between 1960 and 1965. Designed for Australasian outports and North American service, they were hull sisters with a long forecastle and bridge deck positioned well aft. Overall dimensions were 463 x 63ft and tonnage measurements around 7,600gt and 9,200dwt. *Canterbury Star, Montreal Star* and *America Star* had conventional posts and cargo gear, but deck cranes of differing types replaced all but the pair of kingposts abaft the funnel in the final deliveries, *Halifax Star* (originally intended to be *Quebec Star*) and *New York Star**. Main propulsion was by means of an eight-cylinder Clark-Sulzer developing 12,000bhp and giving a sea speed of seventeen to eighteen knots. The last three to be completed were lengthened by 78ft by Framnæs M V at Sandefjord in 1972, tonnage being raised to around 9,200gt and 11,700dwt. *Canterbury Star* and *Montreal Star* were broken up at Bombay and Gadani Beach respectively in 1980 and in the same year *New York Star* was transferred to Blue Star-controlled Calamedia SpA di Nav. as *Liguria*. She later changed ownership twice, the last time for a single outward voyage in 1983 before demolition at Gadani Beach. *Halifax Star* went to Chinese breakers in Beilun the same year. The last of the class to go was *America Star*, which was scrapped in Shanghai in 1984 after spending two years as the Panamanian *Golden Princess*. *Timaru Star*, a one-off ship completed by Bartram & Sons in 1967 for the New Zealand trade, was broadly similar in design but was 34ft longer and 2ft broader with the poop extended to the stern. The extra length was due to her well-deck being stretched to accommodate a Stülcken heavy-lift derrick. She was transferred to the Crest Shipping subsidiary in Hong Kong as *Crest Hill* in 1984 and was cut up at Huangpu the following spring. *(Bent V Sorensen)*

Scandinavian developments

The sleek-looking, 5,584gt *Samos* and *Tenos** were open shelter-deckers completed by Elsinore Shipbuilding & Engineering and Mitsui's Tamano yard in 1960 and 1961 for Otto Hillerström's Far East–Australia service. Measuring 455ft oa x 60ft, they had a long forecastle and poop and their cargo-handling arrangements typified modern thinking, with a mix of six 3t Thrige deck cranes and six 5t or 10t derricks, four of which were mounted on a bipod mast that also supported a 35t boom. A nine-cylinder Burmeister & Wain engine developing 7,400bhp, positioned well aft between Nos 4 and 5 holds guaranteed a comfortable sixteen and a half knots in service with two knots in reserve. *Tenos* was sold to Portugal in 1970, becoming *Porto Amélia* and *Samos* to Everett-Orient Line in 1973 with a charter back until 1977, when she was renamed *Pabloeverett*. She was scrapped at Kaohsiung in 1982 whilst her sister, which had become *Pemba* in 1975, was cut up at Gadani Beach in 1986.

Norwegian shipowners Fred Olsen & Company, Det Bergenske D/S and A/S J Ludwig Mowinkels Rederi each ordered a new ship in the late 1950s for the jointly run Norwegian South American Line. Olsen's *Bandeirante** was the first to enter service, in August 1960, and measured 8,189gt and 9,470dwt in the closed condition. She embodied much of her owner's forward thinking regarding cargo handling, with a complete outfit of six 5t deck cranes and some of her holds having triple hatches with the smaller outer hatches serving individual compartments, as in Johnson Line's *Rio de Janeiro* class (see page 123). Her remarkably clean profile incorporated a short forecastle and long poop, the latter including the accommodation block and No 5 hatch. The overall effect was heightened by two light masts, one forward and the other combined with her funnel in typical Olsen fashion. Hull dimensions were 472 x 61ft and a six-cylinder Götaverken diesel rated at 7,500bhp allowed her to maintain a speed of seventeen knots. Bergen Line's *Estrella*, which had a conventional mast forward, followed in 1961 and Mowinkels' all-crane *Norma* two years later. *Estrella* was sold in April 1978 to Uruguayan owners S A Comercial y Maritima Montemar and renamed *Estrella del Mar*. On 8 September that same year, *Bandeirante* sank off Ushant after colliding in fog with the Greek bulk carrier *Maroudio NV*. *Norma* passed briefly into the Wilhelmsen fleet as *Tijuca* in 1980, before joining her erstwhile partner as *Lucero del Mar* in the Montemar fleet and was finally scrapped in Port Alegre in 1987. (*A Duncan*)

Although Wilh. Wilhelmsen was one of the last liner companies to switch from a split-superstructure layout to a single accommodation block, it was one of the first to adopt a near all-aft profile for its five 12,500dwt *Tricolor*-class ships delivered in 1960–1. Designed for either Far East or Australian service, four were built by Eriksbergs M V, Gothenburg but *Tønsberg*, depicted here working cargo off Lisbon, was a 'home' product from Kaldnes M V, Tønsberg. Ships from this yard tended to be a bit special, because Tønsberg was the birthplace of the line's founder. All five ships shared the same dimensions of 510ft oa x 68ft and measurement of around 10,200gt but *Tønsberg* had a more powerful eight-cylinder Burmeister & Wain diesel developing 13,200bhp, compared with ten-cylinder 12,500bhp units in the other vessels, but all could maintain more than nineteen knots in service. Cargo gear comprised a mix of derricks and four 5t deck cranes, whilst 25t and 100t heavy-lift booms were mounted on the fore and main masts respectively. The small hold aft contained deep tanks for the carriage of liquid cargo. *Tricolor* was renamed *Troja* in 1971 and *Tønsberg* was sold to Venezuela at the end of 1977 and renamed *Terepaima*, later passing through two more hands as *Ocean Defiant* and then *Defiant* before becoming the Vietnamese *Truong Son* in 1985. She was finally broken up in Haiphong in 1997, comfortably outliving her sisters, two of which – *Trianon* as *Unique Winner* and *Tarn* as *Halla Partner* – had been scrapped in Kaohsiung in 1983, *Toledo* as *New Dolphin* at Alang in 1984 and *Tricolor* as *Kota Makmur* at Yantai in 1985.

Rederiaktiebolaget Transatlantic's first ship to have her engines placed well aft was the 7,123gt training ship *G D Kennedy* built in Gothenburg by AB Götaverken in 1958. The same concept was also used in five subsequent ships: the 6,725gt *Hallaren* and *Vingaren*, with four holds forward and one aft, which joined the South African service in 1960, and the larger 8,16gt trio *Mirrabooka**, *Parrakoola* and *Goonawarra* (the latter from Lindholmens, Gothenburg) in 1961–2 for the Australia/New Zealand trade, which had an extra hold forward of the machinery. Cargo handling was by six 5t and two 3t electric deck cranes and four 10t derricks in addition to a 100t boom on the forward bipod mast. A service speed of around eighteen knots was maintained by an eight-cylinder Götaverken diesel developing 10,000bhp. In 1971, *Parrakoola* and *Goonawarra* were chartered to Costa Line as *Sestriere* and *Cortina* (the latter being replaced by *Australia Star* in 1974) and renamed *Klipparen* on her return, whilst her sister became *Temnaren* on release a year later. Both were disposed of in 1979, the former to Greece as *Popi* and the latter to Montevideo-based S A Comercial y Maritima Montemar as *Venus del Mar*. *Popi* changed hands again in 1980, becoming *Athinai* and in 1982 *Mirrabooka* was renamed *J C Crane* by Panamanian owners and scrapped in Huangpu two years later. *Athinai* had the letter 's' added to her name for a final voyage to Kaohsiung in 1987. The following year, *Venus del Mar* was renamed *Venus Trader*, then *Sea Trader* in 1989, before being demolished at Alang in 1990. Two smaller versions of the trio, the 6,300gt *Alabama* and *Arizona*, were built by AB Götaverken and Lindholmens Varv. AB in 1960–1 for the owner's North American service.

Swedish East Asia Company's elegant *Nagasaki*, delivered by Nederlandsche Dok Maats., Amsterdam, in 1961, was the first of four new 10,050gt ships with engines placed well aft. *Nippon*, *Nicobar* and *Nara* followed in successive years and *Nippon*, photographed from the Barcelona cable car, had training facilities for twelve deck and twelve engine-room cadets along with two instructors. They measured 521ft oa x 68ft on a deadweight of 10,800t and were driven by eight-cylinder Götaverken diesels rated at 10,000bhp for a service speed of seventeen and a half knots. Following the containerisation of the Far East run in 1972, *Nagasaki*, *Nara* and *Nicobar* were sold to China, becoming *Heng Shui*, *Qing Shui* and *Tian Shui*. The first two were broken up at Sitalpur and Chittagong respectively in 1991 but in the same year *Hengshui* was renamed *Zi Jin* and then *He Sheng* two years later. *Nippon*, which had been trapped in the Suez Canal as a result of the Six Day War, briefly held the name *Marit* in 1974 and then traded for the next decade as Hellenic Lines' *Hellenic Patriot*, before making a final voyage to Qinhuangdao breakers as *Tenon*. The former *Nicobar* outlived her sisters and was broken up at Sitalpur in 1991–2.

US fleet reconstruction

Delivered by Ingalls Shipbuilding Corporation, Pascagoula in 1960, *James Lykes* was the first US cargo ship completed for private owners since World War II and her C3-S-37a 'Gulf Pride' design was in some ways similar to Compagnie Générale Transatlantique's *Magellan* class (see page 130) with a long forecastle, trunked No 4 hatch in the superstructure and engines in the three-quarter-aft position, but she had twin exhaust pipes in place of a conventional funnel. Eight sisters, four each from Ingalls, Pascagoula and Bethlehem Steel, Sparrows Point, followed, and they measured 10,186gt and 11,000dwt and 495ft oa x 69ft. Cargo capacity amounted to 548,848cu ft and special provision was made for the carriage of bulk cargoes, such as grain, iron ore, phosphates and sulphur in addition to tanks for around 1,000t of liquid cargo. The after hold was fitted for both refrigerated and special cargoes. Two sets of General Electric steam turbines geared to a single screw developed 9,900shp for a service speed of around seventeen and a half knots. In 1962–3, four eighteen-knot, C3-S-37b derivations beginning with *Brinton Lykes** were completed by Bethlehem Steel, Sparrows Point, which also shared the construction of the final eight 37c ships with Avondale Shipyards Inc., New Orleans between 1963 and 1964. The nine 37a ships had a 97ft container hold inserted in 1972–3 and *Joseph Lykes* and *Thompson Lykes* were converted to barges as *Lykes Innovator* and *Lykes Enterprise* in 1992 and 1994 respectively. Most were broken up in the mid-1990s, many at Alang, but *Brinton Lykes* lasted in the Reserve Fleet until 2006. The 37b and 37c ships were transferred to the Ready Reserve Fleet under *Cape C–* names in 1984 and began to be broken up from 2007 onwards. Lykes' second generation C4-S-66 *Gulf Clipper*-class ships, starting with *Louise Lykes* from Avondale in 1965, were more conventional in layout and had a speed of twenty knots for transpacific service.

The first ship in Moore-McCormack Lines' $430 million fleet-replacement programme was the 9,207gt *Mormacpride* completed by Sun Shipbuilding & Dry Dock Company, Chester in 1960. *Mormacbay*, seen here off the Brazilian coast, followed in the same year and *Mormaclake, – scan, – cove* and *– trade* in 1961–2. Two more ships, *Mormaccape* and *Mormacglen*, were delivered by Todd Shipyards, San Pedro in 1961. Their C3-S-33a design was based on the experimental *Schuyler Otis Bland* built by Sun Shipbuilding for the US Maritime Commission in 1950. Overall dimensions were similar at 483ft oa x 63ft; however, the 'Prides' were fitted with conventional masts and four pairs of tall kingposts in place of the Ebel rig of the earlier ship. Extensive use was made of aluminium in the construction of the superstructure and the funnel, which was a dummy, with engine exhausts being carried up two tall pipes. Designed for their owners' services to the Baltic and the east coast of South America, they were also fitted with belting for operation in the Great Lakes. Deadweight measurement was around 12,500t and they were propelled at nineteen knots by two sets of GEC turbines geared to a single shaft and developing 12,100bhp. All but *Mormacglen* were transferred to the Reserve Fleet in 1977–8, six in a swap with four of States Marine Corporation's *California*-class ships and all lost their *Mormac* prefixes. Several later saw service with the US Navy, *Mormaccove* and *Mormactrade* being renamed *Northern Light* and *Southern Cross* in 1980 for Arctic supply duty, *Mormacbay* becoming *Vega* in 1981 and being used as a missile carrier, later being returned to MARAD as *Kings Bay* and scrapped at Brownsville in 1999. Finally, *Mormaccape* became the cargo-handling training ship *Cape Catawba* in 1987 and was broken up at Brownsville in 2008.

The partial multi-hatch design pioneered by Johnson Line was taken one step further by US naval architect Jerome Goldman in 1961 with the engines-aft C3-S-43a *Del Rio*, delivered by Avondale Shipyards Inc., New Orleans, to Mississippi Steamship Company for its US Gulf–Buenos Aires service. Apart from a small hold forward, the remaining five holds were divided longitudinally into three sections, each with its own large weather-deck hatch with steel covers, and were positioned between a streamlined navigating bridge mounted on a long forecastle with the main machinery aft. Her three full decks had a bale capacity of 657,200cu ft and cargo gear comprised four 5t revolving deck cranes and a Stülcken mast – the first in the United States – mounting a 75t heavy-lift boom as well as two 10t derricks. Two Westinghouse steam turbines geared to a single stainless-steel propeller developed 10,660shp for a service speed of eighteen knots. *Del Sol** and *Del Oro* were also completed in 1961, tonnage figures for all being 10,325gt and 13,106dwt on overall dimensions of 506 x 70ft. Five similar ships, led by *Delta Brasil* were completed by Ingalls Shipbuilding Corporation, Pascagoula in 1967–8. Slightly longer at 522ft oa, they were fitted with more powerful General Electric engines of 14,250shp giving eighteen and a half knots. The earlier trio were disposed of for demolition in 1985, *Del Sol* going to Recife in Brazil and the others to Spain: *Del Rio* to Ferrol and *Del Oro* to Aviles. (*A Duncan*)

United States Lines started to replace its ageing World War II-built cargo fleet in 1962 with the delivery of the 11,105gt *American Challenger**, the first of eleven twenty-one-knot steamers completed in two batches, five from Newport News Shipbuilding & Dry Dock Company in 1962–3 and six from the Bethlehem Steel Company, Shipbuilding Division, Quincy, in 1963–4. The distinctive Gibbs & Cox C4-S-57a design included a long forecastle, tripled hatches at Nos 3 and 4 holds and a 70t Stülcken derrick. Bale capacity amounted to around 580,200cu ft with a further 30,000cu ft of insulated space and provision was made for the carriage of 1,000t of liquid cargo in lined and heated tanks. Westinghouse cross-compound double-reduction steam turbines drove a single screw and developed 16,500shp in service with a maximum continuous rating of 18,150shp and an overload 21,600shp, sufficient to allow *American Challenger* to set a transatlantic speed record for cargo ships on her maiden eastbound voyage, averaging 24.42 knots. Superheated steam was supplied by two Foster Wheeler bent-tube boilers working at 600psi. Dimensions were broadly similar to the 'Mariner' class at 560ft 6in oa x 75ft and tonnage was 13,500dwt. *American Challenger* was renamed *Pioneer Moon* for Pacific service shortly after delivery and her name was transferred to the second ship, whilst several more were given *Pioneer* prefixes in 1967. United States Lines went into liquidation in 1986 and eight of the class – many of which had served the war effort in Vietnam – were broken up between 1986 and 1988. *Pioneer Crusader, – Contractor* and *– Commander* were still in the Ready Reserve Fleet in 2008. (*John G Callis*)

Farrell Lines had employed C3 tonnage on its South and East African services since World War II but its new C4-S-58a *African Comet* completed by Ingalls Shipbuilding Corporation, Pascagoula, in 1962, marked a major improvement. *African Meteor** and *African Mercury* followed later the same year and *African Neptune, – Sun* and *– Dawn* in the first half of 1963. The C4-S-58a Gibbs & Cox design was around 10ft longer than the 'Mariners' at 572ft oa, equating to the largest British refrigerated ships, on a beam of 75ft and measured 11,309gt and 12,728dwt. A combination of very fine lines and a 16,500shp steam turbine provided a sea speed of twenty knots, which could be easily exceeded and passages at more than twenty-two knots were regularly achieved. Their aluminium superstructure was the largest yet installed in any US freighter and cargo capacity amounted to 688,026cu ft (bale) with a further 28,000cu ft available for refrigerated cargoes. All changed hands in 1980; *African Dawn* went to Central Gulf Lines as *Dawn* and the remainder passed to the US Maritime Administration and were placed in the Ready Reserve Force as *Cape Alava, – Ann, – Alexander, – Archway*, and *– Avinof. Dawn* was laid up in the National Defense Reserve Fleet in 1988.

Further Soviet series

The 14,485dwt *Beloretsk* and *Belovodsk* (seen here entering Cochin) were completed by Denmark's Nakskov Shipyard in 1962. The first of six large Soviet cargo carriers, they had a clean-looking profile with a long forecastle and machinery positioned well aft. Gross measurement was 10,651t on overall dimensions of 526 x 70ft and cargo gear comprised an outfit of six 5t hydraulic cranes and a single Hallen mast mounting two 60t heavy-lift booms. A six-cylinder Burmeister & Wain diesel developing 12,600bhp gave a speed of eighteen and a half knots on loaded trials. The identical *Belitsk* and *Kosmonaut* followed from Burmeister & Wain, Copenhagen a year later and finally the 12,000dwt *Berezniki* and *Biysk* were delivered by the Nakskov Shipyard in 1964. The latter two ships were 2ft shorter and driven by eight-cylinder Burmeister & Wain diesels rated at 12,000bhp but externally they differed from the earlier ships in having a more enclosed superstructure, enclosed crane cabs and a modified type of Hallen mast. *Belovodsk*, *Belitsk* and *Kosmonaut* were broken up in Chittagong in 1987 and *Beloretsk* became *Byron* a year later. This name was shortened to *Ron* in 1989 before she followed her sisters to the breakers at Chittagong. Of the final pair, *Biysk* was renamed *Bisk* for a final voyage to Alang breakers in 1989, whilst *Berezniki* met a similar end in 1995 after trading for her final five years as the Maltese flag *Olvia*.

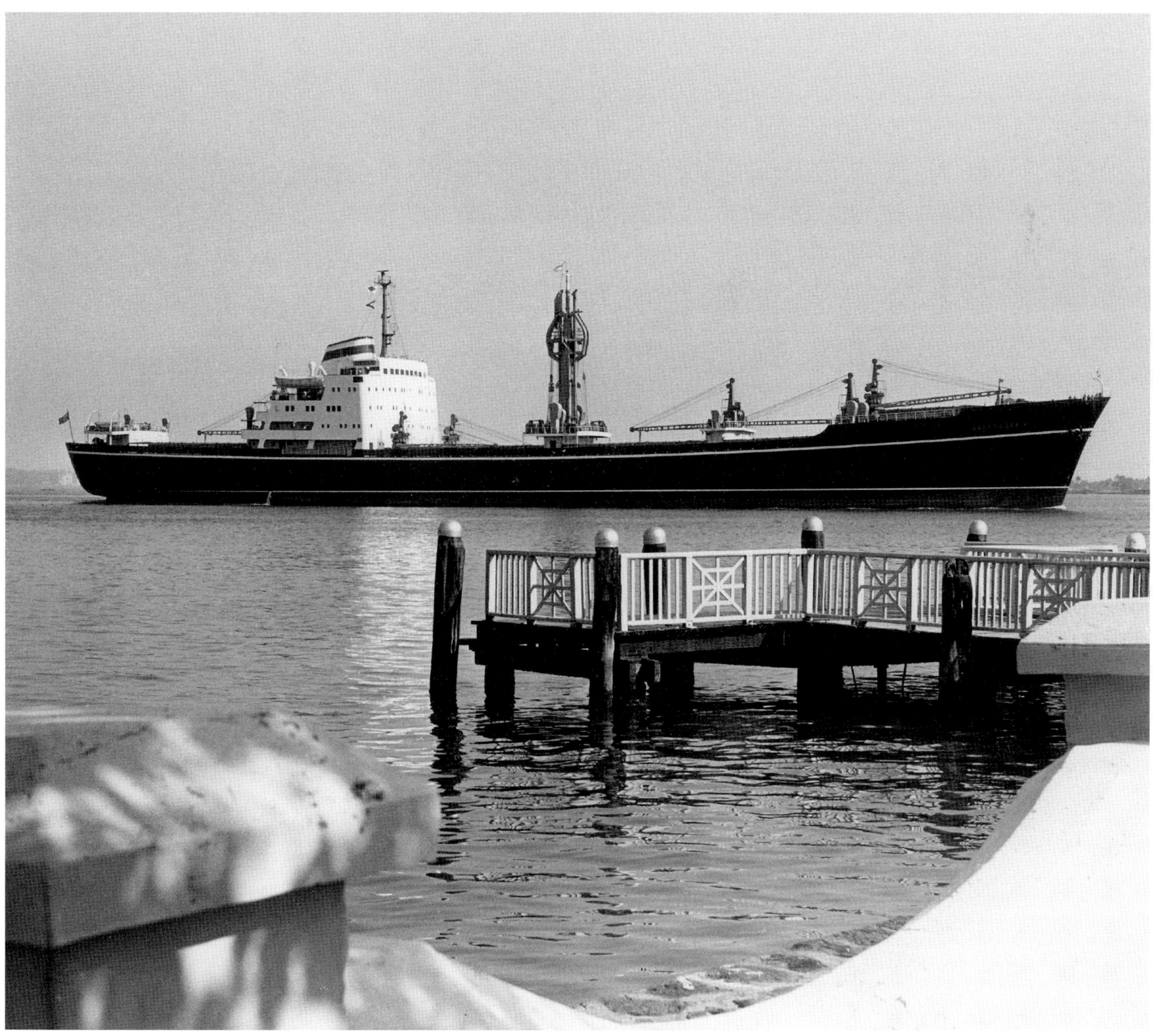

The Soviet Union's new 9,500gt *Poltava*, which came to prominence during the 1962 Cuban missile crisis, caused a stir in Western shipping circles in that she was built on the 'open' principle with twin hatches in the well-deck in addition to having accommodation and machinery aft, both concepts still being in their infancy at the time. A product of the Nosenko Shipyard, Nicolayev, she had a long forecastle and poop on a hull with little hull sheer and a single mast amidships supporting a 60t heavy derrick. Normal cargo working was undertaken by a complete outfit of thirteen 5t deck cranes. Hull dimensions were 510ft oa x 68ft and speed was around seventeen knots, supplied by a six-cylinder Burmeister & Wain diesel rated at 8,750bhp and built under license at Bryansk. After the delivery of *Polotsk* and *Perekop*, the Kherson Shipyard began building a similar series in 1963, starting with *Bezhitsa* and illustrated here by *Pavlovsk*. By 1967, the two yards had built twenty-two ships for the Soviet Union between them, one of which, *Genichesk* (1966), was converted to a space tracking ship and renamed *Kosmonaut Vladimir Komarov*. The final Nikolayev-built ship, *Kapitan Vislobokov*, was damaged by limpet mine in Namibe in May 1986 and was broken up in Valencia later that year. The rest were scrapped between 1988 and 1995 apart from *Balashika*, which had reached a respectable thirty-five years of age when demolished as *Luna I* at Alang in 2000. The design proved popular with other countries and in all thirty-four units were exported from Kherson, beginning with *Eftychia* for Greece in 1965 and ending with *Al Solehiah*, the thirteenth vessel built for Kuwait, in 1974.

The Soviet merchant fleet continued its rapid expansion in the 1960s with several series of cargo liners from yards in Denmark, Finland, Poland and Yugoslavia. Amongst the most numerous was the thirty-strong B-44 *Murom* class built by the Gdansk (23) and Szczecin (7) shipyards between 1963 and 1967. They were stylish-looking ships with machinery aft of amidships, as shown in this view of *Mozhaysk* transiting the Dardanelles. They measured 9,700gt and 12,600dwt on dimensions of 509ft oa x 66ft and a service speed of seventeen knots was provided by a six-cylinder Cegielski-Sulzer engine rated at 9,600bhp. The second delivery, *Mozdok*, was lost in the Black Sea on 13 January 1971 following a collision. The former *Medyn*, which had been sold and renamed *Romashka* in 1991, sprang a leak and was beached on 23 July 1996 north of Bombay. The remaining ships were broken up between 1987 and 1997, twenty of them at Alang, with just a handful having traded for new owners. The B-44s were followed between 1968 and 1970 by twenty broadly similar B-40 ships led by *Kommunist* (507 x 68ft), which had a shorter forecastle and Ebel-type masts in place of bipods combined with a 60t Stülcken serving Nos 2 and 3 hatches.

West Africa trade

The 5,682gt *Ibadan Palm** ushered in the second phase of Palm Line's twelve-ship renewal programme that had started in 1955, her three bipod masts introducing an entirely new look to the fleet. A product of Swan, Hunter & Wigham Richardson, Low Walker, in 1959, she was designed for West African creek work, which limited her dimensions to 460ft oa x 63ft. Sister *Ilorin Palm* followed a year later. Two 1961 completions – *Ikeja Palm* and *Ilesha Palm* – had a modernised superstructure featuring sloping stanchions, echoing that of the slightly longer and faster 'Express Service' ships *Lobito Palm* and *Lagos Palm* built alongside them in 1960–1. The 'I'-class ships were driven by four-cylinder Doxford diesels rated at 4,500bhp for a service speed of fourteen knots, whereas the 'L's were equipped with six-cylinder units rated at 7,500bhp for sixteen knots. *Ibadan Palm* was the first to be sold, in 1978, becoming the Kuwaiti *Hind* but went to Hong Kong as *Arunkamal* a year later and was scrapped at Gadani Beach in 1983. *Ilorin Palm* and *Ilesha Palm* were sold to Greece in 1979 and were registered in Liberia as *Diamant Captain* and *Daphnemar* respectively. The former became *Cap Blanco* then *Sea Venture* in 1982 and was demolished in Chittagong in 1983, whilst the latter was arrested at Mina Saqr in February 1982 and eventually towed to Karachi for scrap in 1984. *Ikeja Palm* was the last of the quartet to leave the Palm Line fleet, briefly becoming the Panamanian *GME Palma* in 1981, before arriving at Gadani Beach for scrapping in October 1982. *Lobito Palm* became Thenamaris Maritime's *Lobito Pal* in 1979 and changed names four more times before being cut up in Chittagong as *Euro C* in 1984. *Lagos Palm* was renamed *City of Lobito* by Cypriot owners in 1981 but was wrecked off Cheung Chau, Hong Kong, during a typhoon in September 1983 and was later scrapped. Nigerian National Line's first new build, *Nnamdi Azikiwe*, completed by Swan Hunter in 1963, was a development of the 'I' series.

Elder Dempster Lines revitalised its fleet between 1961 and 1964 with six 7,700gt 'F'-class ships, which turned out to be its last conventional cargo liners. Beginning with *Fourah Bay*, which carried twenty cadets, and *Falaba* from Scotts' Shipbuilding & Engineering Company, Greenock, the series continued with *Forcados*, *Fulani*, *Freetown* and *Fian* from the company's long-favoured builder, Lithgows, Port Glasgow. *Forcados* is depicted in Tenerife carrying a heavy accommodation barge, which required the construction of a temporary flying bridge. In design terms, they were developments of the 8,586gt *Egori*, a single ship from Scotts', which introduced bipod masts to the fleet in 1957, but they had one less hold aft, the shorter dimensions of 465ft oa x 62ft being necessary for creek working. Deadweight amounted to 8,150t and a single five-cylinder Sulzer rated at 7,400bhp provided a service speed of sixteen knots. *Fourah Bay* and *Falaba* had a 50t heavy derrick serving No 2 hold whilst the others had one 80t and two 30t booms. *Freetown* sailed in Guinea Gulf colours from 1967 to 1974, when she was transferred to Holt's Dutch subsidiary N S M 'Oceaan'. The arrival of new container-friendly ships from Poland rendered the 'F'-class ships surplus and *Forcados* and *Fulani* went to Cameroon Shipping Lines as *Cam Ayons* and *Cam Azobe* in 1975, passing to Greek ownership as *Copper Trader* and *Cotton Trader* six years later. The former was arrested in Mombasa and broken up at Gadani Beach in 1983–4 and the latter met the same fate in 1985 following a fire off Oman on 12 July 1983. *Fian* became the Indian *Mahapriya* in 1975 and was scrapped ten years later in Bombay, the last three spent in lay-up. From 1978, *Fourah Bay* and *Falaba* traded for Mexican owners as *Magda Josefina* and *Leonor Marina* under Ocean management but were sold to Greece in 1980 and renamed *Alexander's Faith* and *– Trust*. Three years later they passed to Cyprus registry as *Lenina* and *City of Zug* and were broken up at Gadani Beach and Chittagong in 1984. *Freetown* became the Greek *Panseptos* in 1978 and two years later the Singapore-registered *Cherry Ruby*. She caught fire in the Malacca Strait after a disturbance aboard in April 1981, was laid-up in Singapore and broken up at Chittagong early in 1982.

The 1955 UNCTAD agreement, which allocated a greater portion of trade from developing countries to be carried in their own ships, led to the establishment of new West African shipping companies. Amongst these was Black Star Line, of Ghana, set up in 1957 in conjunction with Zim Israel Navigation Company, which was also responsible for operations. The company's first new-building programme commenced with the 7,351gt *Pra River* series, six of which were built at Flushing by De Schelde and two, *Otchi River*, seen in the Thames, and *Nasia River*, by Orenstein-Koppel, Lübeck. All eight vessels were completed during 1961–3. Their design incorporated a short forecastle with a sharply raked bow and poop and a cruiser spoon stern. There were five holds, three of which were placed forward of the machinery, which consisted of a five-cylinder De Schelde-Sulzer developing 4,500bhp for a modest fifteen knots. Cargo arrangements varied slightly, the first four ships having 25,000cu ft of refrigerated space whilst the others had four deep tanks for 500t of vegetable oil, but all had sixteen derricks including one of 40t and four of 15t. The first and the last of the series, *Pra River* and *Lake Bosomtwe*, were sold for further trading in 1981. *Pra River* was renamed *Notos* but soon after becoming *Mayon II* was wrecked on 26 July 1983 near Dakar and was later scuttled. *Lake Bosomtwe* became *Charmyl* and was scrapped in Shanghai in 1985. The remaining vessels were all broken up in Spain in 1983–4, three at Aviles, two at Vigo and one at Gijon.

Tramp ships built for liner-trade charter

Liner companies would often charter in tonnage on a time or voyage basis in order to cover shortages and some tramp companies built shelter-deckers with this in mind. Typical of these was John I Jacobs & Company's 12,550dwt *Teakwood*, seen here inbound off Southend wearing the funnel colours of British India Steam Navigation Company, a company which almost invariably insisted on the change of colours, even for a single-voyage charter. *Teakwood*, which normally had a buff funnel with a black top, was completed at Sunderland in 1962 by Sir James Laing & Sons and had a 631,950cu ft bale capacity on overall hull dimensions of 473 x 62ft. Her main engine was a five-cylinder Kincaid-Burmeister & Wain developing 7,800bhp for a normal speed of around fifteen knots. She was sold to Greece in 1970, becoming *Alikrator* and six years later *Med Cape* under which name she traded for a further eight years before being broken up in Kaohsiung. *Teakwood* was followed in 1963 by the similar *Rosewood*, which passed to Scindia in 1968 and sailed as *Jalagirija* until scrapped in Calcutta in 1984.

Another tramping company building shelter-deckers specifically for charter was Denmark's Ove Skou, which, between *Jytte Skou* in 1949 and *Susanne Skou* in 1967, took delivery of twenty-five distinctively streamlined ships. Whilst slowly increasing size and speed, they shared the same design, incorporating a long forecastle and three bipod masts. *Birgitte Skou* and *Maren Skou*, depicted in the Dover Strait in July 1968, were products of Howaldtswerke, Kiel, in 1961–2 and differed from the other ships in having a long poop. Measuring 7,178gt and 9,250dwt on dimensions of 453 x 59ft, they were propelled by a seven-cylinder MAN main engine giving sixteen and a half knots. They were sold in 1979, becoming *Ebel* and *Cherry Crystal*, the former changing to *Desanmar* a year later. *Cherry Crystal*, went to China, which was hungry for second-hand liner tonnage, in 1980 as *Shu Yu Quan*. Her sister followed in 1982, becoming *New Haining* and being scrapped at Huangpu six years later. *Shu Yu Quan* was renamed *Bi Hai 2* in 1994 and is believed to have been demolished in 1999. Skou's final liner tonnage comprised the eight eighteen-knot *Dorte Skou* class completed by Elsinore Shipbuilding & Engineering between 1968 and 1974. Measuring 513ft oa x 65ft, they mounted four bipod masts and had accommodation and nine-cylinder Burmeister & Wain engines placed right aft.

Engines and accommodation aft

Cargo ships with engines and accommodation right aft can be traced back to the Dutch 4,758gt *Van Spilbergen* and *Van Linschoten* of 1953 but the layout was not adopted for larger ships until 1961. One of the first of these was Compagnie Nouvelle Havraise Peninsulaire's 9,847gt *Ville du Havre*, built by Ateliers et Chantiers de la Seine, Le Trait, in 1961; she was the first of a class of four for Havraise Peninsulaire's service to the Red Sea, Madagascar and Indian Ocean ports. *Ville de Brest* was completed in 1962, *Ville de Bordeaux** (identified by an all-round bridge) in 1964 and finally *Ville de Lyon* in 1967. The absence of kingposts resulted in a clean-looking layout and all five hatches were positioned between a long forecastle and poop. Nos 2, 3 and 4 hatches were around 44ft long for heavy cargoes, which could be handled by 120t and 60t jumbo derricks on the fore- and mainmasts (*Ville de Bordeaux* 2 x 60t derricks). Main engines were eight-cylinder Burmeister & Wain units developing 13,200bhp for a service speed of nineteen knots. The first two ships – *Ville du Havre* and *Ville de Brest* – were sold to Greece's Aliakmon Group in 1977 and renamed *Aliakmon Leader* and *Aliakmon Light* respectively. The latter became *Marika* in 1981 and was scrapped in China three years later but her sister, which had become *Apostolos K* in 1982, caught fire on 13 February 1983 off Madagascar and sank four days later whilst under tow. The two later ships went to China Ocean Shipping Company in 1977 as *Tu Men Jiang* and *Hei Long Jiang*. They were renamed *Hang Shing* and *Hang Tone* in 1989 and 1988 and both were broken up in 1992, the former in Calcutta and the latter in Chittagong.

Norway's first all-aft cargo liner was Ivarans Rederi's 4,099gt *Norholt* completed by Nakskov Shipyard in 1961 but Norwegian America Line's 6,300gt *Altafjord* followed from Bergens M V just one year later. Originally ordered by J Ludwig Mowinkels, she had been bought on the stocks and was joined by a sister, *Vigrafjord**, built by Drammen Slip & Verksted in 1963. They were handsome five-hold ships with a short forecastle and long poop that incorporated No 5 hatch forward of the main machinery, which comprised a six-cylinder Sulzer developing 6,600bhp for sixteen and a half knots. In 1969 and 1970, AB Götaverken inserted an extra hold abaft the foremast, which was served by a 5t crane whilst another crane replaced the tall goalpost at the break of the poop. Overall length was thereafter 505ft instead of 461ft on the same beam of 63ft. *Vigraford* was the first to be disposed of, being sold to Indonesia's Djakarta Lloyd in 1975 and renamed *Djatiwangi* and three years later her sister went to Argentine owners as *Punta Norte*. They were broken up at Alang in 1983 and Porto Alegre in 1986 respectively.

Cunard Line embarked on a new series of engines-aft cargo ships beginning with *Media** and *Saxonia* from John Readhead & Sons, South Shields, in 1963 and *Parthia* and *Ivernia* from Caledon Shipbuilding & Engineering Company, Dundee in 1963–4. They measured 5,586gt and 7,500dwt on dimensions of 437 x 60ft and were propelled at sixteen and a half knots by seven-cylinder Sulzer diesels developing 7,600bhp. Their design was stretched by 20ft in three subsequent ships from Cammell Laird, Birkenhead – *Scythia* and *Samaria* in 1964 and *Scotia* two years later. This last was ice-strengthened for winter service to Montreal. Although still relatively new ships, all seven were displaced by Cunard's new ro-ro ships *Atlantic Causeway* and *Atlantic Conveyor*. *Scythia* and *Samaria* became Thos & Jas Harrison's *Merchant* and *Scholar* in 1969, whilst *Saxonia* and *Ivernia* were transferred to Thos & Jno Brocklebank in 1970 as *Mahronda* and *Manipur* and lengthened to 517ft. *Manipur* became the Panamanian *Philippa* in 1977 and was scrapped in Chittagong in 1985, whilst *Mahronda* passed to Singapore owners as *New Deer* in 1978 and was demolished in China in 1983. *Scotia* was sold to Neptune Orient Lines in 1970, serving for seven years in the Singapore Straits–Australia trade as *Neptune Amber* before beginning a third career as *Sri Kailash*, which ended at the hands of Bombay breakers in 1984. The first two ships, *Media* and *Saxonia*, were sold in 1971 and ran for the Western Australian Coastal Shipping Commission as *Beroona* and *Wambiri* until 1978–9, when they became the Panamanian *Palm Trader* and *Rice Trader*, the former being destroyed by fire at Bandar Abbas on 13 October 1983 and the latter demolished at Gadani Beach in 1984. Thos & Jas Harrison's *Merchant* and *Scholar* were sold in 1979 and 1980 and renamed *Sisal Trader* and *Steel Trader*, the latter was shelled at Khorramshahr on 5 October 1980 and hulked. *Sisal Trader* briefly became *Mount Ibech* before being cut up at Gadani Beach in 1986.

Meeting the Ben challenge – more twenty-knot ships

In response to Ben Line's *Benloyal* (see page 131), Nippon Yusen Kaisha introduced in 1962 the twenty-knot, highly automated *Yamanashi Maru*, a 10,119gt motor ship with a more powerful 17,500bhp engine. A product of Mitsubishi, Yokohama, she was followed in 1963 by the radically different 10,467gt *Yamashiro Maru* from Mitsubishi, Nagasaki, which was claimed to have a revolutionary hull form with bulbous bow and an underwater shape resembling an elongated teardrop. Although her overall length of 528ft was the same as *Yamanashi Maru*, she was nearly 7ft broader at 75ft, which increased her deadweight capacity by some 800t to 12,700t, whilst a more economical 13,000bhp Mitsubishi-UEC engine ensured only marginally less service speed and enabled her to reach 22.45 knots on trials, which was hailed as a record. Ben Line later contested this, claiming that its conventional-hulled *Benloyal* had reached 22.6 knots with her steam turbine developing just 11,371shp. Two sisterships *Yamagata Maru*, seen here in Sydney Harbour, and *Yamaguchi Maru* followed in 1965 and all four ran initially in the company's European service. They shared the same layout with a long forecastle and short poop but their machinery was located one hold further aft than in NYK's preceding 'S'-class ships (see page 117). The basic design was continued in the succeeding eighteen-knot 'I' and twenty-knot 'K' classes, the latter eventually being converted to full container ships. After only twelve year's service, *Yamashiro Maru* was sold to Funny Shipping Company, Greece, and renamed *Kyra*, eventually making a single voyage to Alang breakers as *Michele* in 1983. Her sisters became the Panamanian *African Express* and *Brazilian Express* in 1979–80 and were scrapped in China in 1984. A similar type of advanced hull form was adopted for *Oriental Queen* built at Uraga in 1966 for C Y Tung's Orient Overseas Line.

The Holt Group placed orders for four advanced twenty-knot ships in 1960. *Glenlyon** was the first to be delivered by Nederlandsche Dok Maats., Amsterdam, in August 1962, followed by the delayed *Glenogle* and *Glenfalloch* from Fairfield Shipbuilding & Engineering Company, Govan, and finally *Flintshire* from C van der Giessen, Krimpen, in January 1963. Their layout included a short forecastle and poop together with six unstayed stump masts, but elements of traditional Holt design by Harry Flett, who died during construction, could still be seen in the upright superstructure and funnel. To obtain high speed, the hull had a very fine entry with a bulbous forefoot (the Group's first) together with a clear-water stern frame and rudder. Tonnage measurements were 11,918gt and 10,550dwt on dimensions of 544ft oa x 75ft beam. The superstructure was constructed of aluminium and cargo capacity amounted to 636,700cu ft plus around 80,000cu ft of insulated space in No 4 hold. In addition, some 1,700t of liquid cargo could be carried in eight edible-oil tanks in the poop. The prime mover was a nine-cylinder turbo-charged Sulzer diesel conservatively rated at 16,600bhp for twenty knots but later up-rated to its full 18,900bhp to give twenty-one knots. On trials, *Glenogle* recorded 22.3 knots in light conditions on the Arran mile. *Flintshire* was transferred to the Dutch 'Oceaan' subsidiary in 1974 and three years later all four ships adopted yellow funnels for service under Ben-Ocean/Elder Dempster management. This proved short-lived and *Glenogle* and *Glenfalloch* were sold in 1977, becoming the Hong Kong *Harvest* and China Ocean Shipping Company's *Qing He Cheng* respectively. The following year *Glenlyon* and *Flintshire* went to Univan of Singapore as *Emerald Express* and *Orient Express* and were scrapped in Kaohsiung in 1978. *Harvest* followed her sister into Chinese ownership in 1979, taking on the name *Yang Cheng*, and both were believed to be still in existence at the turn of the century; however, efforts by British interests to locate and preserve one of these proved fruitless.

Mærsk Line, which usually played its cards close to the chest, had also been working on the development of high-speed cargo liners and, in 1962, took delivery of the powerful 9,050gt *Trein Mærsk*. She had been towed to Copenhagen for completion by Burmeister & Wain due to industrial action at A P Møller's Odense shipyard, which delivered sisters *Thomas Maersk** and *Tobias Mærsk* in 1962–3. Measuring 11,100dwt on overall dimensions of 527 x 74ft, their layout incorporated a long forecastle with five holds forward of the machinery and an even longer poop carrying the accommodation block and No 6 hatch. Cargo gear comprised twenty derricks of either 10t or 5t, in addition to 60t and 25t heavy-lift booms mounted on the foremast. Their newly designed nine-cylinder Burmeister & Wain diesels developed a maximum of 20,150bhp, allowing them to operate at twenty-one knots if required and they were deployed in Mærsk Line's New York/US west coast/Far East service. After some twenty years of service, latterly carrying an increasing number of containers, they were sold in 1981 to Panamanian interests and renamed *New Stallion*, *Sarika B* and *Sibuyan Career* respectively. The first two were broken up in 1982 (*Sarika B* in Kaohsiung), and the last at Yantai in 1986.

Nederland Line's first twenty-knot ships, *Neder Rijn** and *Neder Rhone*, were completed in 1962 and 1963 by Howaldstwerke, Hamburg, which had produced a more competitive bid than Dutch shipyards. Conventional in appearance, they had a long forecastle and no bulbous bow, relying on powerful main engines to maintain their high service speed. The two ships differed in machinery, *Neder Rijn* having the first Stork large-bore engine, an eight-cylinder unit de-rated from 18,500 to 15,000bhp, and her sister a nine-cylinder Sulzer. They measured 537ft oa x 71ft and tonnage figures were 10,300gt and 11,718dwt. Cargo capacity amounted to 620,000cu ft, in addition to 24,000cu ft of insulated space, and handling gear comprised a comprehensive array of twenty-four derricks, mostly of 10t capacity, but including no less than three 80t jumbos, two of which could be used in tandem for lifts up to 160t. Although placed in Far East service, they were designed to operate on other routes if required. They passed to Royal Nedlloyd in 1970 and in 1977 changed their *Neder* prefix to *Nedlloyd*. Five years later they were sold to Saudi National Lines and re-christened *Saudi Ambassador* and *Saudi Al Madirah* (changed to *Saudi Al Madina* in 1983). The former was scrapped in China in 1984 and the latter demolished in 1987.

New heavy-lift ships

Thos & Jas Harrison entered the heavy-lift market with the 8,971gt, engines-aft *Adventurer** delivered by Wm Doxford & Sons early in 1960. She was the first British cargo liner to have a Stülcken mast, serving extra long hatches at Nos 3 and 4 holds and which, at 180t capacity, was briefly the world's largest. Her design bore some similarity to Hansa Line tonnage but she had two holds forward of the separate bridge house and one aft of the machinery space. A vessel of 10,920dwt, she measured 490ft oa x 65ft and was propelled by a six-cylinder engine from the shipyard rated at 6,900bhp for a speed of fifteen knots. She was followed in 1961–2 by two modified sisters, *Custodian* and *Tactician*, which had 110t derricks, more streamlined funnels and no poop. The poop was reinstated in the Charles Connell-built *Inventor* of 1964, which had cranes in place of derrick posts, a generally stiffer appearance and a 150t Stülcken. Harrison's final pair of heavy lift ships, the 11,100dwt eighteen-knot *Magician* and *Historian* completed at Doxford's Pallion Yard in 1968, had their bridge moved aft and combined with the superstructure. Their Nos 2 and 3 hatches were extremely wide, measuring 54 x 43ft and the 150t Stülcken mast was especially low to allow transit of the Manchester Ship Canal. *Adventurer* was sold to Greece in 1979 and renamed *Eleftheria* and was broken up at Gadani Beach in 1985.

Delivered by Caledon Shipbuilding & Engineering Company in 1963, the 10,294gt *Benarty* was Ben Line's only purpose-built heavy-lift ship and was fitted with a Stülcken mast capable of lifting 180t. Unlike the four former Ministry of War Transport heavy-lift ships the company had been operating for some fifteen years, *Benarty* was fitted with tweendecks and her hatches and tank tops were specially strengthened for carrying Centurion tanks. Deadweight measurement was 12,61dwt on overall dimensions of 509 x 67ft and her main machinery consisted of a six-cylinder Rowan-Sulzer diesel developing 9,000bhp for a sea speed of seventeen and a half knots. Her five holds had a total bale capacity of 661,540cu ft. and somewhat unusually her boat outfit included a small 'Shadowfax'-type hydrofoil for use by the captain. After eighteen years in Ben Line service, she was sold in May 1981 to Pacific International Lines of Singapore and traded for a further five years as *Kota Petani* until broken up in Kaohsiung in 1986.

New designs for Australasian reefer trade

The 13,086gt *Port New Plymouth*, delivered by Swan, Hunter & Wigham Richardson in 1960, and the similar 14,972gt *Port Nicholson**, completed by Harland & Wolff in 1962, were the largest and fastest refrigerated ships yet delivered to Port Line and were fine examples of the consistently high standards set by that company. Built to a three-island design, they had long forecastles and very long bridge decks; *Port Nicholson* could be distinguished by her more substantial funnel. Overall lengths were 560ft for *Port New Plymouth* and 573ft for *Port Nicholson*, whose beam was two feet greater than her sister's at 76ft. Insulated capacities, which included provision for the carriage of chilled cargoes, amounted to 567,000cu ft and 594,000cu ft respectively, this latter finally eclipsing the record held since 1934 by Blue Star Line's converted passenger liner *Avelona Star*, which had been lost in June 1940. Twin screws drove them at more than eighteen knots, power being supplied by two six-cylinder Burmeister & Wain engines. In *Port New Plymouth*'s case these produced a combined output of 14,000bhp, whilst *Port Nicholson*'s engines developed a more substantial 17,000bhp, which gave her a slight edge in speed. The ships were still in their prime when containerisation was introduced to the UK–Australia trade in 1969 but they soldiered on for another ten years before making final voyages out to Kaohsiung breakers, *Port New Plymouth* under the shortened name of *Plymouth*, and both arrived within days of each other in October 1979.

Shaw, Savill & Albion Company's large, twin-screw refrigerated carriers *Megantic* and *Medic** not only marked a complete break from a standard layout that began with *Karamea* in 1928 and evolved right through to *Iberic* of 1961, but also introduced a new grey hull livery with a white line, emulating the company's passenger ships *Southern Cross* and *Northern Star*. Delivered by Swan, Hunter & Wigham Richardson's Neptune yard in 1962–3, they had a long forecastle and combined bridge and poop with fully air-conditioned accommodation set slightly aft of amidships. They measured 12,226gt and 13,400dwt on overall dimensions of 538 x 71ft and refrigerated capacity totalled 581,050cu ft with a further 83,650cu ft available for general cargo. Twin seven-cylinder opposed-piston turbo-charged Harland-Burmeister & Wain diesels with a maximum output of 16,000bhp developed 13,600bhp in service for a comfortable eighteen knots. In addition to a comprehensive outfit of derricks, cargo-handling gear included two deck cranes of 7t and 3t capacity located aft. They were sold in 1979–80 and placed under Greek flag, *Megantic* being renamed *Dimitrios Ventouris* and *Megantic* becoming *Odysefs*. The former went to Taiwan breakers in 1980 and her sister made a final voyage as *Magy* to Gadani Beach early in 1987 for demolition.

South American trade

Houlder Brother's final refrigerated ships for the River Plate run were the 10,338gt (9,700dwt) *Royston Grange** and *Hardwicke Grange* completed on the Tyne by R & W Hawthorn, Leslie in 1959–60. A lack of sheer gave them a slightly hogged appearance, despite which they were fine-looking ships, and marked the culmination of some fifty years of development. The very long combined forecastle and bridge of the company's previous tonnage had been extended to the stern, producing a third complete deck to which a short forecastle was added. Dimensions were 489ft oa x 66ft and the six refrigerated holds were divided into three compartments on each deck. MacGregor steel hatch covers were fitted on both the weatherdeck and tweendecks. Propulsion was by two sets of double-reduction steam turbines with an output of 8,500shp, which drove a single screw for a sea speed of sixteen knots. On 11 May 1972, the outbound *Royston Grange* collided with the Liberian tanker *Tien Chee* in fog off Montevideo and, in the ensuing fire, all seventy-four on board perished. The hulk was towed to Montevideo, then on to Spain for scrapping. Meanwhile, her sister, *Hardwicke Grange*, became the largest ship to call at the small Sussex port of Newhaven and, in 1975, was transferred to Shaw, Savill & Albion management. Sold in 1977 and renamed *Jacques*, she was broken up in Kaohsiung two years later.

Cap San Nicolas was the first of six distinctive ships completed for Hamburg-Südamerikanische DG's Brazil–River Plate service in 1961–2. She and *Cap San Antonio* came from Howaldtswerke, Hamburg, whilst the yard's Kiel facility was responsible for *Cap San Marco** and *Cap San Augustin*. Deutsche Werft, Hamburg built *Cap San Lorenzo* and *Cap San Diego*. Designed by celebrated naval architect Caesar Pinnau, they were known as the 'White Swans of the South Atlantic' and their long combined forecastle and bridge deck was unusual for this type of tonnage and more reminiscent of some of the small refrigerated fruit carriers built in the 1940s and 1950s. The sloping top to the bridge was painted red to give the impression of a dummy funnel, whilst the actual exhausts were carried up two tall uptakes at the rear of the superstructure. In addition to a normal outfit of derricks, they carried a 50t heavy-lift boom and single cranes fore and aft. Hull dimensions were 523ft oa x 70ft and tonnage figures were 7,421gt and 8,500dwt in the open condition. A service speed of twenty knots was achieved by a nine-cylinder MAN diesel developing 11,650bhp. *Cap San Antonio* was seriously damaged by fire in the Dover Strait in November 1973 and her appearance was altered after a subsequent rebuild in Bremerhaven. *Cap San Nicolas* and *Cap San Lorenzo* were scrapped at Gadani Beach as *Nicola* and *Lorenz* in 1982. *Cap San Diego* and *Cap San Antonio* sailed for Ybarra y Cia, without their *Cap* prefix, from 1981–2 until 1986, when they headed for Chinese breakers under the St Vincent flag as *Sangria* and *San Miguel*. The former was saved from demolition by the City of Hamburg and is one of the world's few remaining cargo liners preserved in working order, still making the occasional trip down the Elbe from her permanent city mooring. *Cap San Augustin* became Van Uden Shipping's *Coolhaven* in 1983 and the following year was delivered to Chittagong breakers as the Maltese *Haven*. This left *Cap San Marco*, which had made a single round voyage to New Zealand in 1969, to be the last of the class to sail to South America in 1985 before heading to Qingdao for demolition as the St Vincent-flagged *Marco Polo*.

Koninklijke Hollandsche Lloyd's 6,792gt *Amstelland*, shown passing Lühe in the River Elbe, was completed by Scheepswerf Verolme, Alblasserdam in 1962, for service between northern European ports and the east coast of South America. Although a single ship, her design owed much to the preceding *Montferland*, *Kennemerland* and *Zaanland* built by Blohm & Voss in 1956–7. *Amstelland* differed from these earlier ships in having a raised poop and dropping the pairs of posts on the forecastle and right aft. Her deadweight tonnage was 9,513 and she was propelled by a seven-cylinder Sulzer diesel rated at 8,400bhp for a service speed of seventeen and a half knots. Koninklijke Hollandsche Lloyd was taken over by Koninklijke Nederlandsche Stoomboot Maats. in July 1970 but *Amstelland* retained her KHL livery. This phase was brief and she was sold to Saudi Arabian owners in 1982 and operated by Saudi Europe Lines as *Saudi Al Taif* until demolished in China in the summer of 1984.

North Atlantic and Central America trades

The 8,724gt, engines-aft *Manchester Commerce* was the first of three sisters built for Manchester Liners' Great Lakes service by Smith's Dock Company, Middlesbrough, in 1963, *Manchester City* and *Manchester Renown* following in 1964. Unlike the preceding *Manchester Miller* of 1959, which had a separate bridge, they all had their accommodation placed aft but retained the twin exhausts mounted abreast. Deadweight measurement was 10,653t on dimensions of 502ft oa x 62ft and they had a short forecastle and long poop incorporating No 5 hatch. The main engine was a six-cylinder turbo-charged Clark-Sulzer with bridge control, developing 9,600bhp for a service speed of seventeen knots. Closed-circuit television was installed for navigating the St Lawrence Seaway. The lead ship was sold to Chinese-controlled Yick Fung Shipping & Enterprise Company and renamed *Ber Sea* in 1971, then passed to China Ocean Shipping Company as *Yang Chun* four years later, and was finally gutted at Khorramshahr by Iraqi shellfire during the Iran–Iraq war in October 1980 and broken up locally in 1985. *Manchester City* and *Manchester Renown* went to Korea Shipping Corporation, Pusan, as *Korean Winner* and *Korean Challenger* in 1971, the former becoming Jin Yang Shipping's *One West No 8* in 1978 and being scrapped at Pusan in 1985. *Korean Challenger* hoisted the Greek flag as the Panama-owned *Edessa* in 1978 and was broken up in Kaohsiung in 1984 after being gutted by fire at Trincomalee. (*John G Callis*)

Compagnie Maritime Belge replaced its ageing Victory ships on the North Atlantic service in 1963–4 with four 'Painter'-class cargo liners from NV Cockerill-Ougrée. *Jordaens*, seen here in the Elbe estuary, and sisters *Breughel*, *Rubens* and *Teniers* measured 10,687gt and 12,700dwt on dimensions of 517ft oa x 66ft and were propelled at sixteen and a half knots by eight-cylinder Sulzer engines rated at 9,000bhp. Early in 1967, they were altered by their builder to accommodate 150 x 20ft containers but this was found to be insufficient and they were soon converted to full containerships with a 303TEU capacity. As with all cargo-liner conversions of this sort, stacked containers sat unhappily with conventional masts and posts, making the ships appear top heavy. *Rubens* was renamed *Memling* in 1972 and they were all disposed of in the early 1980s, *Jordaens* being the first to go in 1980, becoming *Char Ning*, then *Nafeesa* in 1982 and finally *Tripos No 2* in 1984 shortly before being broken up in Kaohsiung. *Teniers* was renamed *Santa Clara* in 1981 and was scrapped in Shanghai three years later. *Breughel* became *Treasury Alpha* in 1982, *Tamaki* in 1984 and was demolished the following year in Qingdao. *Memling*, the last to leave Belgian ownership, briefly held the name *Christina* in 1983, before being broken up in Yantai a year later.

Holland-America Line's *Gaasterdyk* class were built in pairs by Rotterdam Drydock Company and Wilton-Fijenoord NV, Schiedam between 1960 and 1963 for the Central American trade. Measuring 7,200gt, they had a short forecastle and their machinery was positioned well aft between No 5 and No 6 holds, representing a complete break from the preceding 5,634gt *Kinderdyk* class. Hull dimensions were 534ft oa x 68ft and they were driven at seventeen knots by an eight-cylinder Stork diesel developing 10,400bhp. The Wilton-built pair went to Hellenic Lines as *Hellenic Sky* and *Hellenic Grace* in 1974, the latter ship capsizing in Suez Bay on 16 April 1984 and being broken up at Gadani Beach in 1985. *Hellenic Sky* was briefly renamed *Nic* before sailing to Bhavnagar for demolition as the Maltese *Berlenga* in 1987. *Gaasterdyk* became the Panamanian *Good Herald* in 1978, had the suffix *II* added to her name in 1982 and was broken up at Kandla in 1985. *Grotedyk*, which had spent some time on the North Pacific service, was partially destroyed by fire at Tampico, Mexico, on the first day of 1980 and was subsequently towed to Kaohsiung for scrapping. The quartet described above were followed by *Moerdyk*, which was delivered by Rotterdam Drydock Company in 1965; she was similar in appearance to the previous four ships, but was slightly larger at 546 x 59ft. She was not only the company's last conventional ship, but also the last to carry its traditional funnel colours, as seen in this Thames view. Her engine was a larger-bore six-cylinder Stork with an output of 14,000bhp for a speed of eighteen knots. She was sold to Portugal's Companhia Portuguesa de Transportes Maritimos as *H Capelo* in 1975 and briefly carried the name *Aveiro*, before being broken up at Nantong in 1986.

Automation for Indian trade

Thos & Jno Brocklebank's 6,867gt *Markhor** and *Mahout* not only brought a new look to the Brocklebank fleet but also were its first motor vessels since the *Lycia* of 1924. Completed by Alexander Stephen & Sons in 1963, they had a three-quarters-aft profile with forecastle and poop and measured 480ft oa on a beam of 63ft. *Mahout* was one of the first British ships to have bridge control of the main engine, which was a seven-cylinder Sulzer rated at 10,000bhp for a speed of sixteen and a half knots. They were both transferred to Cunard-Brocklebank in 1968 and the following year their hulls were repainted white with a blue band. *Markhor* was sold to Eggar Forrester, London, with a charter back in 1976 and both subsequently spent short periods of lay-up in the River Fal. *Mahout* was sold to Greek owners in 1978 and renamed first *Aglaios* and *Evagelia S* two year later. She was bombed by Iraqi aircraft twenty-five miles from Bandar Khomeini on 12 September 1982, was beached and abandoned. Meanwhile, *Markhor* had become the Panamanian *Kara Unicorn* in 1981 and was broken up in Dalien in 1984.

Far East trade developments

Italian ships were noted for their style and Lloyd Triestino's 6,956gt *Palatino* class owed much to contemporary Italian passenger-liner design, especially in their bow shaping. They were built in four different yards in order to guarantee delivery in 1963. *Palatino* was the first to be completed by Riuniti dell'Adriatico in June and the others following at monthly intervals, *Viminale* from Ansaldo, Leghorn, *Esquilino* from Navalmeccanica, Castellammare and finally *Quirinale*, depicted here entering Venice, from Cantieri Riuniti, Palermo. They represented a development of *Isonzo*, built a year earlier, which herself was an improvement on *Aquilea* and *Piave* completed in 1955. Notable for their four tall bipod masts, the *Palatino* class measured 503ft oa x 66ft on a deadweight of around 10,000t and they operated a monthly service from the Mediterranean to the Far East. Main machinery consisted of an eight-cylinder Fiat diesel with an output of 9,600bhp providing a speed of eighteen and a half knots. Unusually, none of the class was sold for further trading and they all went for demolition in 1985, *Palatino* and *Esquilino* to Shanghai and the others to Porto Nogaro.

Koninklijke Paketvaart Maats. took delivery of four fast, 10,500gt cargo liners for its Royal Interocean Lines Far East/South Africa/South America service in 1963–4. *Straat Frazer**, – *Freetown* and – *Fremantle* (1964) were built by P Smit Jr, Rotterdam, and *Straat Franklin* by Verolme, Alblasserdam. Of conventional appearance, they continued a line of development that could be traced back to *Straat Bali* in 1953 and were broadly similar to the preceding *Straat Magelhaen* class of 1958–60 but without a poop. They measured 514ft oa x 67ft and fine lines enabled a nineteen-knot service speed to be achieved with six-cylinder engines developing only 12,100bhp, those of *Straat Frazer* and – *Freetown* being large-bore Burmeister & Wain units, whilst the other two ships had Sulzer engines. Deadweight measurement was 12,090t and bale capacity totalled 502,541cu ft with a further 60,486cu ft being insulated in ten compartments. In 1972–3, all had a container hold with crane inserted forward of the bridge by Nippon Kokan's Asano yard, increasing overall length to 580ft and tonnage to 10,794gt and 15,175dwt. Between 1973 and 1975, *Straat Frazer*, – *Freetown*, and – *Fremantle* were chartered to the Asian Australian Express Service, being renamed *Asian Endeavour*, – *Ensign* and – *Enterprise* and in 1977–8 all four had the *Straat* prefix replace by *Nedlloyd* after being absorbed into the Royal Nedlloyd Group. They were sold in 1983, *Nedlloyd Fremantle* becoming the Panamanian *New Bear* and the others Pacific International Lines' *Kota Wangsa*, *Kota Wijaya* and *Kota Wirawan*. The latter was scrapped at Alang in 1987 and the other three in 1988, *New Bear* in China, *Kota Wangsa* at Kaohsiung and *Kota Wijaya* in Shanghai. Four modfied 'F'-class ships, beginning with *Straat Futami*, were built in Japan in 1965–6 but they differed in layout, having a single mast and six deck cranes in addition to having bulbous forefoots.

Following on from its engines-aft *Bogota* and *Ayuthia* classes (see page 123), Denmark's East Asiatic Company built two experimental single ships, beginning with the unique-looking *Andorra** in 1964. Although sharing the same dimensions as *Ayuthia*, she had her midship deckhouse placed one hatch further aft between Nos 3 and 4, and this was joined to the poop by accommodation passages running either side of the trunked Nos 4 and 5 hatches. Tonnage measurements were 7,610gt and 10,273dwt in the open condition and hull dimensions 523ft oa on a beam of 67ft. Insulated space was provided in No 5 hold tweendecks and she was fitted with two 5t Asea cranes and a 60t heavy-lift derrick, whilst the 12t derricks could be yoked together to lift 24t. The main engine, which could be run unmanned at night, was an eight-cylinder Burmeister & Wain, developing 12,000bhp for more than eighteen knots in service. She also had a controllable-pitch propeller and a bow thrusters. *Andorra* was sold to Indonesia's PPS Trikora Lloyd in 1979 and, after briefly holding the name *Trikora Lloyd*, was re-christened *Padang* and broken up in Chittagong in 1984. *Ancona*, the second of the single ships, which followed from Nakskov a year later, was longer at 540ft oa and had her accommodation placed aft on a longer poop. A combination of fine lines and a 15,000bhp main engine ensured a service speed of more than twenty knots. Experience gained from *Ancona* was incorporated in the subsequent *Azuma* class ships (see page 165).

The 11,902gt *Bendearg*, completed by Charles Connell & Company in June 1964 and photographed here at Hong Kong two years later, marked a change in Ben Line thinking. Despite lacking the fine lines and sophistication of the *Benloyal* class (see page 131), she was still capable of nineteen knots in service and had a much larger deadweight of 16,450t equating to a capacity of 800,000cu ft. Designed to operate a secondary service alongside the express Far East service, she had engines placed well aft and measured 533ft oa x 70ft. Motive power was supplied by a six-cylinder Sulzer engine developing 13,800bhp. Her success led to an improved sister, *Benstac* (12,011 gt), which followed from Connell in 1968 and which could be distinguished by her single masts in place of the paired posts forward, a taller funnel and a longer poop extending to the bridge front. *Bendearg* became the Singapore-registered *New Panther* in 1981 and was scrapped in China in 1985. *Benstac* was chartered to Barber Lines, whose colours she wore until sold to Greek owners in 1982 when she was renamed *John P*. Her subsequent career was brief and she sank in the South Atlantic off the Brazilian coast on 17 April 1985 after springing a leak.

CHAPTER

10

Apogee and Decline as Containerisation Spreads

The cargo liner reached the peak of its development during the latter half of the 1960s. Speeds were higher than ever with some ships capable of sustaining twenty-five knots thanks to advances in hull design and new, more powerful engines, which became increasingly automated, often with bridge control, thus enabling crew numbers to be reduced. Manoeuvrability was increased by the use of bow thrusts and cargo handling was made easier by multiple hatches, flush 'tweendecks for use by fork-lift trucks and new types of crane derricks. Development in the heavy-lift sector saw the introduction of Stülcken masts capable of lifting 300t. Despite all these advances, however, productivity in port remained exasperatingly slow, with ships still spending as much of the year in port as they did at sea. The answer, however, lay just over the horizon.

Malcolm McLean had been quietly developing his container idea under the Sea-Land banner in the US coastal trade and in 1966 he caused a stir by launching the first transatlantic container service with the converted C3 *Gateway City*. Many European shipowners were openly sceptical but a number of forward-thinking British liner companies had been watching the development of containerisation with interest and had formed consortia to design a new breed of fully cellular container ships. Parallel work was also being undertaken in Japan as well as in the United States, whilst Scandinavian owners were working on designs for large transatlantic roll-on roll-off (ro-ro) ships. These new ships began to enter service from 1968 onwards and it quickly became apparent that their mode of operation greatly reduced the time spent in port, allowing them to make several more voyages a year than the traditional cargo liners.

Containerisation started in the transatlantic and transpacific trades, spread to the Europe–Australia trade in 1969 and three years later to the Europe–Far East trade. Each container ship effectively displaced a number of conventional ships, some of which were still fairly new, and these were either converted to semi-container ships by the insertion of one or two new cellular holds or sold for use in non-containerised trades.

With the major lines henceforth concentrating on building container and ro-ro ships, cargo-liner development could be said to have passed its peak; however, ships of this type continued to be built for a further ten years, mainly for emerging nations. These were increasingly 'container friendly' with squared-off holds and large flat hatches and their general appearance became more functional, with little thought given to aesthetic features such as sheer and rounded sterns. Even the term 'cargo liner' was replaced by the more prosaic 'multi-purpose' or 'break/bulk' ship.

Note: An asterisk in a caption indicates the vessel shown in the photograph.

Second-generation US ships

United States Lines was still receiving units of its *American Challenger* class (see page 142) when *American Racer*, the first of its 11,200gt C4-S-64a 'Challenger II' class, was delivered by Sun Shipbuilding & Dry Dock Company, Chester, in 1964. *American Rover* was completed in the same year and *American Ranger*, *American Reliance* and *American Resolute* followed in 1965. They shared the same 75ft beam of the earlier ships but were somewhat shorter at 535ft oa and their hulls had a more pronounced bulbous forefoot. In addition, a more streamlined superstructure extending around No 5 hatch plus a combined mast and funnel gave them a distinctly racy appearance, as depicted in this Solent view of *American Resolute*. Extensive use of automation in the engine room together with bridge control resulted in a reduced complement of thirty-four, some 25 per cent less than the Mark I version. A 70t heavy-lift derrick mounted between two thick masts served Nos 3 and 4 holds, which were accessed through triple hatches. Main machinery comprised two GEC single-plane geared steam turbines fed by high-pressure steam from two Babcock & Wilcox boilers and rated at 18,750shp for a sea speed of twenty-one knots. In 1969, *American Rover* and *American Resolute* became Farrell Lines' *Austral Pilot* and *Austral Patriot* and eleven years later passed to Moore-McCormack Lines as *Mormacmoon* and *Mormacdawn*, the former being renamed *American Moon* in 1983. *American Ranger* and *Mormacdawn* were broken up at Brownsville in 2004–5 and *Mormacmoon* at Sparrows Point in 2005. Two similar ships, *Prudential Seajet* and *Prudential Oceanjet*, were delivered to Prudential Lines in 1966 by Bethlehem Steel, Sparrows Point.

The $10 million *Mormacargo* was the first of Moore-McCormack Line's C4-S-60a 'Constellation' class of very fast freighters, which could maintain a sea speed of twenty-four knots. Completed by Ingalls Shipbuilding Corporation, Pascagoula, in 1964, she was followed by five sisters: *Mormacvega*, – *lynx*, – *rigel*, – *altair**, and – *draco*, the last two in 1965. Their hull design incorporated a long forecastle and bulbous bow, whilst the large dummy funnel and tall exhaust pipes echoed the earlier *Pride* series (see page 141). They measured 10,599gt and 12,763dwt on overall dimensions of 551 x 75ft and bale capacity totalled 627,544cu ft with a further 40,000cu ft provided for refrigerated cargoes. All thirty-five crew were accommodated in single-berth air-conditioned cabins and there were three staterooms for twelve passengers who had their own lounge and bar. Holds Nos 3 and 4 were tripled and the design allowed for the carriage of 350TEU containers. Cargo gear included a 70t Stülcken derrick and a single crane positioned between hatch Nos 5 and 6. Engine and boiler functions were automated with bridge control of the engine, which comprised two GEC steam turbines with an output of 19,000shp for a normal sea speed of twenty-one knots. *Mormaclynx* averaged 24.63 knots from Buenos Aires to Hampton Roads, including a day's run of 624 miles equating to twenty-six knots. In 1976, the last three ships to be completed were lengthened by the insertion of a 115ft cellular hold with three 18t cranes, increasing container capacity to 649TEU. The remaining three ships were similarly modified in 1982 and in 1983 all six were sold to United States Lines and renamed *American Argo*, – *Vega* etc, but *Mormaclynx* became *American Reservist* because United States Lines already had a containership named *American Lynx*. Three years later, *American Argo* and *American Vega* went to Lykes Lines as *Stella Lykes* and *Allison Lykes*, the former changing her name to *Magellanes* in 1989. *American Altair* was converted in 1990 to the crane ship *Green Mountain State* for the Ready Reserve Fleet. The remainder were broken up, *American Draco* in 1991, *American Reservist* as *Corpus Christi* in 1992 and *American Rigel* at Alang in 1997.

Fast ships for South America

*Republica de Colombia** was the first of six advanced 12,450dwt cargo liners for Flota Mercante Grancolombiana. She led a trio from Stülcken Sohn, Hamburg, in 1964, *Ciudad de Bogota* and *Republica del Ecuador* following in 1964–5, whilst *Ciudad de Bucaramanga*, *Ciudad de Cucuta* and *Ciudad de Buenaventura* came from the Astilleros de Sevilla 'Elcano' yard in Seville in 1965–6. Adhering to a three-quarters-aft layout, they had five holds forward and one aft of the machinery, the after two containing three conveyor belts apiece for handling refrigerated cargoes such as fruit, mainly bananas, or meat through side ports, whilst Nos 2, 3 and 4 holds had two elevators for lifting containers. In addition, special tanks were fitted for the carriage of dangerous liquid cargoes and two other tanks for normal liquid cargo. Cargo-handling arrangements included eighteen 10t derricks mounted on four pairs of kingposts and a 80t Stülcken. Sea speed was nineteen knots provided by a nine-cylinder Sulzer diesel developing up to 14,000bhp. The lead ship was renamed *Rio Cauco* in 1982 but was broken up in Cartagena following collision on 21 March 1984, sister *Ciudad de Cucuta* also being scrapped locally two years later. Three went to Far East breakers, *Ciudad de Buenaventura* and *Ciudad de Bucaramanga* to Kaohsiung in 1985 and 1988 respectively and *Ciudad de Bogota* to Shanghai in 1989. *Republica del Ecuador*, which had become *Ciudad de Quito* in 1986, survived the longest, not being demolished until 1994 at Alang.

Completed by Ishikawajima-Harima, Aioi, in 1965, Compañia Sud-Americana de Vapores' *Aconcagua II** was the first South American twenty-knot cargo liner. Sister *Imperial II* followed at the end of the same year and *Maipo II* and *Copiapo II* in 1966. The *II* suffix was required until old C2 tonnage bearing the same names could be disposed of. With a long forecastle and engines in the three-quarter-aft position, the new ships measured 10,869gt and 11,900dwt on dimensions of 553ft over the bulbous bow by 72ft and were driven by General Electric steam turbines with a maximum output of 15,000shp, equating to Ben Line's *Benloyal* (see page 131). Cargo-handling gear consisted of an improved Ebel rig with a 35t lift together with an 80t Stülcken serving Nos 3 and 4 hatches. Bale capacity amounted to 530,000cu ft with 110,000cu ft set aside for refrigerated cargoes in No 5 hold, which was fitted with three vertical conveyors for boxed fruit and bananas. Employed in the Chile–US east coast trade, they again had the *II* suffix added in 1980 when their names were allocated to other ships and all were broken up at Gadani Beach the following year, only *Imperial II* being renamed *Alliance Success* for the delivery voyage.

Speed rivals to the Far East

Delivered by Blohm & Voss, Hamburg, in December 1964, the 8,097gt *Westfalia* was Hamburg-America Line's first high-speed cargo liner. She was followed by the class name ship *Hammonia* in 1965 and five other sisters ending with *Thuringia* in 1967, whilst the hull of *Borussia* was subcontracted to Boel & Fils. Overall length was 539ft on a beam of 73ft and they had a long raised forecastle and six holds, five of them forward of the machinery which consisted of a nine-cylinder MAN diesel rated at 18,900bhp for a speed of twenty-one knots. Bale capacity totalled 680,000cu ft with an additional 24,000cu ft of insulated space and the comprehensive handling outfit of twenty-four winches and derricks was supplemented by an 80t Stülcken. They operated on Hamburg-America Line's Express Far East service until 1972, when they were gradually replaced by the large new container ships built for the TRIO consortium made up of Hapag-Lloyd, Nippon Yusen Kaisha and Overseas Container Line. *Alemannia* was the first to be disposed of, becoming the Bolivian-flag *Bolivia* in 1979, and the lead ship became the Saudi Arabian *Saudi Jamal* in 1983. They were broken up at Xingang in 1986 and Kaohsiung in 1985 respectively. The remaining five sisters served out their years with Hapag-Lloyd, having been altered to become more container friendly, and were eventually scrapped in 1987, *Hammonia* and *Thuringia* at Huangpu and *Borussia*, *Holsatia** and *Bavaria* at Kaohsiung.

Such was the pace of competition that barely two years elapsed between the delivery of *Benarmin*, last of the *Benloyal* class (see page 131), and the 11,898gt *Benledi**, the first of a radically improved quartet of ships for Ben Line's express Far East service. Completed by Charles Connell & Company, Glasgow, in 1965, she had her machinery placed well aft and measured 563ft over the bulbous bow on a beam of 75ft. Her hull featured a long forecastle and poop whilst her hatches at Nos 3 and 4 holds were tripled to expedite cargo handling. She had a mix of derricks and five 5t cranes as well as a 2.5t Carron transporter serving the poop 'tweendeck via side ports. Sisters *Benwyvis* and *Benalbanach*, which followed in 1966–7 had even longer forecastles incorporating No 2 hatch. All three were propelled by nine-cylinder Sulzer engines developing 20,700bhp for a service speed of more than twenty-one knots. The final unit, *Bencruachan*, completed in 1968 and modified to carry a few containers, reverted to turbine propulsion and, although designed to be the *Cutty Sark* of her age, was arguably less graceful due to a lack of sheer and the twin funnels mounted abreast. She hit the headlines in 1972 when her bow was bent downwards by wave action off the southeast coast of Africa. After very short service with Ben Line, the three motor ships were sold to Italia Line in 1972 and placed in Mediterranean–west coast of North America service as *Da Noli*, *Da Recco* and *Da Verrazano* respectively. They looked good in Italia colours but *Da Recco* caught fire at La Spezia on 4 June 1979 and was later broken up. Despite the oil price rises during the 1970s, the turbine-driven *Bencruachan* survived until 1980, when she was broken up in Kaohsiung; in the same year the remaining sisters became the Panamanian *Tina B* and *Rea B*. They were laid up in Greece two years later and *Tina B* subsequenty bore the names *Bello* then *Tina* but was wrecked in August 1987 whilst en route to India for scrapping. *Rea B* was renamed *Razorbill* in 1985, shortened to *Bill* two years later but she finally went to Alang breakers as *Glint* in 1988.

South African trade contrasts

In 1965, Union-Castle Line took delivery of two unique vessels, the 10,538gt *Southampton Castle* and *Good Hope Castle**, which were designed to operate alongside the mail ships in a new accelerated schedule requiring the high service speed of twenty-two and a half knots. Built by Swan, Hunter & Wigham Richardson's Wallsend shipyard, they measured 593 x 77ft 6in. Their three-island design incorporated six holds with No 4 hatch placed at the forward end of the bridge deck between a Hallen mast and a short superstructure surmounted by a very large pear-shaped funnel topped by a short radar mast. Power was supplied by twin eight-cylinder Sulzer diesels developing a massive 34,720bhp, which made them the most powerful cargo liners ever built and gave the lead ship more than twenty-seven knots on trial, although unsubstantiated reports allude to speed of more than thirty knots being achieved in emergency. Accommodation for twelve passengers was added at the after end of the boat deck in 1967 to cater for additional calls at the islands of Ascension and St Helena. The long-standing Cape mail service was finally wound up in 1978 and they were sold to Genoa-based Costa Line for South American trading, becoming *Franca C* and *Paola C* respectively. The *C* suffix was dropped in the final year and they were broken up at Dalian and Shanghai in 1984.

Depicted off Lühe in the River Elbe wearing South African Lines funnel colours, Globus-Reederei's 10,527gt *Tugelaland* was completed by Deutsche Werft, Finkenwerder in 1967 for service to East African ports. Apart from having a more substantial superstructure which accounted for her greater gross tonnage, she was basically a sister of *Tabora*, *Talana* and *Taveta* delivered to John T Essberger's DAL – Deutsche Afrika-Linien in 1965–6. All four shared the same dimensions of 511ft oa x 67ft and their design incorporated a long forecastle and poop with machinery placed one hold further aft than in previous ships. A six-cylinder MAN diesel developing 9,600bhp assisted by a prominent bulbous bow provided a speed of eighteen and a half knots. Cargo-handling equipment included 150t and 85t heavy-lift booms, together with another eighteen derricks of varying capacities. *Tugelaland* was renamed *Concordialand* for one year in 1972 but had the prefix *S A* added to her original name in 1974 after Globus had been acquired by South African Marine Corporation. In 1977, she was transferred to German registry and a year later was sold to China Ocean Shipping Company and renamed *Lu Cheng*. *Taveta*, which had become the Greek *Nicos* in 1975, also went to China Ocean Shipping in 1977 as *Dai Bai Shu* and in 1993 both ships were renamed, *Lu Cheng* becoming *Dong Ru* and *Dai Bai Shu* becoming *Wan Long*. Their ultimate fate is unknown but both were still in existence at the turn of the millennium. *Tabora* was sold in 1974 and renamed *Artico* and a year later *Talana* became the East German *Georg Handke*. After several further changes of name they were demolished at Gadani Beach in 1987 and 2003 respectively.

South African Marine Corporation placed orders for new fast refrigerated cargo liners in 1965, including three from the Dutch Verolme Group. *S A Van der Stel*, pictured in the North Sea, was the first to be completed, at Heusden in 1966, followed by *S A Weltevreden* at Alblasserdam and *S A Nederburg* at Cork Eire, in 1967. Tonnage figures were 9,500gt and 12,400dwt on overall dimensions of 542 x 75 feet and they had five holds. Their heavy-lift masts were unusual, the lead ship having two and the others just one. Fine lines and a bulbous bow guaranteed a twenty-knot service speed from a six-cylinder MAN diesel developing 13,800bhp. In 1974–5, they were lengthened by Tamano Shipyard by the insertion of a new No 4 hold with twin hatches served by a Stülcken derrick. *S A Van der Stel* was sold to Kaohsiung breakers in 1984 but *S A Weltevreden* ran as Springbok Shipping Company's *Safocean Weltevreden* between 1977 and 1981, before passing to Greek owners in 1982 as the Maltese-registered *Agia Marina*. Laid up at Eleusis, she underwent several more changes of ownership before being demolished at Kaohsiung in 1988. The third sister, *S A Nederburg*, emerged as *Safocean Nederburg* with three Stülcken derricks following alteration at Shimonoseki in 1980 and was briefly renamed *Nederburg* seven years later, before sailing as *Anro Adelaide* for a further two years. She was then sold to the Philippines, becoming briefly *Sinbad Explorer* and then *Pul Sentosa* but had to be towed the last part of the journey to Chittagong breakers after catching fire off the west coast of Thailand in September 1990.

A Yugoslav-built series for the Soviet Union

The Soviet Union's 10,109gt *Pula** was the first of a series of thirty fast ships built in Yugoslavia between 1965 and 1970, twenty by Brodogradiliste Uljanik, Pula, and ten by Brodogradiliste III Maj, Rijeka. They measured 525ft oa x 70ft on a deadweight of 14,200t and were driven at a comfortable eighteen knots by either eight-cylinder Uljanik-Burmeister & Wain or III Maj-Sulzer engines rated at 12,000bhp. In 1979–80, four of the Uljanik deliveries, *Novikov Priboy, Ivan Kotlarevsky, Konstantin Paustovsky* and *Gamzat Tsadasa*, were converted to 704TEU fully cellular container ships by Jurong Shipyard, Singapore, overall length being increased to 587ft. Around a dozen of these ships had careers lasting more than thirty years including *Pula*, which was amongst a number sold for further trading. She became *Astra* in 1991 and was broken up in Chittagong in 1996.

Scandia ships

The Scandia ship design resulted from collaboration between Svenska Ostasiatiska Kompaniet (SOK), Rederi A/B Transatlantic and Wilh. Wilhelmsen. Each ordered four ships for delivery in 1966–7, the latter from Uddevallavarvet and the others from Eriksbergs. SOK's *Hondo**, *Hokkaido, Hirado* and *Hakone* measured around 10,650gt and 13,100dwt on dimensions of 511ft oa x 70ft and were driven at nineteen knots by an B&W eight-cylinder B&W diesel developing 12,000bhp. Twin hatches served Nos 2 to 5 holds and cargo gear included seven cranes and a 65t heavy derrick. The other ships differed slightly., Transatlantic's *Killara, Waitara, Woollahra* and *Talarah* having had an extra crane in place of the mast amidships and a taller bridge whilst Wilhelmsen's slightly smaller, single-funnelled *Torrens, Taronga, Tamerlane* and *Tirranna* had a poop and a heavy mast forward with 40t and 200t derricks, the first two having cruiser sterns and the last two being driven by 13,000bhp Pielstick diesels. *Killara* was trapped in the Suez Canal for eight years from 1967 by the Six Day War and in 1970–71 *Talarah, Woollahra* and the Wilhelmsen ships had a cellular container hold inserted. *Waitara* became Polish Ocean Lines' *Pulawy* in 1973 and the rest were sold in the late 1970s and early 1980s, serving under many flags, including those of Bangladesh, France, Greece, Spain and Uruguay. Four, including lead ship *Hondo*, survived until scrapped at Alang in 1994.

Heavy-lift developments

Blue Star Line made a spectacular entrance to the heavy-lift market in 1965 with *Australia Star*, which was fitted with a 300t Stülcken derrick, the largest yet seen. Built by Austin & Pickersgill, Sunderland, she proceeded to Hamburg after launching to have her mast fitted before returning for fitting out. Her general layout included a long forecastle and a pronounced bulbous bow. Measuring 10,915gt on overall dimensions of 526 x 70ft, she had five holds, four of which were positioned ahead of the machinery. Nos 2 and 3 were fitted with extra long hatches and those of Nos 3 and 4 were twinned. In 1972 she was chartered to Christian Haaland and renamed *Concordia Gulf* but was sold two years later to Costa Line and renamed *Cortina*. In 1984 she again changed hands, becoming the Panamanian *Candy Ace* and was scrapped in Shanghai a year later.

F C Strick & Company first adopted a three-quarters-aft design with *Turkistan* in 1963 but she was basically a development of the preceding *Farsistan*-class ships with machinery moved one hold further aft. The next two ships after *Turkistan*, the 9,469gt *Shahristan** and *Floristan* delivered by Readhead & Son in 1965, introduced an entirely new look with cranes instead of derrick posts, and with minor changes this was continued for the company's final four ships. Although having the same overall length as *Turkistan* at 503ft, they were 2ft greater in beam at 68ft to allow sufficient stability for the operation of the 180t Stülcken derrick. The 8,985gt *Serbistan* and *Registan*, which followed in 1966, were similar but 4ft narrower on account of having a conventional stump mast and heavy jumbo derrick in place of the Stülcken. All four ships were propelled by a six-cylinder Doxford diesel rated at 10,000bhp for a service speed of sixteen to seventeen knots. Their management was transferred to the newly formed P&O General Cargo Division in 1972 and they were purchased by P&O a year later. In 1975 they were renamed – *Shahristan* becoming *Strathappin*, *Floristan* becoming *Strathalvie*, *Serbistan* becoming *Strathangus* and *Registan* becoming *Strathanna* – and given corn-coloured hulls. *Strathalvie* and *Strathappin* were sold to Greece as *Alexandra* and *Irenes Ideal* late in 1978 and early in 1979, the former was towed to Kaohsiung for scrap in 1983 following a serious engine-room fire at Luanda the previous November, whilst the latter became the Maltese-flag *Ideal* in 1982 and was demolished at Chittagong three years later. The 1966 pair were both sold to Hong Kong Islands Shipping Company as *Kelett Island* and *Tsing Yi Island* in 1978, the latter going to Kaohsiung breakers in 1987 and her sister, which had become the Panama-registered *Golden Bear* in 1983, a year later. Strick's final pair of ships came from Swan, Hunter in 1969 and 1970, *Tabaristan* resembling *Shahristan* with a Stülcken mast, whilst *Nigaristan* carried two extra cranes in its place. They measured 510 x 70ft, and could make seventeen and a half knots thanks to bulbous bows and 12,000bhp engines.

In 1966–7, Hansa Line built a series of six ships at A G Weser, which were all-aft developments of its earlier *Wartenfels*-class ships. Their hulls featured a long forecastle and measured 9,099gt and 12,991dwt on overall dimensions of 500 x 67ft. *Crostafels* and *Schönfels* were completed at the end of 1966 and had seven-cylinder MAN engines developing 10,800bhp for nineteen knots but the 1967 deliveries, *Falkenfels*, *Birkenfels*, *Hohenfels** and *Kybfels*, had uprated 11,200bhp units for twenty knots. Cargo-handling gear included two 5t electric cranes and a 150t Stülcken heavy-lift derrick. They were all disposed of in 1978–9, *Crostafels*, *Schönfels*, *Birkenfels*, *Kybfels* going to China and renamed *Da Long Tian*, *Da Qing Shan*, *Wu Yi Shan* and *Da Hong Qiao*. *Falkenfels* and *Hohenfels* went to Greece as *Aias* and *Hohenbels*, and were both scrapped at Alang in 1985. Of the Chinese ships, *Wu Yi Shan* was broken up locally in 1993, *Da Hong Qiao* and *Da Long Tian* at Calcutta in 1996 and 1997 after dropping the *Da* prefix for the delivery voyages but the fate of *Ta Ching Shen* are uncertain.

A style change for Federal/New Zealand Shipping

The refrigerated motorships *Westmorland*, *Taupo*, *Tekoa** and *Tongariro* introduced an entirely new look to the Federal Steam Navigation Company and New Zealand Shipping Company and fleets. Gone were the traditional masts and pairs of heavy kingposts and in their place were four bipod masts and eight Hallen crane derricks ranging from 10t to 30t capacity, which could be individually controlled by one man. Another innovation was the *eau-de-nil* hull colour in place of the former black and Federal funnel colours were common to all despite the three 'T' ships being registered to New Zealand Shipping. *Westmorland*, which was the correct county spelling compared with earlier ships, was first to be delivered, by Lithgows, Port Glasgow, early in 1966, with the first two 'T's following from Bartram & Sons, Sunderland, later the same year and *Tongariro* early in 1967. They measured 10,983gt and 11,866dwt in the closed shelter-deck condition on overall dimensions of 528 x 71ft. Insulated capacity was around 480,000cu ft and they were propelled at twenty knots by eight-cylinder Sulzer diesels rated at 17,600bhp. In 1971, they were transferred to the P&O General Cargo Division and adopted the latter's blue funnel colouring, whilst hulls were changed initially to black and later to corn colour. They changed hands several times within the P&O Group but *Tongariro* was sold in 1979 becoming Seaspeed Maritime Inc's *Reefer Princess* and a year later *Capetan Leonidas* for other Greek owners Platana Maritime Company. The other three were disposed of in 1980; *Taupo* and *Tekoa* were renamed *Mandama* and *Mahsuri* by Vestey Group's Singapore subsidiary Austasia Line, whilst *Westmorland*, after a year as the Lebanese *Fares Reefer*, also joined Vesteys as the Hong Kong-registered *Beacon Hill*. The Austasia ships were broken up at Chittagong and Kaohsiung in 1984 and their former sisters a year later following periods of lay up, *Capetan Leonidas* at Gadani Beach and *Beacon Hill* in Huangpu.

New North Atlantic designs

In addition to its short-sea activities, the Danish shipping company Det Forenede Dampskibs-Selskab (DFDS) had been associated with the liner trades to the east coasts of the United States since 1895 and South America since 1907. These received a considerable boost in 1966 with the delivery of *Nebraska*, the first of eight attractive shelter-deckers illustrated here by *Michigan* entering Rio de Janeiro. They were built in three yards, Elsinore Shipbuilding & Engineering, and Burmeister & Wain, Copenhagen, each being responsible for a pair of vessels with the other four coming from Bergens MV. They measured 4,500gt and 6,660dwt on dimensions of 463ft oa x 62ft and a ten-cylinder Burmeister & Wain diesel developing 12,000bhp ensured a high service speed of nineteen and a half knots. Competition from container and ro-ro ships caused the New York service to be dropped in 1967 and greater emphasis to be placed on the US Gulf trade. In 1972, *Nebraska*, *Alberta* and *Wisconsin* were sold to Italia Line, becoming *D'Azeglio*, *Mazzini* and *Crispi* respectively; all were scrapped at La Spezia in 1985. In 1978, *Ontario* went to India as *Marhaba* and was broken up at Bombay in 1988. The remainder were sold in 1980, *Missouri* and *Michigan* going to Prodromos Lines as *Ermioni* and *Zanet*. The former became the Maltese *Fair Runner* in 1989 and was scrapped in Chittagong in 1991, a year before *Zanet* was demolished as *Anet* at Gadani Beach. *Manitoba* became the Saudi Arabian *Nour* then *Taibah IV* in 1983 and was broken up at Gadani Beach in 1987. *Labrador* (launched as *Quebec*) went to Dannebrog Rederi as *Viborg* but was abandoned after her engine-room flooded off Cape Finisterre on her first voyage. She was later towed back to Denmark and repaired but in 1981 she was converted in Singapore to a livestock carrier with added sponsons. From 1986, she sailed as the Argentine *El Cordero* under Panamanian flag and was broken up at Alang in 1999.

The 6,031gt *Suffren* and *Rochambeau** were the final conventional ships built for Compagnie Générale Transatlantique's North Atlantic services before containerisation and Atlantic Container Line's new ro-ro tonnage, in which CGT had a share, revolutionised the trade. Built by Chantiers de l'Atlantique, St Nazaire and Chantiers Navale de la Ciotat, Le Trait, in 1966–7, they measured 490ft oa x 68ft and hatches at all but the No 1 position were triples, suitable for the on-deck stowage of containers. Cargo gear comprised four 5t cranes and a 30t heavy derrick in addition to a mix of smaller derricks. A service speed of eighteen knots was achieved by twin sixteen-cylinder SEMT-Pielstick medium-speed diesels developing 12,800bhp and geared to a single screw. The success of the new forms of transportation led to the sisters having short careers with CGT, *Suffren* being sold to Société Navale Caennaise in 1977 and renamed *Dione*, whilst *Rochambeau* became the Italian *Siba Queen* a year later and was converted to a livestock carrier. *Dione* became *Khalij Express* in 1983 and was scrapped two year later at Alang, whilst *Siba Queen* was renamed *El Borrego* in 1988 and then *Al Rayzan I* the following year, and finally foundered in the Arabian Sea on 9 June 1994. (*A Duncan*)

More twenty-knot ships for Far Eastern trade

The Ocean Group's response to Ben Line's *Benledi* class (see page 160) was the eight-ship *Priam** class designed by Marshall Meek, four for Blue Funnel and four for Glen Line. *Priam, Peisander, Prometheus, Protesilaus* and *Radnorshire* were contracted with Vickers-Armstrongs, High Walker, *Glenfinlas* with John Brown & Company, Clydebank and *Glenalmond* and *Pembrokeshire* with Mitsubishi, Nagasaki. Owing to industrial action in the United Kingdom, *Glenalmond* was the first to be completed, in September 1966, and *Radnorshire* the last in 1967. They measured 12,094gt on dimensions of 564ft oa x 78ft and cargo capacity amounted to 708,920cu ft with 20,240cu ft of insulated space and a further 77,800cu ft for liquid cargoes in thirteen deep tanks in Nos 1 and 5 holds. Comprehensive handling gear included a 60t Stülcken, six rail-mounted cranes and twelve derricks. A lifetime speed of twenty-one knots was guaranteed by nine-cylinder Mitsubishi-Sulzer or Burmeister & Wain engines which delivered 18,900bhp and could be run unattended with automatic monitoring. The four Glen ships were transferred to Blue Funnel in 1972–3, *Pembrokeshire* becoming *Phrontis*, *Radnorshire* becoming *Perseus*, *Glenalmond* becoming *Patroclus* (transferred to N S M 'Oceaan' between 1974 and 1978), and *Glenfinlas* becoming *Phemius*. Six of the class were sold in 1978, the original Blue Funnel quartet to C Y Tung and renamed *Oriental Champion, – Merchant – Importer* and *– Exporter* respectively in order of original delivery, whilst the former Glens *Perseus* and *Phemius* also went to Hong Kong as China Navigation Company's *Kwangsi* and *Kweichow*. *Phrontis* became Gulf Shipping Lines' *Gulf Osprey* in 1982, the Iranian *Iran Ejtehad* in 1983 and was scrapped as *Dolphin VIII* at Gadani Beach in 1995. *Patroclus* went to Saudi owners as *Rajab I* in 1982 and was demolished at Gadani Beach in 1984 following a fire at Port Rashid. *Oriental Importer* was hit by an aircraft missile during the Iran–Iraq war in June 1985 and was towed to Kaohsiung for scrapping. Four months later a similar fate and demise befell *Oriental Champion*, which had been converted to a full container ship in 1979. *Oriental Exporter*, which had sailed as *Main Express* from 1981 to 1984, followed her former sisters to Kaohsiung in 1986 as did *Oriental Merchant* as *Om*, having briefly held the name *Om No 1* in 1979. The two ships that had gone to China Navigation Company were demolished in China in 1984, *Kwangsi* having become *Asia Dragon* in 1981 and *Saudi Zamzam* in 1982, whilst *Kweichow* had been renamed *Saudi Kawther* in 1983.

Bremen Maru, seen here in London's Royal Albert Dock, was the first of a quartet of high-speed ships for Mitsui-OSK's North European service. Together with *Bristol Maru*, she was a product of Mitsui's Tamano yard in 1966, whilst *Bergen Maru* and *Barcelona Maru* came from the builder's Kobe facility in 1966 and 1967. Tonnage measurements were 10,431gt and 12,352dwt on dimensions of 544ft over the bulbous bow by 76ft and their accommodation was placed well aft between hatches Nos 5 and 6. Their hull design incorporated a long forecastle and long poop abaft the superstructure but they were unusual for Japanese ships in having three bipod masts whilst all hatches remained single. Working gear included sixteen 6t derricks, a single 30t boom and three 10t cranes. Propelling machinery comprised eight-cylinder Burmeister & Wain diesels in the Tamano-built pair and Sulzers in the others, each rated at 18,400bhp for a service speed of twenty and three-quarter knots. Mitsui-OSK was one of the first lines to adopt containerisation and in 1978 *Bristol Maru* was lengthened to 590ft and converted to a fully cellular container ship. She was scrapped at Kaohsiung in 1985. The remaining three ships were disposed of in 1983, *Bremen Maru* and *Bergen Maru* becoming *Jami* and *Iran Reshadat* and both being destroyed by aircraft missile attack in the Khor Musa Channel, the former at the end of March 1984 and the latter on 24 August 1983, later being hulked at Bushire. *Barcelona Maru* was renamed *Mowlavi* and was into her thirty-first year when she was broken up in Alang in 1998.

The East Asiatic Company followed up its single ship *Ancona* with three further 'A'-class developments. *Azuma** was completed by Mitsui Zosen's Tamano yard in 1966 and was followed by *Aranya* and *Arosia* from the Nakskov Shipyard in 1966 and 1967. *Aranya* introduced the new funnel livery with blue EAC letters shown here on *Azuma*. They were three-deck ships measuring 11,200gt and 13,200dwt in the closed condition on overall dimensions of 540 x 77ft. Five of the six holds were placed forward of the ten-cylinder Burmeister & Wain engine, which produced 15,000bhp for a service speed of twenty and three-quarter knots. Deck gear included five cranes and two pairs of 12?t derricks that could be yoked together for 24t lifts, together with a 60t derrick on the single bipod mast. To aid manoeuvrability, they were fitted with a bow-thrust and controllable pitch propeller but the hull did not have a bulbous forefoot. They sailed to the Far East from northern Europe and later from the Mediterranean after the former route was containerised, whilst *Aranya* sailed to West Africa in her later years. *Azuma* was transferred to Greek registry without change of name in 1979 and six years later became the Maltese *Zenith* for delivery to breakers in China. *Aranya* and *Arosia* were sold to Bombay owners in 1979 as *Rishi Atri* and *Rishi Agasti* and were broken up locally in 1988. *Alameda*, completed at Nakskov in 1967, was broadly similar with no poop and had two bipod masts and tripled hatches at Nos 3, 4 and 5 holds. She was eventually broken up at Chittagong in 1991 after several name changes.

Royal Rotterdam Lloyd and Nederland Line collaborated on the design of a new fast vessel for the Far East trade, each ordering a pair from Nippon Kokan, Shimizu, and which would become their final vessels. *Leuve Lloyd** was the first to be completed, in December 1966, followed by *Neder Linge* and *Loire Lloyd* in 1967 and finally *Neder Lek* in January 1968. They measured just over 9,600gt and 12,000dwt on a length of 532ft over the bulbous bow and a beam of 78ft. The hull featured a long forecastle and a squared-off transom stern as in the Scandia ships (see page 161). Cargo capacities amounted to 680,400cu ft (bale) and 60,700cu ft (refrigerated), and cargo gear included six 5t cranes and a 130t Stülcken heavy-lift derrick. They were powered by large-bore six-cylinder Stork engines producing a maximum 17,000bhp but a service rating of 15,000bhp was sufficient to maintain twenty-one knots. They passed into the combined Koninklijke Nedlloyd fleet in 1970 and in 1977 were renamed *Nedlloyd Leuve, – Linge, – Loire* and *– Lek* respectively. In 1980–1, they were converted to semi-container ships by Asano shipyard, Yokohama, and all went for scrap in 1991, three to Chittagong minus their *Nedlloyd* prefix and the former *Nedlloyd Lek* to Sitalpur. The latter had sailed in the Safocean South Africa–Australasia service as *Safocean Mildura* between 1980 and 1987 and had briefly held the name *Sindbad Voyager* in 1988 before ending her days as *Voyager*.

With its eighteen-knot steamers from the early1950s being outclassed by fast new ships from its competitors, P&O ordered three fast ships from Mitsui's Tamano yard. Delivered in 1967, the 12,539gt 'Super Straths' *Strathardle**, *Strathbrora* and *Strathconon* had a long forecastle and short poop and were distinctive on account of their white livery with buff funnel and a Hallen mast supporting 15t and 30t crane derricks. Holds Nos 2, 3 and 4 had twinned hatches and cargo gear included six 5t and one 15t cranes. Overall length was 563ft on a beam of 79ft 6in and they measured 14,000gt with a capacity of 740,000cu ft.
A nine-cylinder Burmeister & Wain developing 20,700bhp produced 24.46 knots on trial and twenty-one knots in service. They operated the Strath Express Service to the Far East until 1971, when they were transferred to P&O's new General Cargo Division and given a blue funnel carrying the P&O logo. The following year, the Far East service was containerised and they were transferred to the Arab Gulf–Japan trade in place of four British India Steam Navigation Company N-class ships. In 1979, all three sisters were sold to United Thai Shipping Corporation, becoming *Anchan*, *Benjamas* and *Chuangchom*. This last stranded in the Red Sea in May 1980 but was bought by Greeks and after repairs in Piræus traded as *Tzelepi* until scrapped in Shanghai in 1984. A year later, the remaining pair went to breakers in Huangpu and Kaohsiung.

Norddeutscher Lloyd's decision to lengthen and re-engine seven of its 1950s-built cargo liners for nineteen and a half knots in the early 1960s enabled it to postpone the ordering of new fast ships for a while and at the same time to benefit from the experience of other shipowners. Increasing competition on the Far East run, however, ultimately led to the building of six 10,481gt *Friesenstein*-class ships at Lübecker Flender-Werke and Bremer Vulkan in 1967–8. Deadweight amounted to 12,787t and they measured 540ft oa x 75ft, their design differing from Hamburg-America Line's *Hammonia* class (see page 159) in having a shorter forecastle, a short bridge deck and a transom stern. Cargo gear included a mix of four 5t cranes and derricks together with an 80t Stulcken, whilst the main engine was an eight-cylinder MAN developing 18,400bhp for twenty-one knots. In 1974, *Hessenstein* was sold to Ecuador as *Isla Puna*, *Badenstein* and *Sachsenstein** joined Chile's Compañia Sud Americana de Vapores fleet as *Rupel* and *Renaico* in 1978–9 and a year later *Bayernstein* became *South Star* of Singapore. All were demolished at Kaohsiung, the latter in 1983, the two Chileans in 1984 and *Isla Puna* in 1987. In 1980, Thyssen Nordseewerke converted the three remaining ships, *Friesenstein*, *Holstenstein* and *Schwabenstein*, to semi-container ships by inserting a 49ft-long cellular hold forward of the bridge and fitting a 318ft-long blister, which increased their beam to 87ft. The new hold was served by a 28t crane and had a capacity of 322TEU below deck and 182TEU on deck. Speed was reduced to nineteen knots and they were transferred to the Pacific coast of South America route. In 1983–4, they were sold to Tilsamar Inc, Panama, and renamed *Kinaros*, *Karos* and *Karpathos* respectively under the Panamanian flag. *Kinaros* was renamed *Athinai* in 1987 for the Greek South American Line and was broken up at Alang in 1994. Her two sisters changed to Greek registry in 1987 and also went to Alang, in 1984–5.

Dutch Central America traders

The 5,153gt *Mercurius** was Koninklijke Nederlandsche Stoomboot Maats.' largest cargo liner when delivered by Scheepsbouwwerf Gebroeders Pot, Bolnes, in 1966. Built for service to Curaçao, Aruba and Paramaribo, she was joined by sister *Neptunus* in 1967. They had a deadweight of 6,936t in the open condition and measured 477ft oa x 64ft. Cargo handling was achieved by an outfit of eight remote-controlled cranes and four derricks and the hatches at Nos 3 and 4 holds were twinned. A six-cylinder Stork diesel with an output of 8,000bhp ensured a service speed of eighteen knots. *Neptunus* was the first to be disposed of, going to Transytur, Maracaibo, in 1978 and renamed *Elena Altomare* but by 1980 she had become the Greek *Agios Giannis* and a year later *Alexander's Power*. Her final change of name to *Florina* occurred in 1984 and she was scrapped at Nantong a year later. Her sister was sold to Piræus-based Manta Line in June 1980 and traded as *Coffee Trader* until broken up around 1992.

The last conventional refrigerated tonnage

Shaw, Savill & Albion's last and largest conventional refrigerated ships were the 12,227gt *Majestic** and *Britannic* delivered by Alexander Stephen in 1967. They were developments of the 7,750gt, eighteen-knot *Zealandic* and *Laurentic* built two years earlier by Alexander Stephen & Sons and Vickers-Armstrongs and had an additional hold forward of the superstructure. Main dimensions were 546ft oa x 74ft on a deadweight of 14,300t and their eight-cylinder turbo-charged Sulzer main engine, which had a 'Mahout' system of bridge control, had a maximum output of 17,600bhp and a service rating of 15,000bhp for a speed of nineteen knots. In 1974, both were sold to the newly formed state-owned Shipping Corporation of New Zealand and served for four years in the Europe–New Zealand trade as *N Z Aorangi* and *N Z Waitangi*. Sold on in 1978 to Vernicos-Eugenides, of Greece,, they were renamed *Mykonos* and *Serifos* and given white hulls, the former becoming *Mykonos V* in 1992. They were both broken up at Alang in 1995 and 1996. (*A Duncan*)

Blue Star Line's final conventional ships, the 11,300gt *Southland Star* and *New Zealand Star**, were completed by Bremer Vulkan in 1967. They measured 552ft over the bulbous bow by 73ft on a deadweight of 13,470t and their fine-lined hulls incorporated a long forecastle and poop. The hatches serving Nos 3 and 4 holds were twinned and cargo gear comprised two lightweight Stülcken masts, each mounting a 40t derrick, which could be combined for lifts up to 80t, five cranes and eight 3–5t conventional derricks. The main engine was a nine-cylinder MAN developing 20,700bhp for a service speed of twenty-one and half knots and they were amongst the first UK cargo liners to operate with a periodically unmanned engine room. With the spread of containerisation, both were returned to their builder in 1977 for conversion to fully cellular container ships with a new crane at the break of the forecastle; *New Zealand Star* re-emerged from this process as *Wellington Star*. Compared with many ships of their era, they had surprisingly long careers under their original Blue Star colours and were not broken up, in Chittagong, until 1993.

The twin-screw *Port Chalmers** and *Port Caroline* were the last, largest (16,283gt, 19,000dwt) and fastest (twenty-one and a half knots) Port Line ships, as well as being the final products of Alexander Stephen & Sons, which became part of Upper Clyde Shipbuilders between the deliveries of the two ships in 1968. Apart from a heavily flared bow, their hulls were devoid of sheer in order to keep both upper and lower 'tweendecks level to accommodate palletised cargo and as a result they lacked something of the grace of earlier Port liners. Their massive appearance was not helped by a heavy 'rugby post' mast which mounted two 25t Thompson swinging derricks. They measured 612ft oa x 81ft and their insulated capacity of 606,940cu ft out of a total of 820,000cu ft, outstripped all previous outfits. Cargo handling was achieved by means of three travelling 5t Stothert & Pitt cranes forward and two fixed units aft, plus two 15t and four 10t derricks capable of being used singly or in union purchase. The high service speed was maintained by twin Clark-Sulzer turbo-charged diesels with a combined maximum output of 26,000shp. The containerisation of the UK–Australia trade shortly after their entry into service rendered them almost immediately obsolete and they were transferred to Cunard Shipping Services in 1979 becoming Brocklebank's *Manaar* and *Matra* in 1982 and being laid up at Opua, New Zealand, and in the River Fal respectively. Plans to convert them to either container ships or Caribbean cruise ships were considered and abandoned on the basis of cost and suitability. In 1983, they were sold to Kappa Maritime and renamed *Golden Glory* and *Golden Dolphin* respectively, making final voyages to Shanghai breakers in 1985, just seventeen years after completion.

Final designs for Far Eastern trade

Wilh. Wilhelmsen's final conventional cargo liner design had a transom stern and was basically a larger and faster derivative of their earlier Scandia ships (see page 161). Built in Japan by Mitsui Zosen's Tamano yard in 1967–8, *Talabot**, *Taiko*, *Trinidad* and *Taimyr* had a gross tonnage of 12,545 on a deadweight of 15,600t and measured 552ft over the bulbous bow by 80ft. They were capable of maintaining twenty-one and a half knots in service by means of a seven-cylinder Burmeister & Wain diesel developing 16,100bhp and also had bow thrusters. *Trinidad* was renamed *Tamano* under Barber Line management in 1978 and together with *Talabot* passed briefly through Far Eastern hands under Wallem & Company management as *New Sun* and *New Dawn* before being sold in 1980 to Chile's Compañia Sud Americana de Vapores and renamed *Maule* and *Malleco*. *Taimyr* followed a similar path, also becoming *New Dawn* and then CSAV's *Maullin* in 1987. *Maule* was scrapped in Beihai, China, in 1987 and her Chilean sisters at Chittagong in 1992. In the meantime, *Taiko* had been sold to Thoresen & Company, Bangkok (initially under Bruusgaard management), in 1985 and renamed *Hai Lee*. She was eventually demolished at Alang in 1993 after a twenty-five-year career.

A P Møller's seven-ship *Cornelia Mærsk* series was completed in 1967–9, four being built by Bergens MV and the remainder by Kockums in Malmö. Tonnage measurements were 10,928gt and 14,600dwt on dimensions of 560ft oa x 80ft. They were fitted with a bow thruster and were designed to operate at up to twenty-three knots through a combination of an eight-cylinder Akers-Burmeister & Wain diesel rated at 20,900bhp and exceptionally fine lines forward, which led to the same stability problems encountered by *Benloyal* (see page 131) and required permanent concrete ballast forward. During the course of 1980–1 they were both lengthened and broadened by Hitachi Zosen, Innoshima, into fully cellular 1,218TEU container ships. *Chastine* – and *Charlotte Maersk* were sold to China Ocean Shipping Company and renamed *Hui He* and *Tao He* in 1987. The following year, these were joined by *Christian* –, *Clifford* – and *Clara Mærsk** (which had spent two years on charter as *TFL Adams* from 1984) as *Shun He*, *Jian He* and *Yi He*. The remaining two, *Cornelia* – and *Cecilie Mærsk*, were chartered out from 1991 and spent their last years as Montemar's *Paraguay Express* and *Bilbao Express* before being broken up at Alang in 1999 and 1998 respectively. The latter year had also seen *Jian He* demolished at Tianjin and *Tao He* at Xingang, whilst *Shun He* and *Yi He* lasted until 2004. The fate of *Hui He* is unknown.

Holland's United Netherlands Navigation Company adopted a unique design for four fast 'W'-class cargo liners ordered in September 1965 and delivered in 1967–8. The lead ships *Wissekerk* and *Waalekerk* were products of P Smit Jr, Rotterdam, *Westerkerk* came from Wilton-Fijenoord, Schiedam and *Willemskerk** from van der Giessen-De Noord, Krimpen. Measuring around 10,710gt and 13,290dwt on overall dimensions of 547 x 75ft, they were driven by six-cylinder Stork diesels developing 17,000bhp in service for a speed of around twenty-one knots. The design was dominated by a large, unusual-looking heavy-lift mast mounting a 120t derrick. All hatches were of the MacGregor type and those in the well-deck serving Nos 3, 4 and 5 were tripled. Normal cargo gear comprised six 10t and two 3t cranes. On 1 July 1970, they were transferred to Koninklijke Nedlloyd and in 1977 the *Nedlloyd* prefix was added to their names. This was dropped in 1984 and *Waalekerk* went to Kaohsiung breakers in 1986 when the prefix was again added to the other three. *Nedlloyd Westerkerk* followed her sister to Taiwan in 1987 but the two remaining ships were sold to Panamanian owners, *Wissekerk* becoming *Arrow Duke* and *Willemskerk* becoming *Arrow Queen*, finally being demolished at Chittagong in 1988 and 1990 respectively.

Royal Interocean Lines boosted its Far East–South Africa–South America service with four advanced 10,184gt 'H'– class ships in 1967–8. *Straat Holland*, *– Honshu*, *– Hobart* and *– Hong Kong** were products of Nippon Kokan's Shimizu yard and differed from the preceding 'F'-class ships (see page 155) in having the engines placed one hold further aft, whilst No 3 hatch was tripled to handle containers and unitised cargo. Following inconclusive results obtained from the bulbous bows of the previous Japanese-built *Straat Futami* quartet, they reverted to having a conventional fine-lined bow. Total bale capacity was 630,000cu ft and provision was made for carrying ferro silicon in the No 1 lower hold and ore in two special compartments aft. Cargo gear included one 20t, three 5t and two 3t cranes in addition to six 10t derricks. The turbocharged six-cylinder Mitsui-Burmeister & Wain engine was automatically monitored and developed 13,500bhp for a trial speed of twenty-one and a half knots. A Nippon Kokan passive stabiliser system was installed using wing tanks. After a reorganisation in Nedlloyd Lines in 1977, the *Straat* prefix was replaced by *Nedlloyd* and *Nedlloyd Holland* was sold to Saudi Arabia in 1984 becoming *Saudi Al Jubail*. All four were broken up in Kaohsiung in 1983–4.

Transpacific finale

The US west coast-based States Steamship Company took delivery of its final ships, *Colorado*, *Montana*, *Idaho**, *Wyoming* and *Michigan*, from Avondale, in 1968–9. Slated for transpacific service to Japan and Hong Kong via Honolulu, their officially designated C4-S-69b design was new compared with the four earlier *California*-class ships, which were built at Newport News in 1962 using standard Mariner-type hulls. They had long forecastles and four unstayed Ebel masts, which allowed booms to be used like cranes, saving on manpower and speeding-up cargo handling. Tonnage measurements were around 13,050gt and 14,150dwt on dimensions of 588ft oa x 75ft and propulsion was provided by a fully automated steam turbine developing 24,000shp for a fast service speed of twenty-three knots. A pronounced bulbous bow minimised pitching and wave-making, whilst gyro-controlled flume tanks were installed to diminish rolling. They had a large bale capacity of 855,000cu ft with an additional 40,000cu ft of insulated space and hatches 3, 4 and 5 were tripled. States Steamship Company was absorbed into United States Lines in 1981 and the ships were renamed *American Titan*, *– Trojan*, *– Spitfire*, *– Monarch* and *– Spartan* respectively. This last sprang a leak off Diego Garcia in December 1982 and was broken up in Kaohsiung, whilst the others were all demolished at Alang in 1991, *American Trojan* as *Santa Victoria*, having changed name two years earlier.

Commencing with *President Van Buren*, delivered by Ingalls Shipbuilding Corporation, Pascagoula, in August 1967, American President Lines' five C4-S-69a 'Seamaster'-class ships measured 14,760gt and 12,830dwt on overall dimensions of 572 x 82ft and the hull was constructed of high-strength low-alloy steel giving an 18 per cent weight reduction. The three-deck George Sharp design incorporated a long forecastle and poop with a squared off transom providing extra stowage for thirty cars, whilst holds Nos 3 and 4 were served by triple hatches. Cargo gear comprised a full Ebel rig plus a 70t Newport News-type swing-through heavy derrick. Total cargo capacity, including refrigerated space, amounted to 845,000cu ft. A 24,000shp turbine fed by a single boiler ensured a service speed of twenty-three knots that could easily be exceeded, the lead ship crossing from Yokohama to San Francisco in a record seven days and fifteen hours at an average speed of 25.55 knots. Subsequent conversion to full container ships was planned from the outset and all had a new 90ft mid-body inserted by the Todd Shipyards Corporation at Seattle in 1972, emerging as fully cellular 1,140TEU vessels. *President Grant** was lost in September 1976 after grounding twice, the second time in a typhoon, near Keelung and breaking in two. *President McKinley* and *President Fillmore* were sold to Lykes Lines in 1987 and renamed *Almeria Lykes* and *Mason Lykes*, *President Van Buren* following as *Howell Lykes* a year later. The year 1993 brought several changes: *President Taft* went to Kaohsiung breakers, *Almeria Lykes* became Sea-Land Service's *Sea-Land Shining Star* and the other two Lykes ships reverted to their original names, before towed to Alang for demolition. The surviving Sea-Land ship also ended her days at Alang in 1996.

The 15,549gt *Alaskan Mail* series (C5-S-75a) can lay claim to being the largest ever conventional cargo liners. Built by Newport News Shipbuilding & Dry Dock Company to a J J Henry design for American Mail Line's transpacific service, the lead ship and *Indian Mail* were completed in 1968 with *Korean Mail*, *Hong Kong Mail* and *American Mail** following in 1969. Their relatively conventional appearance disguised a deadweight capacity of 22,536t, representing a 50 per cent increase on the earlier *Washington Mail* series, which was based on a standard Mariner hull. They had seven holds, four of them forward of the machinery, and four bipod masts. Overall length was 605ft on a beam of 83ft and bale capacity totalled a massive 1,082,207cu ft whilst, in order to facilitate tweendeck cargo handling, they were fitted with an air-cushion pallet system. Service speed was twenty-one knots provided by two sets of General Electric turbines geared to a single screw. American Mail Line was amalgamated with American President Lines in 1978 and they were renamed *President Adams*, *– Jackson*, *– Taylor*, *– Wilson* and *– Cleveland* respectively. *President Wilson* was chartered to Lykes Lines as *Sue Lykes* in 1987. The following year, *President Adams* and *President Jackson* were sold to the government and placed in the Ready Reserve Fleet at Suisun Bay as *Cape Girardeau* and *Cape Gibson*, both being operated by American President Lines during Operation Desert Storm. In 1989, *President Taylor* was sold to Lykes Lines and which served as *Stella Lykes* until scrapped at Alang in 1995, whilst *President Cleveland* became Sea Lift Inc's *Cleveland*. She was joined by *President Wilson* (renamed *Wilson*) following completion of her Lykes charter in 1996.

Bibliography

Books

Bakke, Dag Jr, *Linjer Rundt Jorden, Historien om norsk Linjefart*, Seagull Publishing, Bergen, 2008.

Boyer, Friedrich, *Alles über ein Schiff*, Herder, Freiburg, 1962. A detailed description of Hamburg-Süd's *Cap San* series.

Clarkson, John, Fenton, Roy and Munro, Archie, *Clan Line*, Ships in Focus Publications, Preston, 2007.

Cooper, Malcolm, Harvey, Bill and Laxon, Bill, *Glen and Shire Lines*, Ships in Focus Publications, Preston, 2005.

Craig, Robin, *Steam Tramps and Cargo Liners* 1850-1950, HM Stationary Office, London, 1980.

Critchell, J T and Raymond, J, *History of the Frozen Meat Trade*, Constable, London, 1912.

de Kerbrech, Richard P, *Harland & Wolff's Empire Food Ships*, Coach House Publications, Freshwater, 1998.

Detlefsen, Gert Uwe, *Schiffahrt im Bilde Linienfrachter*, 2 vols, Hauschild, Bremen, 1999 & 2004

Dunn, Laurence and Heaton, P M, *Palm Line*, P M Heaton Publishing, Abergavenny, 1994.

Goldberg, Mark H, *The Hog Islanders*, American Merchant Marine Museum, New York, 1991.

Haws, Duncan, *Merchant Fleets* (Hereford). Many chronological fleet histories with scale drawings. Continued under the same title by Middlemiss, Norman L, Shield Publications, Gateshead.

Hyde, F E, *Blue Funnel*, Liverpool University Press, Liverpool, 1957.

Jaffee, Capt Walther W, *The Victory Ships from A (Aberdeen Victory) to Z (Zanesville Victory)*, The Glencannon Press, El Cerrito, CA, 2006.

Jordan, R, *The World's Merchant Fleets 1939*, Chatham Publishing, Chatham, 2000.

Kinghorn, Captain A W, *Before the Box Boats*, Kenneth Mason, Emsworth, 1983.

Kolltveit, Bård and Crowdy, Michael, *Wilh. Wilhelmsen 1861–1994*, World Ship Society, Kendal, 1994.

Laxon, W A, Farquhar, I, and Kirby, N J, *Crossed Flags*, World Ship Society, Graveend, 1997.

Laxon, W A and Perry, F W, *B I – The British India Steam Navigation Company Limited*, World Ship Society, Kendal, 1994.

Mitchell, W H and Sawyer, L A, *Empire Ships of World War II*, Sea Breezes, Liverpool, 1965.

Sawyer, L A and Mitchell, W H, *From America to United States: Parts I–IV. The history of the merchant ship types built in the United States of America under the long-range programme of the Maritime Commission.* World Ship Society, Kendal, 1986.

Somner, Graeme, The *Ben Line*, Ships in Focus Publications, Preston, 2009.

Spong, H C and Dobson, J, *Port Line*, World Ship Society, Windsor, 2004.

Stewart, I G, *The Ships that Serve New Zealand Vol 1: British & European Lines*, A H & A W Reed, Wellington, New Zealand, 1964.

Strachan, Michael, *The Ben Line 1825–1952*, Michael Russell Publishing, Norwich, 1993.

Woodman, Richard, *Voyage East*, John Murray, London, 1988. A fictitious cargo liner voyage based on fact.

Periodicals

The Marine Engineer & Naval Architect
Marine News
The Motor Ship
Sea Breezes
Shipbuilding & Shipping Record
Ships in Focus
Ships Monthly

Registers

Lloyd's Register of Shipping
Starke-Schell Registers
Miramar Ship Index

Index

Dates of build have been included where names are duplicated and to identify ships where the name has been used more than once in a particular company. Warships referred to in the text have been excluded except in cases where ships served as such during their careers.